This Happy Isle

The Story of Sea Island and the Cloister

Harold H. Martin

Sea Island Company
Sea Island, Georgia

Design, Ken Faulkenberry,
typography, Conni McDonald,
Kaufmann Associates.

Library of Congress Cataloging in Publication Data

Martin, Harold H
  This happy isle

  Includes index.
  1. Sea Island, Ga. Cloister Hotel
I. Title
TX941.C48M37   647'.94758'7   78-14320

*To all those who for fifty years
have come here to find Howard Coffin's
"place of peace and play and freedom"
and to those who made them welcome,
this book is dedicated.*

"It may be we shall touch
the Happy Isles . . ."

Tennyson's "Ulysses"

"Here care ebbs out with every tide,
And peace comes in upon the flood;
The heart looks out on life clear-eyed,
And finds it good."

Carlyle McKinley,
Confederate soldier

Contents

PREFACE

Two hundred and sixty-one years ago, in 1717, Sir Robert Montgomery, a Scottish laird with a flair for real-estate promotions, distributed throughout London broadsides that would have filled a modern advertising man's heart with envy. He spoke of the great flat plain that is now coastal Georgia and of the islands that protect it from the sea. Here, he said, was "our future Eden . . . in the most delightful country of the universe." Here he hoped to establish a feudal fiefdom which he would call the Margravate of Azilia, with himself, of course, as the margrave, or chief lord. Nothing came of the venture—possibly because Sir Robert could only offer the Lords Proprietors a penny an acre, plus a fourth of whatever gold or silver might be found.

But in truth, Sir Robert's hyperbole was not too far-fetched. God indeed had created here, where the mainland meets the sea, a very special place, a second Eden. On the flow of mighty rivers, pushing in the wake of subsiding seas, He brought down rich earth from the hills, and over this dark silt He laid the sands from the sea. With wind and water He formed shapes and textures, and He called in the sun for warmth, and over all He wove a binding cover of oaks and palms and pines and waving grasses. Between the rivers, where they met the sea, lay the dunes and the broad white beaches. Toward the mainland stretched the green-gold plain of the tidal marshes. And everywhere there were creatures, bearing fur or fins or feathers or scaly hides.

Eons passed and men finally came. First the red tribesmen, hunting with tools of shell and bone, leaving behind huge mounds of oyster shells that mark their place of habitation. And after them the Irish, Norse, and Welsh seafarers came, leaving only a legend of their passing. And then came the Spaniards, carrying cross and sword and fruit trees and building missions that predated by two hundred years the first missions of Spain in California. With the Spaniards came the French, building no missions, founding no lasting colonies, but taking back to King Louis's court cargoes of sassafras, deer and beaver skins, and wild turkeys for the royal table, long before the Pilgrims ate turkey at their first Thanksgiving.

At last came the English: Oglethorpe, the settlers, and the soldiers who turned back the Spaniards at Bloody Marsh, making safe at last the colony of Georgia, until a third of a century later, when the colony would join her sisters in a rebellion for independence from the king. The end of the Revolution marked the beginning of a golden period that lasted nearly a hundred years — the era of the plantation worked by slaves, growing rice and sugar and, above all, Sea Island cotton, for lords of the land who prospered far more greatly than ever Sir Robert Montgomery could have dreamed.

But another rebellion ended that era, the revolt of the slave states against the free, and the freeing of the slaves ended forever the plantation system. Then the loggers came, felling the great trees and floating them down the rivers to vast mills on Saint Simons. After a few years the sawmills too were gone, and the land went back to nature again, lying wild and tangled under the sky, the old fields grown up, the great houses fallen in ruins, the marshes lonely, the beaches empty. And for generation after generation, the land stayed that way, untouched and unproductive. Men of greater wealth than the old planters ever knew came in and quietly bought up the old islands, but they used them only as hunting preserves, or as an occasional refuge from the cares of a troubling world.

Then at last came two men with a different dream and a different goal. Howard Earle Coffin and his young cousin Alfred William (Bill) Jones were to make of one of these islands a very special place. Seven main islands face the sea in a golden chain that lies along the Georgia coast, but to nearly every Georgian, and to thousands of other Americans, there is only one Sea Island. To them it is "th'island," as if there were no other. And indeed it does have an ambience all its own, a shining peace. Sea Island is a place the benison of sun and sand and sea and sky, all the less combative sports, and the friendship of like-minded folk may be enjoyed in surroundings of understated elegance. The island is still as Jones and Coffin visualized it half a hundred years ago—a place where natural beauty and manmade comforts blend to cast a gentle, gracious, happy spell upon the spirits of young and old alike. Fifty years is only a tick of the clock as historians measure time, but in that brief space, Howard Coffin, until his tragic death in 1937, and Bill Jones in the four decades thereafter, were able to turn a lonely wilderness into one of the fabled hotel and cottage colonies of the world—a Shangri-la not only for quiet gentlefolk and their young, but for queens and princes, poets and playwrights, and presidents of the United States from Calvin Coolidge to Jimmy Carter.

The story of how Sea Island became the memorable place that it is today is more than the story of Howard Coffin and Bill and Kit Talbott Jones, and their concept of what a year-round resort ought to be. It is also the story of their efforts to preserve the entire Georgia coast for the highest and best use for all the people, for those who work as well as for those who play. It is the story, too, of the men who helped them on the management level over the years; of T. Miesse Baumgardner, the landscape architect; Jim Compton, the money manager; Irv Harned, the innkeeper; Dick Everett, the historian. And equally important, it is the story of the chefs and bellmen, the waitresses, housekeepers, and maîtres d'hôtel, now going into their third generation, who have given Sea Island and the Cloister Hotel a special aura of friendliness, an atmosphere of "ladies and gentlemen being waited on by ladies and gentlemen." It is the story, too, of a new generation of Joneses, Bill Jr., and Howard, and of their own stout helpers, Dewey Benefield, Dennie McCrary, and Ted Wright, all of whom are determined that the Sea Island of the future will have the same strong appeal to a new generation of Americans that it had to the families of years gone by.

In the main, it is a story of high courage and of high hope fulfilled; at times, too, it is a litany of tragedy and deep sorrow. Perhaps the best place to start this story would be on that October evening in 1928 when Howard Coffin's "friendly little hotel," the Cloister, first opened its doors to a throng of welcome but somewhat startling guests.

This Happy Isle

1

HOW IT ALL BEGAN

In the office of Dewey Benefield, vice president and secretary of the Sea Island Company, hangs a yellowed parchment, delicately illuminated like a medieval manuscript. On it is a coat of arms showing a castle, a leaping fish, and a running deer, and around the border are drawings of flying ducks and Spanish dancers, a golfer at the top of his swing, and a blonde in a bathing suit, poised like a sea gull on a piling. And in a script Olde Englyshe, in both calligraphy and content, it bears the following message.

YE FIRSTE PAGE IN YE HISTORY OF
YE CLOISTER
1928
On ye night of October, it being ye day twelve—in ye darke of ye moone, at Brunswick Towne was gathered ye sages, ye roisterers and their ladyes faire in assembly—Up spake ye leader, "Tomorrow morne across ye Bloody Marsh shall Ye Cloister ope its doors for ye Public—but we townsmen of Brunswick Towne shall this nighte cross ye marsh again and be ye first to make ye Welkin ring in Ye Cloister Hall"— Ye trek was made across ye marsh and ye assembly gathered

by ye Cloister Door — And darke was ye place. Not a torche
nor a sound.

"What want ye now?" demanded ye Night Watch.

"We want to make ye Welkin ring in yon Cloister Hall" ye
populace cried — and ye leaders advanced and clamored
for ye doors to ope. Ye torche flared. Ye music plaide. Mine
Host Roy Baker appeared and bid ye populace "Caede
Mille Hailthe" — Thus ye Brunswick townsmen and their
ladyes faire laid siege and captured ye Cloister opening for
their very, very own. Testified by ye following present —

More than ninety names were on the list that followed, and
though few of them are still around today, those who are remember
that even though the blight of prohibition was still upon the land,
the welkin did indeed ring that night in Ye Cloister Hall. The
hotel's first manager, Roy Baker, a rotund man, jovial of manner,
opened the door to his guests. Pretending to be surprised, he was
dressed as if for bed, in a nightshirt, a nightcap with a tassel, and
carrying a candle. The official opening, a far more formal affair,
took place two weeks later, on October 27, with more than 400
guests present, all in evening dress. They came from everywhere
in Georgia, with a scattering from Florida and the North, to see
what miracles Mr. Coffin had wrought on the one-time goat
pasture that was first called Fifth Creek by the Indians, then Long
Island, then Glynn Isle, and now Sea Island. This affair was no
quick serve-yourself buffet, but a sit-down dinner of eleven
courses, served with the deft friendliness that later was to become
traditional at the Cloister. An orchestra imported from New York
played background music for vocalists, dancers, and monologists,
and for the ladies there were favors — bronze replicas of the
monastery windows of the hotel's Spanish Lounge. After dinner
the assembly strolled past newly planted palms and oaks to the
Beach Casino, where they danced until 2:00 a.m.

A few weeks later, in November, there was another "opening,"
this one for Mr. Coffin's banker and businessmen friends from

the North, and for a notable array of journalists and columnists. But to the citizens of Brunswick, who themselves had sunk some $50,000 into the new hotel, these events were an anticlimax. To them the Cloister's true opening was the first one, that night of October 12 when they came rumbling across the causeway in their shining boxlike automobiles, horns squonking joyously, car lights gleaming on the green-gold marsh grasses, to rouse the nightgowned manager and make the welkin ring.

Howard Coffin's name is not on the parchment among those to whom Roy Baker on that night bestowed the old Gaelic blessing of "a thousand healths." Although friendly enough, he was a private man, not given to attending purely social events; he was probably on his yacht, or at his "big house" on nearby Sapelo, or he might well have been ill, for he was having desperate trouble with his teeth. But bold among the signatures is that of Alfred W. Jones. Though but little beyond his twenty-sixth birthday, Jones was a man whose vision was as broad as Coffin's, but Jones had a keen awareness of the value of human relationships, of friendship bestowed and welcomed. Coffin was the founding father, the dreamer who could see the high peaks shining in the sunlight far away. Jones was the man who knew how to negotiate the dark valleys that lay between.

The story of the Cloister and the Sea Island Company, and of Jones's and Coffin's joint labors there, really begins in another time and place—in West Milton, Ohio, a little Quaker colony near Dayton. There, Howard Coffin was born in 1873 on a farm bought in 1804 by Jones's great-grandfather. They were cousins, Coffin's mother being Bill Jones's father's oldest sister, though the Coffin-Jones bloodlines had crossed five times before in the 240 years since their Quaker ancestors had arrived in Nantucket. Coffin's father died when he was six weeks old, and he was raised by his Jones relatives—his widowed mother, a bachelor uncle, a widowed aunt, and a spinster aunt—the only child in a severely strict Quaker household. Happily, they did nothing to restrict his genius as an engineer. When he was a small boy he showed remarkable dexterity at fixing a broken piece of farm equipment. Recognizing that his talent for mechanics could carry him far if properly developed, his mother left the farm and enrolled him first in high school in Ann Arbor, Michigan, and then in the engineering department at the University of Michigan. To finance his tuition, she ran a student boardinghouse. Equally convinced of the youngster's talent, Rufus Jones, Bill Jones's father, helped generously with his support, and Coffin himself got a job as a mail carrier, while continuing school on a part-time basis. During this period, he built in his home workshop a one-cylinder steam-driven automobile, which he used to carry him on his rounds, and a two-cycle gasoline engine. In 1902, the year his young cousin Bill Jones was born in Dayton, where his father was prospering in the banking business, Coffin left the university and went with the Olds Motor Works, Incorporated, of Detroit – a young company convinced, like Coffin, that the future of the motorcar lay in the mass-produced low-priced machine.

Here began the fabled career as an automotive engineer that was to make Coffin one of the most famous automobile builders and one of the wealthy Americans of his day. When Olds finally abandoned the idea of making an inexpensive car, he, with his friend Roy Chapin, a financial wizard, and Fred Bezner, a purchasing agent of great skill, set out to find financial backing with which they could build a car of their own. They found their angel in the E.R. Thomas Motor Company of Buffalo, New York, and the car Coffin built for the Thomas-Detroit Company became an instant success. Flushed with this triumph, in 1907 he married his university sweetheart, Matilda Vary Allen, and their union lasted in deepest love and happiness until her death at Sea Island in 1932.

The first decade of the new century was a time of fluxion in the automobile business, of mergers, spin-offs, of new companies forming almost daily. Coffin, with his great skill as an engineer, was at the center of this activity. In 1908 Hugh Chalmers, a former vice-president of the National Cash Register Company, bought half of E.R. Thomas's interest, and the company name was changed to Chalmers-Detroit, with Coffin owning a third of the stock. It was about this time that R.B. Jackson, an engineer, whose wife was a niece of J.L. Hudson, head of Detroit's leading department store, came to Coffin with the happy word that Hudson would be glad to put up money to build an automobile that could be sold to the average man on the street — the customers of his department store. This fitted in exactly with Coffin's long-held dream of a car that would sell for less than $1,000.

Thus, there came into being the Hudson car, brainchild of Howard Coffin, and the Hudson Motor Company was born. Coffin, Chapin, and Bezner sold Chalmers their shares in Chalmers-Detroit; he sold them his interest in the Hudson Motor Company. With Chapin as president, Coffin as chief engineer, and Bezner handling sales and marketing, the company boomed. The first car to bear the Hudson name was a four-cylinder roadster selling for $900, Coffin's "Model 20," designed with a special easy-moving, sliding gear transmission. He went on to design the Hudson Super-Six and a jaunty small car called the Essex.

By the end of 1910 the Hudson Motor Company was worth $5 million, and Coffin had money to invest in other things — in business property in Detroit, residential property in the affluent Grosse Point section, and finally in a far-off Georgia island called Sapelo. And it was here on Sapelo, under the "gloom of the live oaks, beautiful braided and woven," that he first fell under the spell of the Georgia coastal country. Here he had truly found that happy place, the Sapelo a young Confederate soldier named Carlyle McKinley had remembered as his home and had immortalized in a poem that Coffin and his wife, Matilda, learned by heart and often quoted. One verse was particularly meaningful in his first years there:

Here care ebbs out with every tide,
And peace comes in upon the flood;
The heart looks out on life clear-eyed
And finds it good.

Perhaps some deep atavistic impulse brought Coffin to Georgia in the first place. His Quaker family, like that of Bill Jones's had come into this country from England in the 1600s, landing on Nantucket. From there they had drifted south to Pennsylvania, then to North Carolina. Shortly before the revolution they had moved again into the vicinity of Wrightsville, Georgia. From there, in 1804, they moved into Ohio to the Quaker community of West Milton in Miami County. Why they left the South is a matter for debate among historians. Bill Jones feels that it might have been because they opposed slavery, or possibly that they did not have the money to buy slaves. Perhaps it was because they had been sympathetic to the Tory cause during the war, while surrounded by hotheaded Patriot neighbors. At any rate, Coffin was to return to Georgia nearly a hundred years after his ancestors had gone.

Whatever his inner motivations might have been, it was his interest in the automobile that brought him back. In the early 1900s automobile manufacturers liked to test their latest models in bone-jarring races over winding dirt roads. These first were held on Long Island, New York, but racing there soon proved dangerous because of the excited crowds that lined the race course. By 1910 the most famous of the races, the Vanderbilt Cup Competition and the Grand Prix, had moved south, at the invitation of motor-minded citizens of Savannah, to a race course in Chatham County, where the Savannah Road Race soon became famous in its own right. Here Mr. Coffin came with Mrs. Coffin to watch his cars perform. These were vacation trips, in a way, leisurely journeys across the country by train.

His first trip into the South for the races in 1910 fascinated Coffin, and he felt a compulsion to explore the coastal area. By chance the black chauffeur who had been assigned to drive for Mr. and Mrs. Coffin while they were in the city had a brother who owned a fishing boat and fishing camp on Skidaway Island. At his suggestion the Coffins delayed their journey north for a weekend there of rest and fishing. From then on, Coffin was hooked. Georgia's dreamy coastline ever thereafter would be in his blood. Back for the races the following year, he heard from friends in Savannah—notably Mayor George Tiedeman and a young real estate broker named Wayne Cunningham—of a truly wondrous place.

It was an island to the south, unreachable by even the stoutest car, but only seventy miles along the inland waterway from Savannah. Its name was Sapelo, and its history fascinated him. In ages past it had been a hunting island for prehistoric Indians; the "Zapala" of the mission-minded Spaniards; a refuge for French aristocrats fleeing slave revolts in San Domingo and the guillotine in France; and finally, the great Sea Island cotton, rice, and sugar plantation of a remarkable man named Thomas Spalding. And now it was as it had been since the War Between the States, an empty wilderness, used only as a hunting preserve, whose five owners had vague ideas of turning it, like Jekyll Island, into a social enclave for multimillionaires.

Coffin, this year of 1911, had planned to stop at Pinehurst on his homeward journey, but word of foul weather in the Carolinas caused him to change his mind. He turned south to Sapelo instead, guided by Wayne Cunningham, and there he found the place that for two decades would be to him a refuge, a showplace, and a challenge. From the five families who owned it, he bought for less than $150,000 the 20,000 acres of marsh and highland that made up Sapelo. His purchase was to result, indirectly, in a happy North-South union. Mayor Tiedeman came down from Savannah with his family to visit Coffin. Roy Chapin was also a visitor there; he and the mayor's daughter, Inez, met, fell in love, and in time were married.

For a dozen years Coffin divided his time and his attention between his interests in the North and his hideaway on the Georgia coast. His fascination with the automobile and its engineering problems did not diminish, though he long since had turned over the details of manufacturing to others. As president of the Society of Automotive Engineers and author of the indispensable *Engineering Handbook,* he became known as the man who contributed most to the perfection and standard-ization of motor vehicle design. At his urging the industry agreed to a process of cross-licensing that permitted the pooling of patents for the common good of all.

Coffin's vision of what the future would demand, not only in automobiles but in airplanes and weapons of war, was of tremendous value to the country when war at last did come. In 1915 he was appointed by Secretary of the Navy Josephus Daniels to serve on the Naval Consulting Board under Chairman Thomas A. Edison, who named Coffin chairman of the board's Committee on Production, Organization, Manufacture and Standardization. He also was named chairman of the Committee on Industrial Preparedness by President Woodrow Wilson. In this post, he would carry out his own idea that an inventory be made of every manufacturing concern in the United States which did business of more than $100,000 a year. This inventory would determine which of these could manufacture munitions for the government. More than 30,000 companies were catalogued and classified by five engineering firms which Coffin persuaded to serve as he served, on a dollar-a-year basis. When something needed doing quickly, and no dollar-a-year man could be found, Coffin picked up the tab himself. His services were of such value that he was described by Secretary of War Newton D. Baker as being "a man who has done perhaps the greatest service that has been done for America by any private citizen in the last fifty years."

Coffin and Roy Chapin, in a large degree, were responsible for converting Army transport from the mule to the motortruck. When General Pershing was chasing Pancho Villa along the Mexican border, and his trucks kept breaking down, Coffin and Chapin went down to investigate the trouble. What they learned there about the maintenance of trucks in the field made possible the motorized army that went to France in World War I. While in Mexico, Coffin got word from President Wilson that he had been named a member of the Advisory Commission of the Council of National Defense, which was, in effect, Wilson's war cabinet. From then until the end of the war, neither Sapelo nor his home at Grosse Point saw much of him. With Mrs. Coffin, he moved into an apartment in Washington, where they lived for the duration, devoting all his energy, time, and thought to the war effort. His interest in aviation now was strong, and he was to a large degree responsible for the design of the highly effective Liberty engine, the first successful American-made motor for American-made planes.

Out of his experience with war planes grew his strong belief in the future of commercial aviation. After the war, he was sent to Europe as part of a mission to study aviation plans in effect or in prospect in England, France, Italy, and Germany. The mission's report outlined with prophetic vision the development of a worldwide system of air transportation. Coffin, for one, was quite willing to practice what he had prophesied. He became chairman of a committee to organize the National Air Transport which would operate nationwide, without government subsidy. Coffin's main job was to persuade his wealthy friends to buy stock in his $10 million enterprise, which was soon to become the biggest privately owned airline in the world. Coffin served for two years as president and chairman of the board of the company, which later was to become United Air Lines.

Although for a decade these national interests occupied the mind of Howard Coffin, he had by no means forgotten Sapelo, to which he always insisted on giving the old colonial spelling *Sapeloe.* (His yacht he called *Zapala,* the island's Indian name.) Each year, except in the busiest of the war years, he spent some time there, creating a comfortable vacation retreat on the foundations of the tabby concrete mansion built by Thomas Spalding more than a hundred years before.

Spalding for his time was as great a visionary, as great a seeker after better ways to do things, as was Coffin. He used sassafras rods to strengthen the mixture of lime, sand, and oystershell which was his building material — the first example, probably, of the use of reinforced concrete in America. In many ways, the interests of the two men were curiously parallel. Spalding advocated a transcontinental railroad, just as Coffin, generations later, was to sponsor an international airline. Spalding's interest in engineering was as keen as Coffin's. He harnessed the tide to provide power for grinding his sugarcane, established a remarkably effective system for drainage of the island's low places, and, most important of all, introduced the Sea Island cotton culture on which vast plantation fortunes would be built.

Just as Coffin was interested in organizing American industry to support the military, Spalding had used his plantation as a center of logistics, supplying the Navy and Merchant Marine with cattle, hogs, and live-oak timbers for the building of ships. He worked nearly a thousand slaves, many of them newly arrived from Africa. He sent them in small groups to the fields to scratch around cotton plants with a blunt stick, in imitation of a trained worker with a hoe, for a new slave could not be trusted with a sharp instrument until he had become adapted to plantation life. On the Spalding plantation, so the legend goes, life was remarkably gentle, so much so that humanitarians held it up as an example of how bondsmen should be treated. He was no absentee owner like his neighbor Pierce Butler, who left the management of his plantation to the harsh action of whip-cracking overseers, and even Fannie Kemble could have found little fault with him. In the War of 1812, he did one unheard of thing, which his neighbors considered highly dangerous. He armed 300 slaves with muskets, which was against Georgia law. They repaid his confidence by turning back a foray by a British gunboat. Other islands were laid waste, but after that, Sapelo was left in peace to grow and prosper for more than fifty years. Then came the Civil War, and Union forces destroyed all that Spalding had built. His tabby mansion was burned, leaving only the thick walls standing; dikes were destroyed, fields flooded, and the slaves freed and dispersed. It was the end of the great Scottish family of Spaldings on Sapelo. After the war some members came back to live briefly in the ruins of a wrecked sugar mill, where they were fed by their former slaves.

When Coffin arrived in 1912, only one of the Spalding bloodline remained on Sapelo. Sarah Spalding McKinley, granddaughter of Thomas Spalding, was postmistress there, and her husband, Major A.C. McKinley, was a Confederate veteran. Both died in 1913, and both in their great age remembered the days before the war when Sapelo was a lush productive land.

Howard Coffin, student of history as well as a visionary, knew this story. He was well aware of Spalding's achievements, and his inner voices told him that it was his destiny to make Sapelo bloom again, with the labor of free men, as Spalding had made it bloom during plantation days. To help him in that tremendous task, he turned to his young kinsman, his cousin Bill Jones, thirty years his junior, who over the years had become to the childless Coffins as cherished and as trusted as if he were their son.

2

FOR MAN AND ISLAND –
A NEW BEGINNING

In Sapelo's long history there had been one previous incident where a kinsman had hired a kinsman, and that arrangement had ended in tragedy. In the days just after our Revolutionary War, five families of Royalist Frenchmen had bought the war-wrecked island and had set up a communal ownership and cultivation of the land. One of them, Jean de Boisfeuillet, hired a nephew, Pouillain duBignon, to act as his agent in buying a plantation and managing his affairs. Boisfeuillet soon grew disenchanted with the way duBignon was handling things, and in a duel he shot and severely wounded the younger man. The commune broke up, and duBignon left to buy Jekyll Island, which remained in his family until 1886, when it was taken over by the Morgans, the Vanderbilts, and the Goulds for their island hideaway. Of the French families, only the Boisfeuillets and the duBignons remain in Georgia today. The others, including the Marquis de Montelet, who used to lead a pig on a leash over Sapelo, hunting for truffles, have all disappeared into the mists of history.

There was little likelihood that Bill Jones and Howard Coffin would come to such a parting of the ways as had their French predecessors. Though they were only cousins and there was nearly thirty years difference in their ages, they and their families had long known and respected each other. Jones's father, Rufus Jones, had helped young Coffin through college, an obligation Coffin did not forget in his relationship with young Bill Jones. To Jones, Coffin was not "Cousin" but "Uncle" Howard, and before too many years had passed, they were on a first name basis. There was a father and son element in their relationship, too. Jones was a sickly youngster, and once, when he was seven and going through a particularly puny spell, Mrs. Coffin, Sr., and his mother took him off to Saint Augustine, Florida, hoping the warm climate would restore his health.

The weakness persisted throughout his high school years, though he doggedly tried to overcome it. The year 1920, his last year in high school, was a turning point in Jones's life. Early that year, the illness that had occasionally plagued him was diagnosed as chronic appendicitis, but since he was in no pain at the moment, he went off to Ontario on a canoe trip with some friends. One night, lying in his tent, the thought occurred to him that if he should suffer an attack of appendicitis there in the deep woods, it would take a day and a half to get him back to a hospital in Toronto. That seemed to him a risky gamble. Quietly he packed his gear, climbed in a canoe, and made his way back to Dayton. He went, unannounced, to his father's office, told the startled gentlemen that he did not want to spend his life worrying about his appendix, and went immediately to the hospital and had it out.

While he was recuperating, a distinguished visitor came by to see him. Newspaper publisher James Cox, governor of Ohio during all of Jones's earliest days and Democratic nominee for the presidency, visited the hospital on the night that he received the nomination, pausing en route to a huge victory celebration. As the campaign drew near, Cox invited Jones to come along with his son, James Cox, Jr., who was young Jones's best friend, on his speaking campaign into the West. Both had traveled happily with the elder Cox on his gubernatorial campaign, but curiously young Cox did not make this trip. Being the son of a presidential candidate attracted attention from the press and from clamorous well-wishers, which embarrassed and annoyed him. He remained behind, while young Bill Jones traveled with the candidate on the campaign trail.

That year, too, marked Jones's first visit to Sapelo, a quick trip with his mother to visit the Coffins there. The next summer he went to Detroit for the summer, working for Howard Coffin in his office, not doing much of anything, and that fall he enrolled in the Wharton School of Business, at the University of Pennsylvania. The next year, 1922, he did the same thing. By now he was deeply involved in Detroit's high-flying social life. A handsome smiling twenty year old, a good dancer, good talker, and tireless so long as the music played, he was on every debutante hostess's list. Working all day, playing all night, he went back to the University of Pennsylvania for his junior year and collapsed. His trouble was now a matter of medical record. He had tuberculosis. He left school, planning to undergo the usual therapy of that time—a long rest in one of the sanatoriums in the dry hot climate of the West, and briefly he tried this. To Howard Coffin, though, there was no better place on earth to rest, relax, and recuperate than on his happy island off the Georgia coast. In the dead of winter, Jones left for Sapelo.

It was 1923 and he was twenty-one. Quickly the island began to work its magic. In the mornings he would get up early, walk the beaches, feel the warm sun, watch the great cloud galleons sailing by. In the afternoons, obeying doctors' orders, he would snooze, then rise to stroll the sand roads beneath the moss-bearded oaks. All around him things were happening, people were busy clearing the fields and horseback trails, planting pastures for beef and dairy herds, bridging creeks and digging artesian wells. Soon both his mind and his hands grew restless. He still took his afternoon naps, but in the hours between, he began to work at whatever needed to be done.

It was, indeed, a time when every pair of hands was welcome. Howard Coffin was just starting on the plans for construction of a great mansion at the south end, where Thomas Spalding's house had stood before the Yankees burned it. One tabby wall, with its oxeye windows still intact, formed a starting place for the new house. A guest house was built on the tabby foundation of what had been the ruins of Spalding's sugar mill, which itself had stood on the site of the original Spanish mission, San Francisco de Zapala, which gave the island its name. Coffin, an impatient man, would have no truck with architects or with building contractors. He could see in his mind's eye the house he wanted, and he entrusted its construction to a huge Swede named Arthur Wilson. Whatever Coffin wanted, Wilson would build, tear out, and build again at Coffin's whims. In three years the great house was finished, including a south wing, which young Bill Jones was to make his bachelor quarters. Although more than fifty years have passed, and the State of Georgia now owns Sapelo, "the big house" is still a place of marvelous beauty and comfort. A winding drive of pines and moss-hung oaks leads from the deep-water dock toward the tall white pillars of the mansion's Georgian facade, which faces the sea. A fountain plays in the center of a huge tree-shaded swimming pool in which the fluted columns are reflected. Broad green lawns, sun dappled, lead to a formal garden reminiscent of the Hermitage at Leningrad. Marble statues of nymphs and naiads of amazing beauty peer from leafy bowers and admire their images in reflecting pools. Huge greenhouses serve the gardens with new plants and fresh cut flowers for the house.

Inside, the life of the house centered around the high-ceilinged living room, heavily beamed in the Spanish manner, where Coffin loved to entertain with a lavish hand as did his predecessor, Thomas Spalding. Off this room, with its massive stone fireplace, lay the indoor swimming pool, where Coffin would take his morning cold-water plunge; the dining room with its huge refectory table, reminiscent of a Spanish monastery; a billiard room; and a library. Over the mantel in the living room stretched a Spanish map, drawn in 1720, which showed Zapala and the adjacent islands with the depths of their waters, and some insulting comments by the Spanish cartographers about the habits of the English usurpers who prowled these coasts. In the library was a letter that Coffin liked to show to visitors. It was from Benjamin Franklin to a Coffin kinsman, telling him that Franklin was sending him some candlesticks and candlesnuffers as tokens of his esteem. Off the living room were two master bedrooms, and upstairs was a huge ballroom, which also could be used as a movie theater. Downstairs, in a vast stone-floored rough-beamed basement, was one of Howard Coffin's favorite rooms, designed like a ship's cabin. Here was a huge brick fireplace with ovens beside it, and around it hung ancient weapons and navigation instruments, charts, flintlock muskets, swords, a sextant, a compass, ship models, and the wheel of some long-forgotten ship. Rum bottles reminiscent of pirate days lay about, and the chairs and hearthside stools were fashioned of old ship's water kegs padded for comfort.

Bill Jones lived in his austere bachelor quarters in the south wing, but he would often come to this lounge to listen while Coffin sat by the fire and talked of his dream of bringing back to Sapelo the glories of its ancient past. His ambition was to make of the island a self-sufficient place, where he and those around him might live in peace and comfort no matter what happened in the world outside. And Bill Jones, sharing this dream, soon found himself deep in labors for which no special training had prepared him, except an inborn capacity for doing things right, for building things and making them work, and for persuading others willingly to share his own ideas. Perhaps his most striking attribute though was his ability to keep an eye on the small but highly important details that Coffin, with his head in the clouds, was inclined to overlook.

It was, as Jones remembers now, truly a time of wine and roses, these few years before the crash. Everybody was rich, and enjoying their riches. Coffin, from his investments in automobile stocks, airplane stock, and Detroit real estate, had an income of roughly $800,000 a year. He had some 200 people working for him on Sapelo, and he was spending a quarter of a million dollars a year there. Jones soon found himself becoming more and more deeply involved with the management of the plantation. The island needed roads, and he laid out new ones and bossed their construction, curving them around the fine old trees, which he was careful to preserve. Coffin, an aviation buff, wanted a place where planes could land. There was no airfield as such, but Jones cleared the plantation fields that had grown up in brush, so that they might serve both as pasture and as landing place. On one of these, Charles Lindbergh, en route to Mexico after his famed Paris flight, safely put down after the cows had been chased off. It was a memorable visit for Sapelo, and a memorable trip for Lindbergh, for in Mexico City he met the ambassador's daughter, Anne Morrow, whom he later was to marry.

When Jones came down to Sapelo, he found another young man already there, doing his best to juggle a multitude of jobs. When Coffin decided to restore the island's old drainage system, he tested a new ditching technique developed by Du Pont. They sent in a Georgian named Walter B. Alford, a noted ditch blaster, to supervise the job, and he brought with him a young explosives expert named Paul Varner. In a few hours they had cleared with dynamite the old silted-up drainage ditches that had been dug by

Thomas Spalding's slaves. Young, eager, and ambitious, Varner did this job so promptly and thoroughly that Coffin, much impressed, hired him. First he did a little of everything, then, when Coffin decided to start a shrimp and oyster cannery on the island to give work to the women there, and later when he bought another cannery near Darien on the mainland, Varner was put in charge of the operations. Varner went on from there to become Coffin's principal land buyer, a job he finally left after a disagreement over his handling of company funds. He went on then to law school, and later became the local lawyer for Richard J. Reynolds.

Jones, from the beginning, took on any job that Coffin handed him, learning by doing as he went along, knowing that Coffin, his mind on higher things, would not berate him if he failed. He had no title, but he did have authority. To the Sapelo hands, most of them descendants of the Spalding slaves, Mr. Coffin was "Boss." And since Mr. Jones lived at the big house with the Boss, he, naturally, in the slurred Gullah speech became "Lil' Boss."

Whatever Jones needed in the way of workmen, materials, or money, all he had to do was ask. When the bills came in, he would sit down and dash off a note to Lena Carle, secretary-treasurer, and Charles Wright, prominent attorney and a director of Coffin's Realty Investment Company in Detroit, from which, in that booming time, all blessings flowed. Whatever Jones might ask for — $10,000, $20,000, $50,000 — back a check would come, no questions asked.

Coffin's bland disregard for the cost of things applied to Jones's own finances. It did not occur to Coffin that Jones might have needed any money for himself, and for quite a while after he came to Sapelo, he was on nobody's payroll. Coffin did provide, indirectly, for Jones's needs. In the early 1920s, Coffin had given Rufus Jones, Bill's father, some Hudson Motor Company stock, which he later exchanged for 6 percent notes of Coffin's Realty Investment Company. In return for this gift, Rufus Jones was to take on the responsibility of the West Milton farm and the support of Coffin's two old aunts and the bachelor uncle who had helped raise him and who were still living there. By 1927 both Howard Coffin and Rufus Jones felt that this task could safely be passed on to the next generation, so $300,000 in Realty Investment Company notes were transferred to Bill Jones. Using these resources, young Jones continued to look after the farm and the old people, until the last aunt died in 1942 and the farm was sold. Meanwhile, during his Sapelo years, he used whatever was not needed at West Milton to live on, financing an occasional trip to Detroit and Dayton to dance at a wedding or attend a debut party. This gift from his father also played an important part in saving Sea Island Company from disaster during the depression.

Jones, as time went on, found himself with almost the entire responsibility of running Sapelo. He had under his charge twenty-seven boats and barges, each of which had a maddening tendency to break down. Among them were Coffin's 124-foot power yacht, the *Zapala*, with a crew of seven, and several shrimpboats and speedboats. Jones had never milked a cow in his life, and he knew nothing of raising beef, but he had general supervision over a dairy herd of Guernseys, which Coffin had bought from a doctor in Sandersville, and a huge herd of purebred Aberdeen Angus. The dairy herd gave more milk than there was a market for on the mainland, so the milk was given away to the workers on the island. (Jones's Ohio aunts did not trust his prowess as a dairyman. Once, when they came down for a visit, they brought their own crocks of butter from the Joneses' farm in Ohio.)

Jones was also responsible for running a machine shop, a marine railway, a carpenter shop, and for keeping happy and busy and honest all the people who worked in them, from the laborers who lived at Hog Hammock on the island, to the white supervisors, most of whom lived ashore and went home on weekends.

He made an occasional mistake, of course, and one that he

recalls was a beauty, a political gaffe that caused both him and Coffin deep embarrassment. Howard Coffin was profoundly interested in ecology, even in that day, and he had the idea that some place should be set aside where deer and game birds could be raised and shipped out for stocking other areas in Georgia. In line with this thought, he had persuaded the State of Georgia to transfer isolated Blackbeard Island to the federal government so that it might be put off limits to all hunters as an area for biological research. This was done, and Coffin took over, at his own expense, as caretaker for the island, putting guards ashore there to protect the game from poachers. In the ten years he served as caretaker, he spent some $20,000 on Blackbeard, but it was worth it, for by doing so he also was protecting Sapelo's game and oyster beds from poachers sneaking across the narrow waterway from Blackbeard and from the tick-infested cattle that still roamed there, a danger to Sapelo's own herds.

Liaison between government departments was no better then than now, and in the fall of 1924 a couple of south Georgia congressmen got a permit from the Navy Department to take a party of Georgia and Washington VIPs there on a two-day deer hunt. The Navy had had no authority on Blackbeard since the 1850s when ship's timbers were cut there. The island had then gone under Treasury Department jurisdiction, serving as a yellow fever quarantine station, which had long since been abandoned. Coffin was away from Sapelo at the time, and Jones, feeling responsible for protecting his boss's status as caretaker, pointed out to the hunters that hunting on Blackbeard was prohibited. They were, he told them, welcome to hunt on Sapelo, where the deer were equally plentiful, but they refused. Jones then called on the sheriff of McIntosh County to stop the hunt, but the hunters ignored him, knowing that a Georgia sheriff had no authority on federal land. They continued the hunt, killing a number of deer and wounding several others on their two day foray. The whole thing ended in a great row. The congressmen were embarrassed and wrote an angry letter to Coffin, complaining about Jones's action. Coffin wrote an apologetic letter in reply. The upshot was that Coffin resigned his role as caretaker until Blackbeard could be conveyed from the Treasury Department to the Agricultural Department, which immediately set up a program under the Bureau of Biological Survey, with Coffin again named to guard and protect the property.

Jones, looking back on it now, saw his action as a young man's error, a situation that he probably would have handled differently later on. At no time, though, did Coffin criticize Jones for what he had done, nor did he comment on all the trouble it had caused him. This did not mean that Coffin was not interested in what Jones was doing or in what was happening at Sapelo. He still kept his office in Detroit and spent a great deal of time there, but he would come down to Sapelo periodically, arriving unexpectedly, to look into every detail of what Jones and the house builder, Arthur Wilson, had done during his absence. Frequently, particularly in dealing with the house, he would order what had been built torn down and done over again. As a result, the house was built and rebuilt about three times, Jones recalls, before Coffin was finally satisfied. The gigantic fluted columns were a particular problem. They were designed by Coffin, but Jones had the responsibility of getting them built and moved to the island safely.

Scribbling on the back of an envelope, Coffin would lay out a work schedule for the next two or three months, and Jones and Wilson would have to take it from there. Jones's job was to purchase the materials, to have them transported to the island, and to coordinate the work schedule so that the workers would not spend their days standing around and with nothing to work with. He spent half of his time, he remembers, trying to keep the work boats, the tugs and barges, in running shape, and to this day he has no great confidence in marine engines. Nor has he ever had any desire to own a yacht. Coffin's feelings toward boats were exactly the opposite. The big house on Sapelo was a place of beauty and luxury, but Coffin was equally happy when he boarded the yacht *Zapala*. He loved boats and liked the company of boatmen, and he built a house on Sapelo for the yacht's captain and for the chief engineer.

By the mid-1920s most of Coffin's plans for Sapelo had been realized. The old fields had been restored to productivity, roads wound their way from the south end dock to the ancient shell mound at the north, a circle 12 feet high and 300 feet across, laid down by some prehistoric people 2,000 years ago. Coffin's experiments in oyster growing supported an oyster cannery, which gave employment to the island women. (Bill Jones could never understand why the black oyster shuckers and shrimp peelers would take off their aprons and go next door to the commissary to buy a ten-cent can of Portuguese sardines for lunch.) Coffin financed, for the Department of the Interior, search expeditions to Central and South America seeking game birds that might thrive in Georgia. In Guatemala the researchers discovered the chachalaca, whose descendants fly over Sapelo today. Thus he carried out, on Sapelo and Little Sapelo, the idea he had urged the federal government to put into effect on Blackbeard — the establishment of a breeding ground where deer and birds could be raised for stocking elsewhere. Coffin hired an English kennel master and gamekeeper to supervise the breeding on Little Sapelo of ringnecked pheasants and wild turkey, and to train the Llewellen setters, whose field-trial prize ribbons soon made a colorful display in Coffin's basement lounge.

Coffin, Jones remembers, worked as earnestly to prepare Sapelo for whatever emergency might arise as he had worked a decade earlier to help his country prepare for war. He developed on the island a scientific truck garden in which more than a dozen varieties of vegetables thrived. He grew asparagus, raised ducks on a pond, kept a pen of more than a thousand diamondback terrapins, and raised chickens by the hundreds. All these, along with his dairy cows and beef herds, combined with the wild game and the fish available in the still unpolluted waters to make Sapelo almost completely self-sufficient so far as food was concerned. In fact, to demonstrate how successfully Coffin had carried out his plans to feed his people no matter what might transpire, Jones once asked the cook to serve a different meal of meat or fish every day for as long as possible. They started off with such prosaic entrees as ham and chicken, beef and turkey, and went on to exotic viands that ranged from peacock to possum, and included guinea hen, venison, and terrapin stew. The demonstration lasted for forty days without repeating a dish.

3

DEAD TOWNS LIVE AGAIN

Men's memories are fickle, and over a span of years the order in which great events took place and the role that individuals played in them are likely to become somewhat hazy and confused. But one thing stands out clearly in Bill Jones's mind. In 1923, when he first came to Sapelo to stay, and in the years immediately thereafter, events born of the automobile were beginning to move and stir along the Georgia coast. In Brunswick a group of citizens led by Frank Twitty, Commissioner R.L. (Tige) Phillips, Alf Townsend, Malcolm McKinnon and E.L. Stephens, backed strongly by engineers W.T. McCormick and Fernando J. Torras, was urging the county to build a causeway across the marshes to Saint Simons, the one big island not yet owned in its entirety by rich visitors from afar, and thus the only one to which the public still had access. The same group was backing the Brunswick Young Men's Club in an even bolder enterprise. The Georgia Coast and Piedmont Railroad, a rickety shortline running from Jacksonville through Brunswick and Darien to the clay pits and potteries at Ludowici, had finally gone bankrupt. Its assets had been sold, and a Chicago salvage firm was planning to sell for scrap the steel bridges over which the rails crossed the winding creeks and rivers of the Altamaha delta. To the young men of Brunswick, this was unthinkable, for this would leave their already remote community with no access to Darien except by water, or along the most roundabout and tortuous of sandy trails. Their plan was simple enough. They would buy the bridges from the salvage company, leave them in place, and persuade county, state, or federal governments to put up the money to pave an automobile highway along the old railroad right-of-way. Thus, Brunswick would be joined, first by shell and gravel, then by asphalt, with the much-talked-about and yearned-for Atlantic Coastal Highway, U.S. 17, which was pushing south in increments from New York to Florida.

To Howard Coffin, the message was clear. The future prosperity of America was dependent upon the web of paved highways that was being created to serve the now ubiquitous automobile. If a man who had some money wanted to increase his fortune manyfold, all he had to do was buy land at strategic spots along the prospective route of a new highway. If he wanted to be doubly sure of making a successful investment, he should buy along the right-of-way of a road leading into a recreation area. For it was the nature of the American to use his automobile not only as workaday transportation, bearing him from home to job, but as a means of escape, a magic chariot carrying him to far-off places he had never seen, to lakes and mountains and the ocean shore.

Often, sitting in boots and breeches before a log fire in his house at Sapelo, popping popcorn and cracking pecans after a day in the hunting field, Howard Coffin would talk about these things with young Bill Jones and whatever wealthy visitors from the North might be his guests that night. And in all honesty, for all his innate compulsion to use his money and his talent to serve his fellowman, so far as Georgia beyond Sapelo was concerned,

Coffin at first had no higher purpose than to make a profit. He would buy some acreage and let it sit until it increased in value.

And that was all he had in mind, one morning in May 1923, when he and his friend Eugene Lewis, Detroit automobile axle manufacturer turned banker, set off for Brunswick by boat to take a look at the lay of the land. What they found there was distressing. In a memo prepared twenty-five years later at the request of Bill Jones, Lewis remembered that day. It was hard to find a dock along all that once prosperous Brunswick waterfront that was safe enough to walk on, he recalled. Buildings and docks were all run-down, falling in, or rotting away, and many stores along the main streets were boarded up. It had taken them two and a half hours to make their way along the winding water from Sapelo to Brunswick. From there they traveled another hour back to Saint Simons, linked now with the mainland only by two trudging ferries, the *Emmeline* and the *Hessie*. The ferries were owned by Brunswick bankers who had stoutly but unsuccessfully opposed a bond issue to build the narrow undulating causeway that on July 11, 1924 would bring a joyous motorcade across the marshes from Brunswick in a travel time of fifteen minutes.

But that happy event was still a year away, and Lewis in later years frankly admitted that what he saw on his first visit left him vastly discouraged. He said so to Howard Coffin. But Coffin was not seeing what lay around him—the vast expanse of empty marsh, the almost roadless island of Saint Simons, which was a boarded-up summer resort nine months of the year, and the goat and hog pasture called Long Island, whose fabulous white sand beach was visited only by hunters of turtle eggs. He was seeing what these places could become once the highway had reached this far south and the causeway had been completed. And out of what he was seeing in his mind's eye came the reality of Sea Island, the Cloister, the cottage colony, and all that has taken place on Sea Island since. And much, too, that has happened on Saint Simons over the years, and much that has happened all along the Georgia coast, both in the development of year-round recreation and in industry. For Coffin's confidence and his money triggered an economic renaissance that extended far up and down the Georgia coast, and the effect of it was felt not only in Brunswick, with its crumbling docks and boarded-up stores, but in the sleepy port of Savannah, the dead town of Sunbury, and the almost dead towns of Midway, Saint Marys, and Darien.

In the relatively brief time that elapsed between Coffin's first thoughts of speculating in coastal Georgia land and his first purchase in McIntosh County in 1924, he spent almost as much time studying the colorful history of the lands he wanted to buy as he did in planning their best and highest use. In so doing he brought into being a new concept of the role a rich man could play in an economically backward region. He became not the grand seigneur, shutting himself off in a social enclave or hunting preserve, as did the lairds of Ossabaw, Cumberland and Jekyll—as indeed he himself had reigned at Sapelo. He became, instead, one in spirit with the Georgians of the coast's great days—with the Spaldings, the Goulds, the Hamiltons, the Coupers, the Pages, the Kings—who made their great plantations there before the Civil War. He began speaking with the voice of a Georgian, selling the virtues of his adopted state to the nation and to the world.

Actually, his first purchase beyond the bounds of Sapelo had been not a land speculation at all, but an effort to revive a failing oyster industry. To the little cannery he had started on Sapelo to give work to the black women there, he added another near Darien in McIntosh County. To support this operation, he bought all the oyster-producing marshland lying between Sapelo and Little Saint Simons, 35,000 acres in all, including Egg and Wolf islands. There he began a program of scientific oyster farming, breaking up overcrowded beds where the oysters grew too small to harvest and planting seed oysters in new areas at carefully chosen water depths. This operation was highly successful, so far as growing oysters was concerned. It takes about four years, from "spat", or seed oysters to harvest oysters, but by the end of the third year the promised harvest was so heavy that it attracted the attention of every oyster poacher on the coast. Short of standing guard with a shotgun over the thousands of acres of tidal marsh, Coffin had no way of protecting his oyster farms. After a few years, he gave up the project.

Despite this unhappy experience, Coffin's first purchase in anticipation of the coming of the highway was also in McIntosh County. There, Paul Varner, a shrewd man at sniffing out land deals, bought for Coffin some 700 acres of woods and farmland chosen more or less at random. He also bought two islands on the Altamaha, Black Island and Hird Island.

It was not until 1926, however, that Coffin's land-buying campaign moved from the mainland to Saint Simons and got fully underway. In May of that year, he bought from the Aiken family and other descendants of the colonial owners, the great plantation called Kings Retreat, lying at the southwestern tip of the island where the Sea Island Golf Club stands today. In June followed the Suttles purchase, which included Gascoigne Bluff, the present location of the Sea Island Yacht Club. Both areas were rich in history. In the waters of the Frederica River where pleasure yachts now are docked, French ships lay at anchor 300 years ago, defying the Spaniards as they traded with the Indians for turkeys and sassafras. After the revolution the timbers for *Old Ironsides* were shipped from Gascoigne Bluff, and long thereafter the sawmills there cut the timbers for the Brooklyn Bridge.

The name of Gascoigne goes deep into Georgia history. There, Captain James Gascoigne, Oglethorpe's naval commander, kept headquarters for Georgia's first and only naval force. Spain, of course, could not let such defiance go unchallenged. In 1742 the Spanish governor of Saint Augustine sent a fleet of 51 ships and 5,000 men under orders to land and destroy the place and to move on to Frederica, "devastating, laying waste, sacking and burning." There was not much between Gascoigne Bluff and Frederica to sack, burn, and lay waste; there were, though, the spearlike plant called Spanish bayonet, and the pulpy, spiny prickly pear, which made miserable the lives of the thinly clothed and ill-shod Spanish soldiers. Their road led not to Frederica, though, but into an ambush laid by Oglethorpe's Scottish Highlanders from Darien, a little skirmish that became known to history as the Battle of Bloody Marsh. On July 7, 1742, it ended forever Spanish rule in the "debatable land."

Less than two decades after this, James Spalding, father of Thomas, of Sapelo fame, received a grant from the crown to the land that came to be known as Retreat Plantation. The land was owned next by a South Carolinian, Major William Page, who built it into one of the great Sea Island cotton plantations. Major Page passed it on to his daughter, Anna Matilda, when she married a Massachusetts lawyer, Thomas Butler King. King gave up the law as soon as his wife inherited the plantation, but his interest in farming was secondary to his interest in politics and the public weal. He, like his wife's father before him, traveled widely, and she, though gently bred and schooled in all the eye-fluttering social graces, took over the running of the plantation. She developed a method of selecting the seed and cultivating the long-staple fiber that caused her Retreat cotton to bring fifty cents a pound on the world market when the going price was forty-two cents.

Of particular interest to Howard Coffin was the fact that she also created at Retreat one of America's first great arboretums. Ships from many nations called at Retreat to load cotton, and she asked their captains to bring her rare plants from all over the world. They did, and so did her globetrotting husband, who served as a special envoy of the United States to Europe in the interest of trade. He was collector for the Port of San Francisco in 1850, and from 1861 to 1863 he was commissioner of the Southern

States to Europe, seeking to persuade the European governments to recognize the Confederacy.

Neither King nor his wife, Anna Matilda, lived to see the end of that war, which destroyed Retreat and all the plantations in the South. Anna Matilda died in 1859, not long after the death of their eldest son, Butler. Her death, and that of another son, Lord, killed at Fredericksburg, whose body was brought home by a slave servant for burial in Christ Church yard, caused Thomas Butler King's life to fall apart. Penniless and despairing, he died in 1864 and was buried beside his wife and their sons in the little cemetery at Christ Church. Nearby are the graves of Howard Coffin, who in his time, too, was to know anguish and despair, and of his wife, who was also named Matilda. It was not the custom in the 1930s as it was in the 1860s to sum up the virtues of the departed in an inscription on their gravestones. But a line from the carved tribute to Thomas Butler King—that he was a "man who lived faithfully for the public good"—could also apply to Howard Coffin. And of Matilda Allen Coffin, it could also be said, as it was said of Anna Matilda King, that she was "a woman lovely and gracious, upright, tender and true."

The day and the hour can be fairly well pinpointed when Howard Coffin finally realized that it was his destiny to look upon his Georgia holdings not as a quick-buck speculation but as a life's endeavor to serve the public good. In July 1928 he wrote to Governor L.G. Hardman: "My Dear Governor: For nearly 17 years I have maintained a home on the coast of Georgia and both my family and myself have come to love it in all seasons of the year in preference to any other part of the world. It has long been my desire to create here in this territory a distinctive year round sea island home colony where discriminating people regardless of means may enjoy all the advantages of this delightful island. For two years now, I have been quietly working toward this end."

This "quiet work" had indeed begun just two years before, shortly after the purchase of Retreat Plantation. Urged on by his friend Eugene Lewis, an avid though somewhat inept golfer (Coffin was no golfer at all—he thought the game was a waste of time), he turned over to Lewis the task of supervising the construction of a golf course where slaves once planted, plowed, and picked Sea Island cotton. In the fall of 1926, the most eminent golf course architect of the day, Open champion Walter Travis, came over from Jekyll to lay out the first nine holes, to be known as the Plantation Nine. Work began on the second nine on January 11, 1927, when a huge $250,000 dredge, the *Blue Heron* (bought for $55,000 from a bankrupt Florida developer) began pumping and filling on the course to be known as Seaside. Though the weather was raw and cold, the day was one of celebration. Prominent citizens from all over Georgia, including Governor Clifford Walker, came across from Brunswick on the *Emmeline* to drop anchor alongside the *Blue Heron.* Bands played, a quartet sang, and there would have been toasts drunk if the local prohibition officer had not been among the guests. At 3:00 p.m. all the people on the *Emmeline* went aboard the dredge, and as Brunswick's whistles blew and the people cheered and shouted, the governor pushed a button and the *Blue Heron* began to pump. From then on, the *Blue Heron* and its seagoing sister the *White Heron* (also a bargain at $55,000) became the symbols of Howard Coffin and his vast effort to change the face and the life-style of the Georgia islands. By June the Plantation course was playable, and its construction set the pattern for a continuing development that over the years would give Sea Island and Saint Simons a worldwide reputation as a golfing center. A year after the Plantation Nine was put in play, Seaside was opened. Travis had died, and the famous English firm of Colt and Alison, which redesigned Saint Andrews, designed this layout that required that more than a million yards of dirt be dredged up from the marsh lands. The firm also made some changes in the Plantation Nine, getting rid of the cone-shaped "chocolate drops" that were Walter Travis's trademark.

Once the mood was on him, Coffin spent money with a lavish hand. In November 1927 he bought Cabin Bluff, in Camden County, 60,000 acres of forest land for which he paid nearly $570,000. There, on the site of one of the first hunt clubs in America, he built a fabulous hunting lodge, bringing his total costs to roughly three quarters of a million dollars.

All these things were done in the bright glow of the boom times, when stocks and bonds and real estate values all were going up and up and up, and men's hopes were rising with them. Through the depression of the 1930s and the war that came in the 1940s, no new land was bought and no work was done on the golf courses, other than maintenance. It was not until 1960, therefore, that Retreat, the third nine, was built. Dick Wilson's layout required the moving of a quarter million yards of dirt for fill creating the basins for two beautiful lakes, one of them eight acres in area. Finally in 1974 Marshside was built by Joe Lee, and the Sea Island Golf Course became the place of beauty and of challenge Gene Lewis had visualized nearly five decades before.

Although Howard Coffin cared nothing for golf, his sense of history and his desire to preserve the mementos of times past did leave their mark on the layout and the landscaping of the first two courses. He kept intact the stately Avenue of Oaks, which had led to Thomas Butler King's modest "big house," where John James Audubon had visited, and it is still a magnificent vista today. The golf course fairways, too, were laid out to curve around without disturbing the graves in the old cemetery where Retreat Plantation's slaves were buried.

Knowing that the Spanish friars in the 1500s had brought olives, dates, oranges, figs, and pomegranates to this place, and that Anna Page King had planted iris, oleander, acacias, crepe myrtle, and ninety-five varieties of roses, Coffin insisted that as many as possible of the plants that still remained should be protected. There were mementos, too, of prehistoric times. Workmen laying a water main across the golf course came upon the bones of a prehistoric Indian chief, buried in a shellbank near the first green. Nearby was a rusty Spanish dagger. Coffin ordered that these things, too, be preserved. The most dramatic act of preservation, though, centered around the old corn and fodder barn, a square two-story structure whose strong tabby walls were still standing when Coffin bought Retreat. This structure forms the nucleus of the clubhouse as it stands today. The ruins of the old slave hospital and the chimney of the "big house," which burned in 1910, also were left standing, creating an ambience which the casual visitor, riding a horse or golf cart on a sightseeing tour, finds fascinating.

Once Coffin had set his hand to the plow, so to speak, there was no turning back to his original idea of letting the land lie fallow while it increased in value. He began building roads, and paving roads already built, twenty-two miles in all, which he turned over to the county without cost. There was no direct road from the end of the Brunswick causeway to the pier at the south end of Saint Simons, where the lighthouse towered over the small village that clustered there. The only way was roundabout, along the Gascoigne Bluff Road to Demere Road, across the island, past Bloody Marsh, and on to the old resort settlement formed by ocean and river traffic a hundred years before. So he built Kings Way, through two other old plantations, the Demere tract and the Suttles tract, which he foresightedly bought up in advance, knowing that with the building of this road they would increase in value. Kings Way ran in a direct line from the end of the causeway bridge to the built-up area around Saint Simons pier, and soon he found that he could sell lots for $1,000 up to

$2,500 each in a subdivision he set up at the end of this route. Off Kings Way he built Retreat Avenue, an extension of the Frederica Road. This provided a throughway the length of the island, past Christ Church and Fort Frederica via Couper Road to the northern tip at Cannon's Point on the Hampton River. Here in 1804 John Couper of Scotland had built his spacious home of wood and tabby whose ruins and the land around them are now owned and preserved by the Sea Island Company.

As Coffin moved deeper into his road-building program, his mind turned to the kind of attraction to which these roads should lead. Soon his imagination soared. He employed a noted planner of urban and country communities, Charles Welford Leavitt, to draw up a plan for the south end of the island, where his golf course was already in play. The development would center around a great resort hotel, facing the beach where the King plantation house once stood, and surrounded by gardens, flowers, and a freshwater pool that could be heated in the chilly months. Also included would be a drainage and sewer system and subdivision plans laid out along a pattern of roads where a colony of cottages would rise. Sketching these plans for the hotel and its surrounding areas, Leavitt outlined certain restrictions insuring that historic places and vistas of great beauty would be preserved. A zoning plan would be required, he pointed out, providing for commercial areas to be set back from paved highways by green-belts and restricting the areas of billboard advertising. To Coffin this seemed a good idea, not only for the south end of Saint Simons, but for all Glynn County. At a cost of $22,000, which he paid out of his own pocket, he had a county-wide survey made and zoning laws drawn up which the county promptly adopted. Thus, Glynn became the third county in the United States to have such a law. By now Coffin was beginning to move a little too fast for his old friend Eugene Lewis, the golf enthusiast. Lewis was well-to-do, but no means as wealthy as Coffin, and although he had gone along happily with the development of the golf course, sharing one-fourth of the expense, he soon became aware that he could not keep up the financial pace. The purchase of the two dredges, even at a bargain price, had dismayed him. Also, in addition to paying for the county zoning survey, Coffin used his new dredges and spent his own money to repair the county's new causeway from Brunswick to Saint Simons at places where it was beginning to squash out and sink back into the marsh. He had also filled in the triangle of land where the causeway to Saint Simons left Brunswick, and he had paid half the cost of building the Chamber of Commerce Welcome Center there.

Then Coffin's thoughts turned to the boldest and most imaginative and most costly project of all, the purchase of the little barrier island that lay across the marshland from Saint Simons. Here on this true "sea island," pines and palms and old oaks hung with moss and vines rose above dunes and grasses looking down upon a five-mile stretch of curving beach. The Creek Indians who hunted on this place they called Fifth Creek Island had left no trace of their passing; the Franciscan friars built no missions and planted no olives and oranges here, and although Bloody Marsh was only a cannon's shot away, no blood had been spilled on this little island. In the days of the great plantations, no slaves worked vast fields on this narrow strip of sand and silt; it was hunting ground and grazing land at best.

From the beginning the island had been a beautiful, unspoiled, and lovely place. When James MacKay, colonial settler and one of Oglethorpe's troop commanders, acquired it under grant from George III in 1768, he made no use of it, but passed it on to his sons. In 1814 his heirs sold it to John Couper of Saint Simons, who in the same year gave it to his friend and former partner, James Hamilton. Hamilton in his turn gave it back to John Couper's son, William Audley Cooper, who in turn sold it to his brother James Hamilton Couper for $500. And so it remained in the Couper family until 1888, when it was bought for $10,000 by Frank O'Shaughnessy, the representative of a group of wealthy New Yorkers who liked to hunt. They stocked it with pheasants and partridge and hired a caretaker, Captain Stevens of Saint Simons, who brought his wife over and built the first house on what is now Sea Island. The O'Shaughnessy project was not so enduring as was the club another group of rich men had set up at Jekyll two years earlier. It failed after three years, and from then on, for thirty years, Long Island went back to its near-primeval loneliness, used only by the Taylor family of Saint Simons as a grazing ground for their goats, hogs, and cattle, and visited occasionally by small boys paddling over from Saint Simons hoping to fill their shirttails with turtle eggs. And now and then, on moonlight nights, it provided a romantic haven for young couples from Brunswick on what they called "marooning" parties.

The Early Days

This famous painting of the World War I era has its home on Sea Island. It appeared in color on the cover of Puck Magazine, *May 12, 1916. The editor explained:*

"Our cover this week, depicting America Defenseless, was prepared by James Montgomery Flagg for the use of the Commi·tee on Industrial Preparedness of the United States Naval Consulting Board, of which committee Howard E. Coffin, the well-known Detroit automobile manufacturer, is chairman.

"As part of its great educational campaign to wake up the nation to the immediate need of mobilizing its industrial resources for purposes of national defense, this committee has enlisted the gratuitous service of many of the most distinguished artists, illustrators and cartoonists of America. Mr. Coffin's committee has brought into being almost overnight a corps of more than thirty thousand highly educated American engineers, forming an organization in every state of the Union unique in the world's history.

"In the words of Mr. Coffin, 'War as now waged means that battles are won not alone by the fighting men, but by the fighting industries of a nation, and this superb body of trained men is going forward with its work , not at the eleventh hour, but in time of peace, with their sole method efficiency, and their sole motive Americanism.'

"In thus selecting Puck as the medium for the initial publication of the keynote cartoon in the series adopted by Mr. Coffin's committee, this body has paid tribute to the stand for preparedness taken by Puck from the outbreak of the European hostilities."

ARMLESS

In 1927 on the southwest shore of Saint Simons Island near where Frederica River reaches Saint Simons Sound, Sea Island's development began with construction of the Sea Island Yacht Club and dredging of a yacht basin. The Sea Island Company also paved King's Way and Demere Road (background), first hard-surface roads on Saint Simons.

While the Cloister Hotel was under construction on
Sea Island, early guests in the summer of 1928 were
housed in the three-story houseboat Amphitrite
docked at the yacht club.

Automobiles first reached Sea Island, then known
as Long Island, via a causeway from this turnoff
on Frederica Road just south of the present
Sea Island Stables.

Predecessor of the Sea Island development, this solitary large frame building beside the beach contained lockers on the ground floor and a dance hall above. It stood near the present Sea Island Beach Club.

First automobiles brave the sands of Sea Island Drive in this 1927 scene.

This 1927 aerial photograph shows Retreat Plantation on the south shore of Saint Simons Island just prior to construction of the first holes, known as Plantation Nine, of the Sea Island golf course. Left center is the plantation corn barn which became the clubhouse. Right center, in what is now Retreat Nine, is the construction headquarters.

A polo field was established beside the golf course and with the construction buildings later served as the first Sea Island riding stables.

The tabby corn barn of Retreat Plantation was converted into the golf clubhouse by Howard Coffin, who enjoyed saving old structures and preserving them as interesting, useful resort facilities.

An early sightseer visiting the developing Sea Island was the famous airship Los Angeles, seen passing the golf clubhouse.

This 1930 aerial shows a matured Plantation Nine in the background and the newly-opened Seaside Nine at the edge of Frederica River and Saint Simons Sound.

While the golf course was being built on Saint Simons, site preparation was underway on the south end of Sea Island for construction of the Cloister, soon to rise at center left. At right beside the beach in this 1928 view is Redfern hangar.

"Hoofing it" to the new Cloister, October 1928.

The Cloister received its first guests in October of
1928. Addison Mizner, architect, designed it in the
Spanish style he made famous in his earlier work at
Palm Beach.

The south patio became the favorite place for guests
to enjoy the pleasant Georgia outdoor temperatures.

The Sea Island Casino and a boardwalk were constructed in 1930 for the growing resort development.

An early Sea Island tradition was the alfresco dinner dance held beside the pool at the Casino.

Howard Coffin in the Cloister's south patio with
Cater Woolford, Atlanta, founder of Retail Credit
Company and then owner of Altama Plantation.
Woolford was one of the earliest friends of the hotel
and enlisted the best financial brains of Georgia in
support of Sea Island.

A 1931 aerial view shows the completion of River
House, center left, the administration building and
three early Sea Island cottages.

This early photograph of the Cloister's Spanish Lounge shows Mizner's genius for combining scale with intricate detail.

Afternoon tea in the Spanish Lounge immediately became a Cloister tradition.

Horseback rides began at the Cloister's motor
entrance in the early years.

Mixed foursome displays styles of the opening years at the Sea Island Golf Club. The caddy holds the wicker-basket-topped pin.

Seaside's fascinating fourth hole. Six ghostly sand traps guard the distant green. Bobby Jones (center) has just driven 325 yards over White Heron Creek.

Photo left, Howard Coffin was not a golfer but he enjoyed playing host to champions such as Bobby Jones. Photo right, Charlie Yates of Atlanta, then just 18, won his first major tournament at Sea Island. He later became British amateur champion.

In 1927 aviator Paul Redfern took off from the Sea
Island beach in an attempt to fly non-stop to Brazil.
He was never seen again but his plane was reported
sighted off the Brazil coast.

Airplanes were important to Sea Island's
development. Howard Coffin, one of America's
aviation pioneers, and friends greet a Ford Trimotor
at Redfern Field, today the site of shopping centers
on Saint Simons. The Tabby House, right
background, was part of Retreat Plantation.

A Sikorsky amphibian, chartered by Major
Alexander P. deSeversky of New York, visits the Sea
Island Casino.

William Gibbs McAdoo, secretary of the Treasury
under President Woodrow Wilson, and his daughter
fly in for a visit. They are greeted by Mr. Coffin
and his secretary.

Mr. and Mrs. Charles W. Deeds of Hartford, Conn.,
right, flew their own plane early to Sea Island
and soon owned a house on the island, where they
still live. With them are Mrs. Deeds' parents,
Mr. and Mrs. F.S. Belden.

The Sea Island cottage colony began with this home known as Cottage Number 1, on east 35th Street.

4

THEY CALLED IT THE CLOISTER

By the time Howard Coffin began to shift his interest from Saint Simons to Long Island, that lonely little goat pasture and turtle crawl had already begun to take on a new personality. Between 1924 and 1926 a group of citizens, most of them from Brunswick but a goodly number from other Georgia towns, had put together a stock company called the Saint Simon-Long Island Company (there was no *s* on Saint Simons at this time). They bought up the entire island, some 750 acres of high ground and 150 acres of marsh, for $24,277. They cut a road straight through it, south to north. Along this sandy track, engineer F.J. Torras laid out and J.A. Blanton surveyed a plan for a cottage colony in a street pattern that much resembles the Sea Island layout as it exists today. Elaborate maps were drawn up, and lots along the still nonexistent streets went on sale to stockholders at $100 for an interior lot and $250 for a corner lot on the beach. At first nothing happened. Then, on July 11, 1924, the causeway from Brunswick to Saint Simons was opened, and in December of that year the mud road across the marshes from Saint Simons to Long Island was dredged up. Now the place began to boom. A number of lots were sold by the spring of 1925, and the prices had gone up to $550 for a beachfront lot 75 by 120 feet, and $400 for an inside corner lot. So many people began coming across the causeway, driving their cars along the white sand beach, that the company hastily put together a combination bathhouse and dance pavilion very near the spot where the Sea Island Beach Club now stands. The bathhouse, which was finished first, was only moderately successful; many people preferred to change clothes in their cars rather than pay the modest bathhouse fee. The opening of the dance pavilion, though, was an event long remembered on the Georgia coast. On August 28, 1925, more than 200 automobiles crossed the causeway, loaded with families eager to bathe in the surf and spread their picnic lunches on the beach. In the afternoon at low tide they watched the racing cars roar over a course laid out on the beach to the south, and there was a beauty contest in which belles from as far north as Macon paraded in their bathing suits. That night there was a grand ball, which went on until long past midnight. Twice a week thereafter dances were held at the pavilion (ladies were admitted free, gentlemen paid a dollar), and never again would Long Island be the remote and lonely place it had been through all the quiet centuries past. Coastal Georgia's citizens were happy to come to Long Island to bathe in the surf, picnic on the beach, and dance at the two-story brown-shingled pavilion with its breeze-swept upper veranda overlooking the sea. Unhappily, they were much less interested in building a summer residence there. Though more than a hundred lots had been sold, Long Island Company was broke. In January, John R. Barfield and C.M. Killian, two Georgians who had made some money in Florida real estate, bought the Long Island Company stock for $300,000. Nobody, evidently, suffered great loss. Of the 105 stockholders, only 13 owned more than 10 shares. Among them were such well-known citizens of Brunswick as Millard Reese, Albert Fendig, J.L. Phillips, J.A. Bennett, W.J. Butts, and F.E. Twitty.

Long Island's prospects as a great resort center under this new management proved no brighter than before. Killian and Barfield soon fell to quarreling among themselves and started looking about for a buyer. They did not have far to look. On July 15, 1926, Howard Coffin's newly formed Sea Island Investments, Incorporated, offspring of and dependent on his highly successful Michigan company, the Detroit Realty Investments Company, bought Long Island, exclusive of the lots that already had been sold. The price was $349,485.17 and included not only Long Island but Rainbow Island, an expanse of marshland on the Black Banks River across from Long Island, which brought the total acreage to more than 2,500. It was Coffin's biggest single investment to date. Retreat Plantation had cost $185,900; the Suttles tract, $225,600. And so, after many owners over many generations, Sea Island at last had found the man, and the family, who in the years to come would bring it to its fullest flowering.

Eugene Lewis, who had been Howard Coffin's friend, confidant, and financial advisor, would remain in this role for another eighteen years as vice-president and director of the Sea Island Company. He did not, however, join Coffin in his Sea Island venture. Coffin's plans for the little island, Lewis told his friend, were "far too elaborate to invite the attention of my bank account." He sold his quarter share in the Sea Island Company to Coffin and used the money to buy a "Retreat" of his own—famed Hamilton Plantation, owned first by Captain James Gascoigne, who brought Oglethorpe's first settlers to Frederica, and later by Scotsman James Hamilton, who turned it into a great shipping port for cotton and timber. He also created there what Fannie Kemble called "by far the finest estate on Saint Simons." There Eugene Lewis sought to operate the finest truck farm in the

South, but he soon discovered that he knew more about golf and banking than he did about growing vegetables. He could not compete with the Florida vegetable growers so he gave up the effort and used the great plantation only as a vacation spot, until he sold it to the Sea Island Company in 1946.

Until the purchase of Sea Island in 1926, Bill Jones had spent most of his working days at Sapelo. Occasionally though, he would come down to Saint Simons by boat to ride the roads with Howard Coffin, talking of future plans. He would chat with Paul Varner, Coffin's other bright young man, at the new office the company had opened in Brunswick and en route home he would pause at Darien to pass the time of day with Judge Charles Tyson, the company's lawyer, an elderly gentleman who distrusted secretaries and insisted on personally pecking out copies of deeds and other legal documents on an ancient typewriter.

Coffin, for all his growing interest in Saint Simons and Sea Island, had not forgotten Sapelo. He kept in constant correspondence with the Department of Agriculture about growing oysters and raising ocellated turkeys, currasows, and chachalacas, rare birds with which he was determined to stock his home island. He also kept a fatherly eye on how well Bill Jones was managing the estate, which now included some 200 gardeners, road builders, farmers, herdsmen, and house servants.

One of his chores at Sapelo gave Jones much pleasure. Coffin, as noted earlier, was not much given to purely social doings, but both he and Mrs. Coffin loved to share with their friends from the North and elsewhere the charm and beauty of their great house at Sapelo, and they wanted Bill Jones to feel free to do the same. Frequently, therefore, they would ask him if he would like to have a house party, inviting his friends from Savannah or wherever. He would indeed, for this gave him opportunity to bring down from Dayton Miss Katharine Talbott, known as Kit, a young redhead who had been Bill Jones's sweetheart since their childhood days. Thus, long before the marriage of Kit Talbott and Bill Jones, there began the warm parental relationship between the young couple and the childless Coffins that was to affect profoundly the lives of both families in the years to come.

Among the older visitors welcomed by the Coffins was Carl Fisher, the developer of Miami Beach, who, like Coffin, had made his millions in the automobile business, with the early car lamp called a Prestolite. Hearing that Coffin had become interested in resort development, Fisher persuaded Coffin to come in with him in a huge project at Montauk Point, on the other Long Island to the north. There, Coffin put up the money to dredge a waterway from Long Island Sound to an inland freshwater lake, with the spill forming Star Island, which became a yacht club site. Coffin took his pay in Star Island land, and half a century later, in 1977, Bill Jones finally sold the last of the Star Island lots.

Fisher also persuaded Coffin to abandon his idea of building his big hotel on Saint Simons overlooking the intracoastal waterway. Modern resort hotels were moving to the beaches, their windows overlooking the sea. "You've got the ideal place on this little island across the marshes," he told Coffin. "Go there." Coffin agreed. He hired Schultz and Weaver, architects who had just completed the plans for the new Waldorf Astoria and had designed for the Henry Flagler family the new Breakers, just being finished on Palm Beach to replace the old Breakers on the bay, which had burned. For a $25,000 fee, Schultz designed for Coffin his own "Palace by the Sea," a hotel to stand eight stories high, towering over the tall palms and pines growing in the middle of the island between Twenty-ninth and Thirty-second streets. Around it would grow up a colony of cottages, the nucleus of the great resort Coffin had visualized. Grading of this location with mule teams, for there were no tractors or bulldozers in those days, had already begun, and seven cottages were under construction, when Coffin suddenly started having second thoughts. He sent Bill Jones, Paul Varner, his construction boss Sam Jones, his public-relations man Charles Redden, and cottage architect and land salesman

George Boll to Florida to take a look at beach hotel operations there and to come back with recommendations on what the Sea Island Company should do.

They went and looked and studied and came back with their report. Their recommendation was simply this: the company should take it easy. It should not rush in and build a huge hotel and promote the sale of lots with a cottage colony around it until it could be discovered whom such a resort center would attract and what kind of people they might be. Instead, a small hotel should be built first, a simple comfortable little overnight inn, where people could stay while they took a look at Sea Island and decided whether they liked the place. Fortunately, a Leavitt engineer named Carl Weir had the ideal location in mind. Dredging of the Black Banks River had filled in several acres of marsh and sandy dune at the end of the island, where the causeway came ashore. And this became the site of Howard Coffin's "friendly little hotel," the Cloister, which formed the focal point of the entire Sea Island operation and still sets its mood and spirit today.

The designer of the little forty-six room hotel was perhaps the most noted resort architect of his time—and surely, as a person, the most colorful. Addison Mizner, a huge man weighing three hundred pounds or more, had never formally studied architecture, and he shared with Howard Coffin a vast disinterest in the minor details of a project. But he had an infallible sense of balance and proportion, and he was able to combine with this a wide-ranging scholar's knowledge of the serenely beautiful buildings of Spain and the Mediterranean. In Florida in the early 1920s, he had, in the words of the *Saturday Evening Post*, "transformed Palm Beach from the rich man's Coney Island into a perpetual world's fair of architecture." Then, caught up in the frenzy of the Florida boom, he and his brother, Wilson Mizner, persuaded a covey of millionaires and a gaggle of stage and screen celebrities to back him in what was to become his most famous production—a

17,000-acre development that Mizner visualized would become "the world's premium resort, a happy combination of Venice and Heaven." But at the center of all this grandeur would be a little one-hundred-room hotel, simple in its lines, whose red-tiled roof rambled in every direction, whose windows opened on sunny gardens where fountains played. And around this focal point, Mizner had designed villas of fabulous beauty for the very rich. Thus, it was with some temerity that Alfred W. Jones went down to speak with this great man to ask him if he would consider coming to a little Georgia island and designing there a small and unpretentious hotel, but one with the distinctive Mizner touch.

From Bill Jones's standpoint, the timing was perfect. In January 1926, the Boca Raton Cloister Inn opened with utmost fanfare, with the rich and famous from both the social and the financial worlds in attendance. And throughout the winter, Boca Raton was the "in" place for the Palm Beach and Bar Harbor set. But upon his arrival, Addison Mizner wooed and entertained Bill Jones as if he were seeking a favor from Jones — and not the other way around. For Mizner knew what Jones could only suspect: the Mizner Development Corporation was bankrupt. The frenzied Florida boom was moving swiftly toward destruction, and the Boca Raton hotel, which had cost a fabulous $1.25 million to build, was soon to close. It would open again in time, as the Boca Raton Hotel and Club, and would go on to great success. But in the sale by creditors, the name "Cloister" was abandoned. Thus Mizner not only readily agreed to design the hotel for Coffin and Jones, he designed it in the Spanish motif — the low red-tile roof, the sunlit patios, the grand lounge with its high beamed ceiling and clerestory windows, all reminiscent of the dream hotel he had built in Florida. And out of sentiment perhaps, he persuaded them to name it "The Cloister."

The area where the Cloister was built had been part marsh, part goat pasture, a low and sandy place where only a few pines grew. But it had been filled in with rich dirt from the river bottom, and as Jones and Coffin had been fortunate in finding the ideal architect for their building, they were lucky, too, in having close at hand a landscape architect of equal talent. T. Miesse Baumgardner, born in Lancaster, Ohio, the hometown of General Sherman, made his own march through Georgia in the winter of 1925, en route to Saint Petersburg, Florida, where he took a year off from his studies at Ohio State University to work for a land planner and golf course architectural firm. He finished school in 1927 with his degree in landscape architecture and promptly sent out his resumé, seeking work. One went to Charles Welford Leavitt, who had laid out Coffin's Saint Simons subdivision and had made the Glynn County zoning study, and now, under Coffin's change of plans, was transferring his interest to Sea Island.

And so it was that "Bummy" Baumgardner, age twenty-three, came to work at Sea Island and immediately turned his heart and hand to creating the congeries of palms and pines and live oaks, the vistas of green grass and winding paths and pools, and beds of many different flowers, which frame the Cloister with beauty in any season, soothing the spirit and pleasing the eye. He was not without help in his designing. Although Howard Coffin was bored by financial details, he seemed to be a frustrated landscape gardener at heart. He was constantly looking over Baumgardner's shoulder, telling him to dig up a tree he had just planted and move it somewhere else to improve a background or lengthen a vista. He was particularly insistent that palm trees should be planted as they grew in nature, in clumps, not rows, and the tall palms that grow beside the causeway today were put there at his command.

On Easter Sunday morning, April 8, 1928, the Brunswick paper announced the new and final plans for the hotel to be built on what for a brief period was to be called Glynn Isle. The architecture was described as being Spanish, three stories high with landscaped patios enclosed by arched walls giving the effect of a Spanish cloister where monks might tell their beads and soliloquize. The rooms, however, in no way resembled monkish cells. The announcement stressed the fact that "only the very best beds will be bought." The next day the piledrivers began their rhythmic thumping, and in ten days a singing gang of wheelbarrow pushers, recruited by a coastal boat captain named Thomas Hopkins, began pouring the concrete foundations. A young construction foreman named Sam Jones, no kin to Coffin or Bill Jones but with a fine talent as a building engineer, had overall charge of the project. For supervising the hotel itself, Coffin brought down from Sapelo the big Swede, Arthur Wilson, who had built Coffin's "big house" there.

During 1927, while waiting for the fill to settle on the Cloister site and the plans to be drawn for the hotel, Coffin made sure that even before the hotel was finished there would be something on the island to hold the public interest. The first seven cottages were built between Thirty-fourth and Thirty-sixth streets, designed by George Boll, Coffin's own architect, on lots landscaped by Baumgardner. The streets had also been named by now, by Mrs. Marmaduke Floyd of Savannah; they bear the names of Indians, Spaniards, Frenchmen, pirates, colonists, Revolutionary heroes, and any person who knew the story behind each name would have a complete history of the islands and all that had happened there. In 1927, too, an event, promoted by Paul Varner and designed to draw national attention to the island, ended in tragedy that became a part of history. On August 25, 1927, Paul Redfern, a skilled young pilot trained to fly over the south Georgia swamps looking for moonshiners, took off from Sea Island Beach in an attempted solo flight to Brazil. The plane, the *Port of Brunswick*, was last seen 200 miles off the South American coast.

With cottages abuilding, and the hotel under way, attention

was also focused on the beach. The old pavilion had a modest face lift in 1927. The veranda was widened and extended around all four sides. To encourage dressing inside, instead of in automobiles, which soon were to be barred from the beach, 100 dressing rooms were added to the 160 already in the bathhouse. Then a small white clapboard restaurant was built, which found great favor with those who did not care for picnicking on the sand.

Then in April 1928, just before the piledrivers started thumping at the hotel site, a really large expansion of the pavilion took place. The building was entirely remodeled, the dance hall was enlarged, the outside was stuccoed, and the name was changed to the Casino. A hundred yards down the beach an open-air pavilion was built beside the biggest surprise of all—a freshwater swimming pool. The new facilities were opened on July 11, 1928, in a pouring rain that seemed to dampen nobody's interest in the water sports and the beauty parade. All that summer name bands played at the biweekly dances, and old and young frolicked in the swimming pool. And just a few hundred yards away, the new hotel, finished, but strangely silent and uninhabited, lay drowsing under the August and September sun. Nervous whispers began to go about; was something wrong, the local people wondered? Would the little hotel, now bearing the official name "The Sea Island Cloister," ever open its doors? It was natural that a number of the local citizens should be concerned. When he decided to build the hotel, Howard Coffin, through his Sea Island Company, had formed a small hotel development company and had sold local people $50,000 worth of stock in it; not because he needed the money, for he had plenty, but because he very much wanted the citizens of the community to have a personal interest in what he was going to do.

Something indeed was wrong, but the problem was temporary. The hotel was finished, but the furniture, including "the best beds that could be bought," had not yet been delivered. That logjam soon was broken, and a quiet "come all ye" went to a select group of people. And it was in answer to this happy invitation that on the night of October 12, 1928, the local folk, most of them investors in Cloister stock, came across the causeway to make the welkin ring.

5

AND NOW, IT'S KIT AND BILL

Not long before this happy evening, Bill Jones had made his last journey to Dayton as a bachelor. In the spring of 1928, as Howard Coffin's interest in Sea Island widened and his investments there increased, it became clear to Jones that whatever career lay ahead of him, for the next couple of years at least, his work would be here on the Georgia coast. After that, he assumed that he would go back to Dayton or Detroit. But wherever it was that life might lead him, he knew that he wanted Kit Talbott with him, and happily, he knew that she felt the same way.

The *Dayton Daily News* of Sunday, June 10, 1928, announced the engagement of Katharine Houk Talbott to Alfred William Jones, late of Dayton and more recently of Sapelo Island, Georgia. Miss Talbott, the announcement noted, was the daughter of Mrs. Harold Elstner Talbott of Runnymede, the Talbott family homestead in suburban Oakwood; she was a graduate of Westover School in Middlebury, Connecticut, and was an active member of the Dayton Junior League. In her many varied interests, social, civic, and humanitarian, she was traveling in the footsteps of her mother, also known as Kit, a vibrant and spirited woman, a lover of music and the arts and devoted to the public good.

Mr. Jones, the paper noted, was the son of Mr. and Mrs. Rufus Jones, of the Plymouth Apartments, his father being one of the originators of the idea of the building and loan association. He was a business associate of his cousin, Howard Coffin, and was manager of Mr. Coffin's Sapelo plantation and vice-president in charge of development for Mr. Coffin's Sea Island Company. He had attended the University of Pennsylvania, where he was a member of the Phi Kappa Psi fraternity. The wedding, the story said, would take place in the fall, after which Mr. and Mrs. Jones would take up their residence in Georgia. Another edition of the *Dayton Daily News* carried a somewhat less reverent account of the upcoming nuptials. Bill Jones's friend, Governor James Cox, publisher of the *Dayton Daily News*, had a "Matrimonial Edition" distributed at the announcement party. The headline read, "KIT TO MARRY BILL: Friends Hope Marriage Takes Place Before Squirrels Get Them."

At the bottom of the front page was an alleged advice to the lovelorn column, written by somebody called Beatrice Barefacts. One letter was signed "Anxious Al," denoting Alfred William Jones. The letter read, "Dear Friend in Need: I have been living a lonely life on a very small island. Recently, a very lovely girl stepped into my life. I have come to know her family—eight (8) brothers and sisters, thirteen (13) first cousins, and twenty-five (25) nephews and nieces. Must I give up this dear girl whom I have just learned to love or should I look around for a larger island?"

His decision was to keep the girl, the island, and the family, too. Forty-nine years later in August of 1977, Bill and Kit Jones welcomed the Talbott clan, now grown to 237 members, to Sea Island for a weekend reunion. Their visit, said Jones, was an unending source of pleasure to him: he was glad to see them come, he was glad to be with them while they were there, and he was glad to see them go.

The Talbott-Jones wedding took place on September 6, 1928, at the Talbott home, Runnymede, at an altar arranged before the north windows of the spacious drawing room. Howard Coffin stood up with Jones as his best man, and Kit's older brother, Harold Talbott, gave the bride away.

The Joneses went on their honeymoon to the Talbott family lodge deep in the woods of Ontario. They came back from there to Sapelo for the last night of their wedding trip. The next day, they rode on the beach together until their horses suddenly began to rear and snort and try to run away. There on the sand ahead of them lay the biggest alligator Bill Jones had ever seen. There was no protection for alligators in those days, and the thirteen-foot monster ended up stuffed and hanging over the mantel in the Coffin hunting lodge at Cabin Bluff.

That night, the Joneses traveled by speedboat across the sound to Darien and from there by car to Sea Island, where they took up residence at the white cottage on the beach which had been prepared for them by the Coffins. The next day, October 1, 1928, the directors of the Sea Island Company met at the Yacht Club on Saint Simons. Howard Coffin announced that the business affairs of the company had progressed to the point that the company needed a more active president. He nominated Jones, who was unanimously elected. Coffin moved up to the newly created position of chairman of the board, and Paul Varner, his other bright young man, handed in his resignation.

Before the month was out, Bill and Kit Jones were host and hostess for the formal opening of the Cloister. The guests were mainly from Savannah, Brunswick, and the little towns along the coast, and it was the first of many memorable parties the Joneses would give thereafter at the hotel or at their home. The next came soon thereafter, on October 28, a formal dinner and dance, with distinguished guests from all over Georgia and from the

North and Midwest, filling every table in the dining room and every bed in the house.

The Cloister quickly became the "in" place for local social events. In early November the four brothers of Buford Aiken, descendants of the owners of Kings Retreat, gave a dinner there for their sister, after her marriage to John Horlick. The Young Men's Club of Brunswick and the Cotillion Club held their formal dances there, and a monthly "dinner and bridge at the Cloister" social group soon was formed in Brunswick.

There was plenty for Bill Jones to do other than entertain local friends, though he did this with consummate skill. Over the next few months he welcomed a continuing parade of tycoons, sportsmen, artists, writers, statesmen, and editors from all over the country to what Arthur Brisbane, in his column for the Hearst papers, described as "the sun parlor of the nation." The man responsible for bringing these notables to this new and hitherto unknown resort was a genius at promotion named Charles F. Redden. A friend of Coffin's, Redden had once been a truck manufacturer in Detroit, and when his enterprise went bankrupt, Coffin hired him. Widely known in newspaper circles, he started off by inviting editors, publishers, and the top writers of all the major newspapers, magazines, and wire services to come to shoot deer and turkey at Coffin's newly acquired 60,000-acre game preserve, Cabin Bluff, in Camden County.

Redden's crowning achievement as a public-relations man for the Sea Island Company came in midwinter of 1928-29, when he persuaded Calvin Coolidge to spend his Chrismas holiday with Howard Coffin and to pose for his picture planting an oak tree on the south lawn of the Cloister. Unhappily, T. Miesse Baumgardner, the landscape artist and horticulturist, was away from the island at the moment, and Coolidge was given a water oak sapling to plant, a more fragile tree than the live oak, which reputedly would live 300 years or more. When Baumgardner returned, Coffin ordered him to dig up the Coolidge sapling and put a live oak down. This was done without fanfare and the "Coolidge Oak" is now a towering giant on the Cloister grounds. Pictures of Coolidge planting the tree on Sea Island, wearing a big hat and riding an ox cart on Sapelo Island, and sitting before the great stone fireplace at Cabin Bluff hunting preserve, dressed formally in a business suit, made all the papers.

As a result of all this publicity, the Cloister went into 1929, its first full year of operation, with more bookings than it could handle. To meet this demand, Coffin decided to build more rooms, and in March of that year the Sea Island Apartments, known now as River House, were begun. With Mrs. Howard Coffin putting up the more than $250,000 necessary for the construction, the apartments, designed by Francis Abreu, stood on the riverbank in front of the Cloister, looking westward across the marshes. The building of the apartments was a precursor of things to come. Next came the Colonial Lounge and the ten rooms above it. Through all the desperate years of depression, in fact, the Cloister kept up its standard of comfort and of friendly unostentatious service. Rooms and lounging space, kitchen and dining areas, were added only as money became available, and by following this cautious program, the little hotel managed to survive as a tranquil haven in a struggling and troubled world. In so doing, it was able to carry, through a desperate time, the entire Sea Island Company operation.

When Bill Jones took over as president on October 1, 1928, the original organization had divided like an amoeba. When Howard Coffin first came to Saint Simons in 1926, there were no facilities whatever to serve the kind of resort he had in mind—no electricity, no water supply, no telephone system, and the causeway across the marsh soon proved hopelessly inadequate to accommodate the heavy trucks which brought his supplies over from the mainland. Nor was the Georgia Light and Power Company, or the local telephone company, interested in supplying their facilities to a region so sparsely settled. In the first six months of 1927, these services were provided by the Sea Island Company itself. A subsidiary called Sea Island Utilities put in a diesel power plant and two telephone exchanges; one on Saint Simons, one at the Cloister. Another subsidiary, the Sea Island Construction Company, took over the task of building roads and strengthening the causeway at no cost to the county, remodeling the Casino, and building the hotel.

Two camps sheltering 230 workmen were set up; one at the golf course, east of the Avenue of Oaks, to serve Saint Simons, one at Thirty-sixth Street, at the north end of Sea Island. The golf course site later became the first riding stable. There were barracks, shower baths, and mess halls for whites and blacks, and a commissary, though at times when supplies ran short the men on Sea Island would cheerfully eat only bread and goat meat. Not far away from the Yacht Club site, from April until the hotel opened in October, a floating hotel, the *Amphitrite,* offered somewhat more luxurious fare for those who came to keep the Yacht Club tennis courts busy, to golf at Retreat, or to swim at Sea Island Casino by day and dance there by night. On Sea Island nine cottages were either finished or under construction. By the end of 1927, artesian wells had been drilled, roads paved, and a nursery planted to provide the thousands of trees, shrubs, and flowers that Baumgardner's helpers would be planting in the coming years. And at Saint Simons, the golf course was rapidly shaping up with Hugh Moore as the first professional. Gene Lewis had hired Marion McKendree, a young Camden county cattle dipper who rode up to Saint Simons on a big red horse, seeking more challenging work. McKendree in the following forty-odd years would become one of the outstanding golf-course supervisors in the nation. (One of his early accomplishments was to teach his dog to pull a golf cart.) In 1931, after plowing through more than a hundred applications, Gene Lewis—influenced by strong recommendations from the poet Edgar A. Guest and the Rev. William Lyon Phelps—hired a fellow Michigan resident, Captain W.H. Lewis, as club professional. "Cap" Lewis also went on to national fame in golfing circles.

Even with all that had been done at the golf club, much was still to be done as Bill Jones, with the opening of the Cloister, took over the presidency of the Sea Island Company. The floating hotel, the *Amphitrite,* had served its day and must be disposed of. The golf clubhouse, built around the shell of the old plantation corn barn, had been opened to the public in September, but obviously would be too small when the second nine came into play some time in the fall of 1929. Still further in the future were the skeet range, the 320-foot wall along the Black Banks River, where the apartments were to rise, and the administration building with its square bell tower reminiscent of an old Spanish mission. This would house the company's offices on the filled land at the entrance to Sea Island. There were roads still to be built off Sea Island Drive running eastward toward the ocean and westward toward the marsh, so that many more lots could be sold and houses built.

From the beginning, the company sought to attract a special clientele. It does not encourage those who seek their pleasure at the horse or dog tracks or the gaming tables, or in the more frenetic forms of night life; nor is there any effort made to attract the ultra rich and social who once thronged Palm Beach and Newport to show off their jewels and their furs. The Cloister guests and cottage colonists are far from poverty stricken, as the tastefully elegant "cottages" and the shining cars that pull up at the post office at mail time every morning will attest. And a busy social life does exist, for there is a happy party going on somewhere every night. But the Sea Island visitors' urge to swing a little is served by a placid, twice-a-week bingo game, or by dancing in the clubrooms to the music of an orchestra that knows everybody's old favorites.

The people who feel most comfortable and most content at Sea Island, therefore, are steady, quiet-spoken folk, amazingly similar in manner, dress, and point of view, no matter where they come from. They come year after year, to play golf or tennis, to swim or surf or lie in the sun, or to walk the beach collecting sand dollars, starfish, and shells. In the evenings they may doze before the television sets in the lounges (the Cloister likes for people to mingle, thus there are no television sets in the rooms except by special request.) For music lovers there are harp concerts and piano recitals in the Spanish Lounge, and art shows and lectures on Georgia coastal history, or slide shows on birds in the solarium while live parakeets twitter sleepily from their cages in the corner. For those who need a fourth at bridge, the social director will find one for them, and in the summer there is supervised play for youngsters of all ages, from sand-sculpture contests for the little ones on the beach, to dancing in the Gazebo for the high school and college set. In the summer at the alfresco dances, the family element is particularly in evidence as young boys dance with their mothers and young girls with their fathers, and old couples proudly demonstrate new steps they have just learned from Tom and Nancy Gallagher, the Cloister's dancing teachers and activities directors.

Thus, life goes on much as it always has, but it would be wrong to assume that the Cloister has not adjusted in any way to the greater freedom and informality of the changing times. In the ladies locker room at the Beach Club, there once was a sign saying that bikinis were forbidden. That sign disappeared a few years ago, and in the summers when the young assemble there, the exposure of epidermis on Sea Island beach is as spectacular as at any spa on the Mediterranean.

Lunching at the Beach Club buffet under the umbrellas on the terrace overlooking the sea is still a happily informal thing, with only bathing suits and bare feet frowned upon, but dinner in the Cloister dining room with lamps glowing softly and fresh flowers on every table still has the touch of old-time elegance. Gentlemen who may not do this anywhere else help their wives to rise from the dinner table by pulling back their chairs, and small boys observing this do the same for their sisters. On Tuesday, Thursday, and Saturday nights the ladies wear long dresses, though in recent years pantsuits are often seen. Black ties are still worn by many of the gentlemen on these nights, but most of these are old timers at the Cloister, seeking perhaps to recapture the glow of their honeymoon days.

The clientele actually has changed but little over the years. Summer guests are still, in the main, young families from the South. Autumn brings guests from everywhere, South and North, many who return year after year for the Thanksgiving holiday, when the buffet menu features venison. Winter guests, by and large, are from the North. Many of them have been coming for forty years or more, and they are particularly fond of spending Christmas or New Years at the hotel. Nearly all are elderly, and many, of both sexes, come alone looking for a bridge partner, conversation, or companionship, which the Cloister's social director is pleased to provide. Some couples come who are so far advanced in years that they must lean upon each other as they walk, a touching sight. Honeymooners come at every season, leading to the irreverent observation that the Cloister clientele is made up of the newly wed, the over fed, and the nearly dead.

Be that as it may, voices are seldom lifted in the Cloister halls. Now and then, of course, some member of a "group meeting"—the Cloister avoids using the word "convention"—does get a little upset when told that he cannot enter the dining room carrying a drink from the bar or wearing a shortsleeved shirt without a tie. On rare occasions one of these may become rude, raucous, and rowdy and challenge the maître d' to fisticuffs. Cloister maître d's, from Harry Welch and George Sherer to John Chalfa, Jack Grant and Vance Shaffer, have learned to handle such incidents quickly and quietly.

From the beginning, Bill Jones knew that handling finances would be more difficult than handling people. By the time the Cloister opened, it had cost some $440,000 to build and furnish, and Howard Coffin, in all, had put some $3 million into his Georgia operation outside of Sapelo. This money had come to the Sea Island Company through Coffin's Detroit Realty Investment Company, which raised $1 million of the money through a bond issue handled by the Detroit Trust Company as trustee. And Bill Jones, despite the fact that he had an extremely good head for figures, knew that if he was ever to pay off this debt and turn the Sea Island Company into a profitable operation, he was going to have to have some expert help. James Drake Compton was the one man he knew could do the job. He and Compton had grown up in Dayton, both had attended the University of Pennsylvania, and both were members of Phi Kappa Psi fraternity. Compton now was working for the National Cash Register Company in Dayton. Finally, after mulling over the matter for weeks and at Kit's insistence that he do something and quit worrying about it, Jones got Compton on the telephone and offered him a job.

And so it was that Jim Compton and his wife, Dorothy, and their daughter, Patsy, age four, moved into a Sea Island cottage down the drive a way from the Joneses. It was an association that was to last for more than forty years, with Compton becoming the man whom Bill Jones depended on to serve as his good right hand, as he in turn had served Howard Coffin. Compton and Jones made the perfect team. Jones was the thinker and planner, bringing Howard Coffin's dreams to reality. Compton was the man who knew what everything cost and how to get the most value for every dollar spent. He would never agree to build anything cheap or shoddy, but he knew how to build good things inexpensively. In his relations with personnel, Bill Jones was likely to be a little soft, a little easy going. Compton, who knew how to get the best value out of a dollar, also knew how to get the best work out of an employee. He did this by knowing what every job required, and how it should be done. As a result, even those he had to rebuff respected him and tried to please him. Coffin once told him that every company had to have its SOB, and for the Sea Island Company, Compton was it. But men who worked with Compton will deny this. Compton, they say, could be tough, and he was impossible to fool. But he was usually friendly, and he was always fair.

He, like Jones, was a worker. On Sundays they would meet in Jones's office, a monkish cell in the newly constructed administration building, and talk of what had to be done. They got rid of the *Amphitrite,* and they got the company-owned light and power company on a precarious break-even basis before selling it to Georgia Light and Power. They did the same thing with the telephone company, selling it to Southern Bell. A bus line from Savannah to Jacksonville by way of Brunswick was greatly needed, so they bought six big white buses and put them into service—the first public transportation on that route. When the proper time came, they sold out, for $150,000, to the newly organized Greyhound line, which needed Georgia Public Service Commission rights to the Jacksonville-Savannah run. They even made a little money on that deal.

Howard Coffin gave them a free hand to do what they thought best. It was his nature, once a project was well under way, to look for new challenges, and at public gatherings there was no more eloquent a spokesman for Sea Island and the future of the Georgia coastal islands than he. The first meeting to be held at the new Cloister was the Twenty-ninth Annual Meeting of the Cotton Manufacturers of Georgia. It was held April 25-26, 1929, and Howard Coffin was the speaker. He began by tracing the history of the Georgia coast from Saint Marys River north to Savannah. Here, he said, was the cradle of Christian civilization in the Americas, for here the Spanish friars in the 1500s brought their mission to the Indians. He pushed on then to the modern day, passing briefly over the fact that where his hearers sat had less than a year earlier been a corral for goats, "though I derive no inference from that," he added. He was merely making the point that all that had been done in the past twelve months was a result of transportation. When he first came to Georgia, seventeen years before, there were no motor roads at all along the Georgia coast. Travel was by boat, or, from Brunswick to Darien, aboard a flat-car pushed by a dummy engine. Now the roads were coming, and that was fine, but the roads would bring trucks, and trucks would compete with the trains, and to destroy the railroads in favor of the motor carrier would be fatal. All roads, railroads, and water routes, he argued, should be blended in a cooperative network to serve the region. For he felt the same way the old Spaniards did: there is no place in the United States where such a combination of worthwhile things could be found, all wrapped in a pleasant climate which could be enjoyed every month of the year.

And here, he said, he was determined to create a community that would be a credit to the state. A place primarily for Georgians, but a place where Georgians could welcome people from many far-off places. And this was happening. The Cloister had been built with the thought that it would be a summer hotel serving the people of surrounding states, for when the Cloister was built the area was little known to people from the North and East. He continued,

> Now, I think that I am safe in saying that this Sea Island Beach is being as much talked about today as any other bit of territory in the United States, I know it is becoming well known. To our astonishment, the Cloister has been crowded

from the time it was opened in November, until the present, by the people whom one usually thinks of as going to Palm Beach, Miami, or some of the older well-known places in the South. The impression upon all of these people has been such that most of them made their reservations for next year. One thing, very embarrassing to us, has been that while guests have come here this winter with the idea that they would merely look in and see what this new place was like, and have engaged their accommodations for two or three days only — they have found that this was just the place they have been looking for, and have stayed on to a point where we have had guests hidden away in every cottage we could rent, and have even had them living on the second floor of the Yacht Club, or any place where we could put up a cot. If Saint Simons has made this sort of an impression in its first season upon the very people whom we, as Georgians, want to attract to Georgia — leaders of the financial, industrial and social life of the country — think what we should be able to do next year when our facilities are much more adequate — when the golf course is completed, and when we are really prepared to extend the traditional Southern hospitality. All of this, of course, is helping to advertise Georgia, and after all, that is one of the big things we are all interested in. As I said to Atlantans the other day, I think we have found that instead of boosting Georgia by paid advertising, as municipalities are prone to do when they raise publicity funds, all we need to do is to bring people here, show them what we have, and let them do the best kind of advertising. This plan is certainly working beautifully as far as Saint Simons is concerned. I don't see why it should not apply to other parts of the state. We have a remarkable state, and if we will only pave the highways and let people get around comfortably and see it, Georgia will make greater relative progress within the next five or ten years than any other state in the Union.

In the fall of 1930, in talking to the annual meeting of the Georgia Bar Association, Coffin made more of the same points, speaking as an adopted Georgian. Now, though, he was urging that air terminals and dirigibles and airplanes be added to the transport network of motor roads, rail lines, and waterways. And again he pulled out all the stops in his praise of the coastal islands and was specific in his description of the people he wanted to share them with. They were "the kind of people we want in Georgia — men of energy, vision, money — people who do things," who could join with him in trying to make Georgia a more interesting, a more attractive, a more prosperous place to live. There was, he said, "a bit of philanthropy and a good deal of business" tied up together in this project. And in any big project of this kind, there is bound to be a lean period, when everything is going out and very little is coming in."

His words were prophetic. The great market crash of October 1929 was just a year in the past, and its effect had not yet been fully felt at Sea Island. There were still clients left with enough money to afford a quiet vacation. But the lean years were coming fast, and in their conversations in Jones's office on Sunday mornings, Bill Jones and Jim Compton were talking more and more about how they could meet the payroll.

6

PUT THE MULES OUT TO PASTURE

The payroll was not their only concern. The little hotel, built by the company's own hastily organized construction crew, was very poorly put together. Looked upon as an interim shelter to be used only until a really fine hotel could be erected, it immediately began to need extensive and highly expensive repairs. Despite this, it had a charm about it, and in the first winter, charging $8 single, $15 double, American Plan, it was crowded, struggling to care for some 150 guests in accommodations designed to serve 100. By the winter of 1930 Compton and Jones knew they were in trouble—although they did not yet know quite how bad that trouble was. They tried to anticipate it in every way they could. At the executive committee meeting on December 9, 1929, the decision was made to suspend all development beyond that needed for basic maintenance and to cut back on sales and advertising; in short, in the old country phrase, they decided "to put the mules out to pasture" for a while.

The basic problem was with the Realty Investment Company in Detroit. Coffin, dreaming big as was his custom, had invested heavily in the aircraft business, in various manufacturing concerns, and in all aspects of the transportation business. He was the biggest stockholder in many of these bold young companies, and when they began going down the drain in the crash of 1929, he went down with them. He had a lot of valuable Detroit real estate, but this all had to be sold to make up his deficits in the aircraft investments he had bought on margin. In short, Howard Coffin was rapidly going bankrupt, and his projects all down the line felt the impact of his losses.

By the spring of 1930, Bill Jones could see the future and see it plain, and it was dark. In the year ending December 31, 1929, the little hotel had lost $60,000, nearly all of it in the last six months of the year. A million dollars in Sea Island bonds that had been issued in Detroit in 1929 had been taken care of automatically by the trustee bank, selling the stocks that were backing it up. But Sea Island still owed another $2.5 million to Detroit Realty, and all Detroit Realty's resources were mortgaged to the banks. So Sea Island found itself doing business with the Detroit Trust Company. Thus, there began for Bill Jones a year and a half of almost unremitting anxiety. Once a month for eighteen months, he rode the train to Detroit, thirty-six hours each way, to talk with the bankers, reading financial textbooks at night in his berth, trying to find a way out of his dilemma.

Jones had little formal training in high finance, but his instinct for managing money had been demonstrated early in life. After a year in public high school, he had gone for three years to the Moraine Park School, an early experiment in progressive education. He had been elected class banker, and out of this experience grew an interest in business that took him to the Wharton School of Business at the University of Pennsylvania. His studies were soon interrupted by illness. From there he had come South to Sapelo where his true education into the brutal facts of economic life had begun.

One thing was deeply in his favor. The last thing these Michigan bondholders wanted was to be forced to take over, in a time of deepening depression, a little resort hotel deep in the wilds of Georgia. And they seemed to trust Bill Jones and his attorney, Charles Wright, who was also Detroit Realty vice-president and Jones's guide through the troubled financial waters. With Wright's legal help and with that of Miss Lena Carle, Coffin's secretary-treasurer, Sea Island Company, for nearly three years after the crash, managed to receive enough of Detroit Realty's declining assets to meet its obligations in Detroit and to keep the little hotel in Georgia open and operating. One thing that made that miracle possible was the attitude of the officials in Glynn County. Knowing how desperately Jones and Compton were struggling to keep the Sea Island Company afloat and knowing how many Glynn countians would be hurt if Coffin's enterprise should go under, County Commissioner Malcolm McKinnon and his associates told Jones to forget all county taxes until he was able to pay them. He did pay them, in time, and though under no legal obligation to do so, he also paid off at fifty cents on the dollar the Brunswick folk who had invested in the little hotel company that had built the Cloister.

Howard Coffin's reaction to the rapid crumbling of his fortunes was one of bleak despair. In 1932, just before the gift-tax laws went into effect, he turned over to Bill Jones the management of all his affairs. He also conveyed to him, and members of the Jones family as his natural heirs, all his remaining assets in money and property—and all his debts. Two things occurring in quick succession brought on this action. On February 26, 1932, the weak heart that had troubled Matilda Coffin all her years failed at last. She died at Bill and Kit Jones's house on Sea Island and was buried in Christ Church yard, beneath a great oak tree. Eleven days earlier in that same month, the word had come down from Detroit. There were no more resources left in the Detroit Company. Coffin, whose heart had long been in Georgia rather than Detroit, had used every scrap of Detroit Realty assets in his effort to save Sea Island. The Sea Island Company was now on its own. The combined effect of his beloved wife's death and the confirmation of his own disastrous financial situation crushed completely the spirit of this man of fire and dreams. He was a builder, whether of an automobile or a great mansion or an island haven. When he no longer had the money to turn his dreams into realities, life lost its meaning for him.

Dental problems and a general physical malaise, which no doctor seemed able to diagnose, also beset him and caused him to withdraw further from the world. He moved to New York, where he lived in the solemn surroundings of the Engineers Club. Friends in the textile business, hoping to raise him from his mood of bleak despair, created a job for him as chairman of the board of Southeastern Cottons, Incorporated, at a salary of $30,000 a year. He took it, but Georgia still called him, and he spent much of his time at Runnymede Light, the Joneses' cottage on Sea Island, where they had fixed up an apartment for him.

By the mid-1930s the little company was struggling desperately to survive. While Bill Jones wrestled with the overall finances, Jim Compton worked with quiet desperation to keep the hotel going. Personnel was reduced to a point beyond which the hotel could not go if it hoped to give even reasonably good service to its guests. Wages and salaries were reduced as much as they could be reduced if the hotel hoped to keep any help at all. Bill Jones cut his own pay down to $500 a month, using Kit's own resources to pay the grocery bills, and Jim Compton took only $12,000 a year. Maintenance at the golf course was cut back to the minimum that would keep the layout playable. Rates at the hotel went down to $5.50 single and $11.00 double for a room and three good meals, American Plan. Some young men were invited down at rates even lower than this. A Bachelor's Club of young Atlantans, handsome, mannerly, and good dancers, were brought down to dance with the northern belles who came with their parents during the winter. When cash on hand was almost gone, scrip was issued in denominations of five cents up to five dollars.

The fact that the little hotel had any cash to back up this scrip came about almost by accident. By sheer luck, Bill Jones was in Detroit the day the two big banks there closed their doors. Knowing that if two such powerful institutions as these were in financial distress, the rest of the country must indeed be in bad shape, he left at once for Dayton. There he went to Greene and Ladd, a brokerage house owned by a relative of Kit Jones's, and borrowed $6,000 in cash on his account there. He hurried home to Georgia and turned the money over to Jim Compton. More than 200 employees of the company at that time were being paid in scrip, and so great was the confidence of the community in Bill Jones and Jim Compton and their little company, that every grocery store, drugstore, filling station, and business house in the county honored the Sea Island paper without question. Every dollar that came in, from anywhere, Jim Compton added to the $6,000 Bill Jones had brought home. Thus, when in February 1933 Roosevelt closed all the banks, there was some cash on hand for emergencies, and this in time turned out to be one of the most effective of public relations gestures. Many wealthy northerners on vacation in the South, at the Cloister and elsewhere, found themselves short of cash and with no way of getting any. To their vast delight, they found that the Cloister would accept personal checks for their hotel bills and for enough money to carry them home by train or car. Among them were a few Florida vacationers who got as far as Sea Island before their funds ran out. One such vacationer was Alfred Cluett, the shirt man. Cluett and his wife had many millions of dollars between them, but with the banks closed, neither could lay hands on a penny. When the cashier at the Cloister cheerfully agreed to buy his railroad ticket north for him, Cluett decided he would be foolish to venture into the world outside, where madness seemed to reign. He would stay here in this quiet place and settle down. He did, and two years later he bought a cottage. Several other wayfarers made the same decision, becoming good patrons of the hotel and, later, residents of the cottage colony.

How Bill Jones brought Sea Island Company through the depression years makes a fascinating story, a textbook classic to the student of money management, though too intricate in its details to relate in a general history. The overwhelming need was for cash to redeem the outstanding bonds, and for this Jones turned to his own resources. The $300,000 his father had given him was still intact, in the form of Realty Investment Incorporated notes. The greatest other asset was Howard Coffin's beloved Sapelo. But where could a buyer for Sapelo be found in this depression time? To Jones's vast relief, Richard W. Courts, Atlanta broker with a wide acquaintanceship in national financial circles, had the answer. Richard J. Reynolds, tired of wandering the world on his own freighter and beset by family sorrows, was looking for a quiet hideaway. At the invitation of Dick Courts, he was brought down to Sapelo to see the place and was taken from there to Cabin Bluff on a turkey shoot. To make sure that all things pleased him, his host arranged that he be guided to a special stand set up where turkeys were known to gather in great numbers at dawn each morning. Unhappily, the guides made a mistake. They took two young Atlantans, Bill Parker and Howard Dobbs, to Reynolds's stand, and as soon as the guide gave his squawking call, there came a chorus of answering gobbles and a flurry of wings. Parker and Dobbs killed four turkeys with four shots. Reynolds, on his far-off stand, did not get a shot.

This did not dismay him. Not long after, he agreed to pay Bill Jones $700,000 for Sapelo with another $50,000 added if the yacht *Zapala* was thrown in. With that money, Jones, on the advice of Courts, who served as his trustee, went into the market and began buying up the Realty Investment Company bonds, then selling at about eleven cents on the dollar. These bonds were backed by Detroit real estate and by Sea Island Company properties in Georgia. When he had acquired about half of them, he went to the trustees of the Detroit Realty bond issue and offered them for cancellation, along with his realty notes. Under this arrangement he would receive clear title to the Sea Island properties, and the Detroit bondholders would retain the interest in the Michigan real estate. After huffing and puffing for about a year, the Detroit trustees agreed, provided that they keep 20 percent of the company stock of the Sea Island Company. Jones agreed, and he continued buying up bonds at fifteen, twenty, and even as much as thirty cents on the dollar. It took eleven years, but finally in 1940 Bill Jones went to Detroit with the last of the bonds, trading them for the twenty percent stock interest in Sea Island still held by the trustees. For the first time, the little company owned itself and was out of debt. Many times during these years Bill and Kit Jones had wondered whether they should throw up the whole idea and go back north. Now they knew they would never go back.

In addition to Richard Courts, Jones in these precarious depression years had sound advice from several Georgia capitalists. Cator Woolford, founder of the Retail Credit Company, was a friend and neighbor who had bought Altama, the great plantation in Glynn County formerly owned by the DuPonts. Solely out of a desire to help his friend and neighbor Bill Jones, Woolford agreed to serve as chairman of the Sea Island Company executive committee, and on his advice Jones asked a number of other distinguished Georgians to serve on the board of directors. Among them were Cason Callaway of LaGrange and Scott Hudson and L.W. (Chip) Robert of Atlanta. On the board with Coffin as chairman were Jones as president, Compton as vice-president and general manager, and Charles Wright and E.W. Lewis of

Detroit as vice-presidents. An array of distinguished citizens of Glynn County, including Millard Reese, Potter F. Gould, and William H. Parker, also were on the board.

Even through the darkest times, Bill Jones and Jim Compton were determined to keep on improving services, to keep on building. In 1933, when the hotel had only about seventy-five employees, they hired a young sports director named Irving Harned to take over as director of the Cloister sports program. Harned was a Quaker, like Coffin and Jones's ancestors, with the instinct for innkeeping that the Brethren seemed to possess, and he also was trained at the Cornell Hotel School. He soon justified their confidence in him. Gradually, under a succession of managers—Pancoast, Wannop, Beers—he rose to become one of the nation's outstanding hotel managers. Every year some little improvement to the physical plant was added—a wing over the kitchen, an addition to the dining room, a planting of trees or flowers, a speed-up of laundry service—whatever was needed to make a guest happier or more comfortable. Harned, as he took over the managers post, introduced, and continued as long as he lived, a custom that gave guests from all over the country pleasant memories of him and of his hotel. This was the Thursday evening cocktail party at which he and Stella, his wife, welcomed guests and introduced newly arrived couples to each other. Another thoughtful Cloister custom was that of giving lady guests a corsage of orchids or gardenias on their departure. Guests who left with happy memories of the hotel were likely to come back and urge their friends to join them, and from these "repeaters" the cottage colony was built.

On Sea Island 125 lots were owned by people who had bought back in the pre-Coffin days, when lots were selling for $100, up to $250 for a corner lot on the beach. By now the company had put some $5 million into the hotel, the golf course, and other developments, and all of this had enhanced the value of lots over which the company had no control. Throughout the depression, therefore, the company acted as broker for these privately owned lots, selling them off at a profit to the local owners, to more affluent buyers who would in time put up handsome houses on them. Thus the value of company-owned lots, which were kept off the market, was greatly enhanced.

The depression, as Jones looks back on it now, taught him and his associates lessons that insured the survival and the progress of Sea Island in the years to come. In the 1970s, when banks and REITS and developers everywhere were plunging headlong into multimillion-dollar projects that were destined to fail, Jones was remembering what had happened forty years earlier. In an enterprise like the Sea Island Company, the big money lies in the sale of land, but when the times are such that the land will not sell, then the resort area—the hotel, the beach, the golf courses, the tennis courts, the swimming pools—must be attractive enough to carry the whole load until times get better and land sales increase. Otherwise the whole operation goes under. But all these amenities must be developed on a pay-as-you-go basis. They must be provided without incurring a long-term debt. And that is how Bill Jones and Jim Compton managed the finances of the Sea Island Company during the depression years. As a result, the little company made its first small profit in 1941. But the cautious pay-as-you-go process did not change thereafter. Growth was financed out of income, and as the old bonded debt finally was paid off, Bill Jones and his family, with Jim Compton and his family as minority stockholders, at last owned the Sea Island Company free and clear.

Howard Coffin did not live to see this happy issue out of its financial afflictions. In 1937, lonely and morose in New York, he had met and married a young woman named Gladys Baker, a free-lance journalist. The wedding was in June, and Coffin soon realized that he had made a mistake. Leaving the new Mrs. Coffin in New York in their apartment on Fifth Avenue, he moved back to Georgia in early November, taking up residence with the Joneses at their new home on Seventeenth Street. On the morning of November 21, 1937, Bill and Kit Jones were on their way home from New York, where they had gone at Coffin's request to talk to his new wife about arrangements for a quiet separation and divorce. On the way home by train, in Rocky Mount, North Carolina, Bill Jones got a message telling him to call Jim Compton. In a few minutes he had the tragic news. Howard Coffin was dead. Seeing no way out of his troubles, he had taken his own life with a rifle.

Bill Jones hurried home to Sea Island. There he quietly and effectively handled all final arrangements. He settled with the new Mrs. Coffin and her lawyer on the amount of the widow's compensation she should receive until her own death or remarriage. He arranged for the funeral to be held at Runnymede Light, the Joneses' cottage. Howard Coffin, after a brief graveside service, was buried beside his first wife, Matilda, in the old cemetery of Christ Church on Saint Simons. The passerby today may note the somewhat unusual placing of the graves. The Coffin plot is a square, forty feet on each side, enclosed by a tabby wall two feet high. The simple gravestones lie flat, and they are not parallel with the walls but lie on the diagonal. This reflects a curious quirk in Coffin's thinking. In life, whenever possible, he slept with his head to the north, for he believed that if he did not, the rotation of the earth had a deleterious effect on the circulation of the blood.

Though born on an Ohio farm, Howard Coffin in his quarter-century in the south had become a true Georgian in his heart, and the people of his adopted state were quick to recognize and honor this quality in him. He was an advisor to governors; and three Georgia universities—Mercer, Oglethorpe, and Georgia Tech—awarded him honorary degrees. Less than two years after his death in 1937, the citizens of Brunswick and Glynn County paid him a particularly fitting tribute. At Brunswick, the Howard E. Coffin Recreational Center was dedicated. Planes from McKinnon Airport on Saint Simons, whose land Coffin had given to the county, circled overhead, and from one of them Mayor W.E. Allen of Augusta dropped a memorial wreath. Major Clark Howell, publisher of the *Atlanta Constitution*, spoke in tribute, saying of Howard Coffin that "he was in some respects a greater Georgian than many of us native sons, for he had the vision to discern and develop what our state possessed when we perhaps were less observant, less audacious, and less willing to gamble on our judgment." Through Coffin's vision, Howell said, "new energy, new life, new appreciation for our Georgia will emerge for an innumerable company," in years to come, as young and old alike come to enjoy the park and playground. Inviting his hearers to look about them, "to feel the pulsing freshness and vitality of this scene," he told them that Howard Coffin's "dynamic influence, his creative mind and understanding spirit will be found here so long as a single child remains to play, or a weary soul to seek refreshment."

Thirty years later, in 1969, another lasting memorial was dedicated to Coffin, the Howard E. Coffin Physical Education Building at Brunswick Junior College. John Gilbert, lawyer for the Sea Island Company and member of the board of trustees for the Brunswick Junior College Foundation (of which A.W. Jones, Sr. was president) was as eloquent in his tribute to Coffin as Clark Howell had been. He struck the same note as he spoke of Coffin's contributions to coastal Georgia, notably to the near-wilderness that before his coming had been Saint Simons and Sea Island. Now, he said,

> we have·but to look around to possess the legacy he left us. His handiwork is visible throughout Glynn County. For here we have lived by his tenets ... we have saved our natural beauty...

we have grown and built but refrained from destroying or cluttering . . . and as he predicted, we have prospered. Because he loved and appreciated what nature has bestowed upon us, he recognized that others would want to share with us our natural heritage.

To describe that heritage, he closed with a line from a poem Coffin himself had often quoted:

> Here care ebbs out with every tide
> And peace comes in upon the flood.
> The heart looks out on life clear-eyed,
> And finds it good.

7

ENTER, MRS. CATE

Though Matilda Coffin died in 1932 and Howard Coffin in 1937, leaving no children of their own, they had lived long enough to come to know and to fix their hearts and treasures upon a second generation of Joneses. Early on the morning of January 3, 1930, an important event occupied the minds of Bill and Kit Jones which had nothing to do with meeting payrolls, or quieting querulous bondholders. The evening before, following a dinner party at their first little cottage on Twenty-sixth Street, they drove quickly to the hospital in Savannah. There, around one o'clock the next morning, Alfred W. Jones, Jr., arrived.

He was also to be known as Bill Jones, and he would grow up to share his father's feeling for the beauty of Sea Island, the "glooms of the live oaks" where the deer walked, the high sky piled with sunset clouds, the many voices of the surf on the long Sea Island beach, and the glow of the sun on the marshes. His acquaintance with the marshes began early. Once when the Jones family was en route to Savannah on a friend's yacht, they put in at Sapelo to have dinner with the Coffins. The 230-foot craft drew too much water to get up to the main dock, so Kit and Bill Jones followed nervously at the heels of a surefooted sailor, who walked a long narrow plank in the darkness, swinging at his side a basket in which young Bill Jones burbled happily.

Growing up with nature all around him, his earliest interests were in the earth and its products of timber and foodstuffs, game, fish, and waterfowl. After completing prep school at Millbrook in New York, he came home to continue his education at the University of Georgia. There he enrolled in the schools of forestry and agriculture. Like Howard Coffin, he did not particularly care for the social gatherings by which Bill Jones, Sr., so graciously introduced the Sea Island colony to prospective citizens, and this for a while troubled his father. But soon the senior Jones began to realize that young Bill's way, though different from his own, represented just as deep an interest in the future of Sea Island. He too was determined that it remain a place for which many people from many places could feel a very special affection.

The qualities of outgoing uninhibited personal friendliness and amiable bonhomie were well represented in the Jones family by the second son, Howard Coffin Jones, known as Howdy. As manager of the Beach Club, he basked in the spotlight during the summer when he introduced swimming coach Percy Walters's swimmers and high divers in spectacular demonstrations around the swimming pool, where guests dined alfresco by the light of Japanese lanterns.

Two other Jones children, who were born on the island and grew up loving it, now serve on its board of directors along with their father and brothers. They are Marianna, whose husband, David Kuntz, for many years had come with his family from Dayton to their Sea Island cottage, and young Katharine, known as Kappy, who is Mrs. Paul O'Connor of Milwaukee. They in turn have multiplied happily, and now a third generation of the Jones-Talbott blood is closely linked to Sea Island.

Bill, Jr., and Betty Macdonald Jones's children are Ann

Macdonald, A.W. Jones III, and James Macdonald; Howdy's are Margaret Ann and Melanie Elizabeth; Marianna and David Lee Kuntz's are David, Jr., Katharine Jones, Charles Edward, and Judith Ann; Kappy and Paul O'Connor's are Katharine Isobel, Marianna Teresa, Elizabeth Ann, and Sarah Talbott. The older ones among them sit in on directors meetings, and by the tenor of their questions indicate that they share their grandfather's and grandmother's feelings toward the place.

Thus for some time to come, the Jones name and the Jones instinct for creating a peaceful carefree place where "the heart looks out on life clear-eyed and finds it good" will be synonymous with Sea Island and the Cloister, and with similar developments yet to come.

While the Joneses and the Comptons, the Harneds and the Baumgardners made the top-level decisions that gave Sea Island its direction and set its mood, there were many who by their own varied talents gave it special ambience. One of the earliest of these was Mary Wylie McCarty, wife of Edwin McCarty of Atlanta. Mrs. McCarty, who was Mary Wylie Jones of Waycross, a schoolteacher when Cator Woolford called her to Atlanta to handle his philanthropic bequests, came to Sea Island in 1930 to take over as director of advertising, promotion, and publicity. She succeeded Charles Redden, who was a brilliant public-relations man, but whose $75,000-a-year budget was more than Jones and Compton felt the little company could bear during parlous times. Redden's proposal that Sea Island be turned into a second Jekyll, a club limited to 350 persons who would pay an entrance fee of $10,000 each, also did not materialize, so at the end of January 1930 his contract was terminated.

Coffin, Jones, Compton, and others soon discovered that Mrs. McCarty, in her quiet way, was as effective at publicizing the Cloister as her sponsor, Cator Woolford, had predicted she would be. She came to have a particularly warm rapport with Howard Coffin, who greatly admired the way she handled *Cloister Bells,* a picture magazine showing the great and the near great as they played or relaxed at the Cloister. Mindful of Jim Compton's admonition to do things well but to do them inexpensively, she made a deal with the Ruralist Press in Atlanta, which printed the Salvation Army *War Cry.* When the *War Cry's* pressrun was finished, McCarty would come in immediately with her *Cloister Bells* text and pictures to be printed on the same paper by the same rotogravure process. As a result of coming in on the end of the *War Cry* run, she got her printing for practically nothing.

The pictures were beautifully done, and Mrs. McCarty was careful to give the reader a good pictorial mix combining dreamlike scenery with notables of the political, social, financial, literary, and sporting world doing interesting things with rods, guns, tennis rackets, and golf clubs against a primeval background. She also discovered that the element of surprise was invaluable. A picture of Bobby Jones, not on the golf course, but playing leapfrog on the beach, made all the papers in the country.

She got along very well with the press, maintaining a particular rapport with the society editors of the national dailies. Some twenty of them put her on their correspondent payroll at ten dollars a month for the season, at a time when ten dollars was a lot of money. In return, she sent them stories of the doings of their local people at Sea Island. As a result, on many Sundays she had a story in the society section of nearly every big city paper. She also was helpful to the editors in other ways. She would invite them down to the Cloister to see for themselves what kind of place it was, and by such methods she got a tremendous amount of free publicity for the hotel in its opening days. The Cloister could not afford paid advertising in its lean years unless the fee could be paid for by providing guest accommodations, which some papers were happy to accept. Among the earliest honeymooners, in fact, were young reporters and their brides, given due bills at the Cloister as a wedding present from their publishers.

Though paid ads were too expensive, Mary Wylie devised a plan of her own that brought in a great deal of business. She would pay society editors a nickel a piece for names and addresses of prominent people in their city who habitually went to Florida for the winter. Then she would write these individuals a warm and welcoming note, inviting them to stop off at the Cloister on their way down or back. She would also take a *Who's Who* to bed with her, making lists of people she felt would find Sea Island a pleasant place. She managed to lay hands on the membership rosters of a number of golf, tennis, gun, yacht, and social clubs, and she would write these individuals letters slanted to their particular interests. To these she added those listed in the New York Social Register, and in time she had built up a file of several thousand names.

It took some doing, this struggle to get a new and unknown resort off the ground in the middle of a depression, and it went on for years. As a result of her deft salesmanship, though, the Cloister in the worst of times kept nearly all of its rooms filled. In 1933, for example, it turned away 1,000 guests for a lack of room while other resort hotels were empty.

In 1935, despite urgings from Coffin, Compton, and Jones, Mary Wylie McCarty decided to retire to Atlanta and a lifetime of private good works. In his farewell letter to her, Howard Coffin spoke of "how very greatly we all appreciate your long term of service. If you have been one-half as happy in this association as we have been to have you, then certainly the combination has been a successful one." Thirty-three years later, in 1968, in a letter to Mrs. McCarty at her home on Habersham Road in Atlanta, Bill Jones wrote his thanks for a book she had sent him, and he added, "I'm sure you realize how much we continue to appreciate the great job you did in those early years in getting us 'off the ground". In looking back, it was really quite exciting when we were all feeling our way along. Now that we are what I guess would be termed a mature resort, we don't really have the day to day excitement, with the multitude of problems. Our real problems now are just a few big ones, and sometimes I think that perhaps we are a little too conservative, but I'm afraid it'll take the next generation after I'm gone to make any drastic changes in our basic policies."

Mrs. McCarty was followed by a succession of young ladies, each in her own way highly effective at publicizing the Cloister. Her immediate successor was Elizabeth Thompson, who in turn was followed by Mary Hurd Hillyer, Louise Ferguson, Rita Van Pelt, Nancy Beyer, and Eunice Rein. There the female line ran out, and the job of publicity and advertising was taken over by ex-newspaperman Sig Kaufmann.

One of the most effective publicists of Sea Island and the Cloister was not a professional in the field but a historian and teacher, Mrs. Margaret Davis Cate. Knowing that Howard Coffin was fascinated by Georgia history and that he wanted Cloister guests to share his enthusiasm, she, along with Mary Wylie McCarty, saw to it that Sea Island, which had no real history of its own, was tied in with all the areas around it which were rich in records of the ages past. Leopold Hazzard, Fannie Kemble's old boatman, was still alive, and his stories of the old days led Coffin to order that boats be built of hollow logs in the old plantation way, and that races be held in the Black Banks River where it flowed by the Cloister Apartments, with the boatmen singing the old racing chanteys as found and recorded by Mrs. Maxfield Parrish. One of the boats may still be seen on the Cloister grounds, along with a huge iron syrup kettle, a relic of plantation days.

Mrs. Cate was widely known in Georgia as one of the more remarkable local historians of her day. On the death of her husband, Dr. G.V. Cate, of Brunswick, she moved to Sea Island in

1932, and soon thereafter she began her series of lectures, telling of Spanish mission days, of Aaron Burr taking refuge at Butler's Point, of Audubon at Kings Retreat. In 1943, through the good offices of Bill Jones, she was made postmistress of Sea Island, which gave her a livelihood while she pursued her hobby of historical research. One of her outstanding contributions was the publication, with Dr. Orrin Wightman as photographer, of a remarkable text and picture history, *Early Days of Coastal Georgia.* Published in 1955 by the Fort Frederica Association, with an introduction by Bill Jones, it is still a classic history of the region.

Her interests, however, lay not alone in preserving old records or telling old stories; she was equally interested in the preservation and, to the degree it was possible without violating historic truth, the restoration of all the historic places in Glynn, Camden, and McIntosh counties. All these were of interest to her, but Fort Frederica on Saint Simons, Oglethorpe's valiant little fortified town, was her obsession. In 1935, at her urging, Howard Coffin had gotten a bill through Congress making Fort Frederica a national monument of the United States Park Service, but no money was provided for the acquisition of the land. In 1941, four years after Coffin's passing, the Fort Frederica Association was chartered and organized with Judge Price Gilbert of Atlanta as its first president. On the association's executive committee were Bill Jones, Mrs. Frank F. Jones, representing the Colonial Dames, and H.J. Friedman of Glynn County. From these and other sources, money was raised to purchase eighty acres around the ruins of the old fort, and the Sea Island Company, through Bill Jones, gave a tract adjoining the area of the fort. So at last, in 1947, the old fort became a national monument. Judge Gilbert again was named its president; Alfred Jones, vice-president; Potter Gould, secretary-treasurer. Attorneys Frank Scarlett and Charles Gowen of Brunswick were especially honored for their great service in tracing land titles back through musty records to the earliest days. Mrs.

Cate was made official historian, a duty she fulfilled with infinite zest. She developed records that guided the Park Service in its research until the entire little town could be laid out. The tabby foundations of all the little houses revealed exactly where they had been when Oglethorpe himself walked these streets. In 1951, with Bill Jones presiding, and Charles Fairbanks, archaeologist of the National Park Service, looking on, she lifted the first shovel of earth and leaf mulch that over a period of two hundred years had covered the town site. And just as she had predicted, she uncovered the foundation of the first two houses built at Frederica. She insisted on absolute historical accuracy in all restorations. When "Bummy" Baumgardner, landscape architect for Sea Island and the Frederica Association, planted a certain variety of azalea in the vicinity of the fort, she snipped the blossoms off. This variety of azalea did not grow there, she said, sending Baumgardner back to the woods to find the proper wild azaleas. Thousands of Cloister guests over the years remember the lectures given in the Spanish Lounge by Mrs. Cate, and thousands, too, were saddened by her death in 1961.

For the Cloister it would be unthinkable to be without a historian, and there happened to be one close at hand. Richard (Dick) Everett in the Cloister reservation office—a nephew of "Dutch" Everett, the Saint Simons grocer who had helped the hotel make it through the lean years by cheerfully accepting the scrip with which Sea Island Company paid its employees—had come to work at Sea Island in 1934. Everett had worked first as a storeroom clerk, then as a steward, and later as a purchasing agent. After serving in World War II, he had come back to the Cloister, where Jones, Harned, and Compton all realized that here was a man singularly gifted at handling people. He soon worked up to the position of resident manager in charge of reservations, where he displayed an exquisite talent for finding space for those people the Cloister wanted and for turning away those it did not want. In all his early years he found no chance to complete his formal education, but he had an insatiable desire for knowledge, and he spent his spare time reading the essays in the *New Yorker* magazine, looking up in the dictionary the words he did not understand. This developed in him a most remarkable vocabulary and an extremely sophisticated sense of humor. These he coupled with an insatiable curiosity about the history of the hotel where he worked. As a result, his lectures, illustrated by lantern slides, were as factual as Mrs. Cate's, but they had a spark and glisten all their own. Dick Everett died of a heart attack in 1975. Now the Sea Island history lectures are given by Mary Burdell, and they too are soundly researched and warmly delivered.

Whatever could contribute to the enjoyment of its guests, the Cloister had always striven to provide. As well remembered by Cloister guests as were Margaret Cate and Dick Everett is the famed harpist, Artiss de Volt Zacharias, whose concerts in the Spanish Lounge over the years have brought to many an experience of beauty they had never known before. Artiss de Volt's talents, not only as an artist on the harp but as a teacher and arranger of musical events, have made the Cloister a mecca for musicians and lovers of good music from far beyond the islands. In 1978 she ushered in the spring season with a program of seven harpists, a flutist, three ballerinas, and a talented young pianist. Sea Islanders on the program were Willou Smith, Mrs. de Volt's first pupil and the wife of Bill Smith of the company's real estate division, and their small daughter, Leigh Ann. A mother and daughter trio came from the cottage colony, Mrs. Harton Semple of Pittsburgh and her daughters, Heather and Cherry, also played in the harp recital. Beaming proudly from a front row were two generations of Joneses, listening raptly as a third generation member, James Macdonald Jones, age seventeen, son of Bill and Betty Jones, performed under the eye of his piano teacher, Mrs. Clyde Smith, of Brunswick. For Kit and Bill Jones, Sr., it was a nostalgic moment, for young Jim was displaying a talent inherited, perhaps, from his great grandmother, Katharine Houk Talbott, who was herself a pianist of concert quality.

8

CHURCHILL'S DAUGHTER, HOLLAND'S QUEEN

Harp concerts and historical lectures, no matter how rewarding to the mind and spirit, were not the main attraction that Sea Island had to offer in its early years. In thousands of letters couched in glowing prose, sent out to prospective guests all over the nation, the overall charm of the place was extolled. The point was strongly made that here at this new resort the person of modest affluence could bask in the same winter sun that warmed the multimillionaires on nearby Jekyll Island, feel the same cool breezes, watch the same seagulls swirl and dip above the same blue sea, and stand mute before the glory of the same sunset clouds. To all this natural beauty was added the best of all sports—golf, tennis, skeet, deer and turkey shooting, horseback riding along forest trails, cycling, swimming in surf or pool, or sailing. For restless youngsters there was an activities director to organize all sorts of games—croquet, archery, badminton, crabbing, bowling on the green, and hunting for turtle eggs. And for the lonely elderly of both sexes there was a social director quick to arrange a game of golf or bridge or merely to provide a sympathetic listening ear to those who wished to pour out their troubles. For lovers of all ages, there was alfresco dancing on the moonlit patio, and for the more than modestly affluent, there were places to dock their yachts as they broke their journey to and from Florida to dine and dance at the Cloister. The letter stressed two points — the opportunity for activities from tennis to turkey shooting, or the equal opportunity to do nothing at all, to laze the golden days away in utter relaxation. The latter point seemed to have the greatest appeal in the troubled decade of the 1930s.

One letter, signed by Howard Coffin on January 10, 1931 and sent to more than 2,000 members of the Detroit Athletic Club, had a particularly poignant meaning in light of what the future held for him. On the letterhead of the chairman of the board, he wrote:

> Not for years have those of us who carry the responsibilities of business been in such need of a good old-fashioned, simple rest. Nerves, minds and bodies need the complete relaxation that rebuilds. We need to get away from all the noise and strain of life — to get the cobwebs of unreality out of our brains and build into ourselves again those qualities of clear thought and initiative which have enabled us to achieve in the past.

> We need days and nights of normal living, exercise, good food, restful sleep with the sound of waves on the beach and the smell of pine forests in the air. We have all been living too fast and too hard, and over-spending ourselves for things which have seemed worthwhile.

> Years ago I sought and found a refuge of my own among these sunny Isles of the Georgia coast. This is a country, lovely and unspoiled, and it will do for you now what it has done many times for me.

> Here you will find a wealth of romance and history to charm your mind while nature mends your jaded nerves. Here you can enjoy every worthwhile sport — or you can laze away your days just sitting in the sun. For forty years, leaders in the financial and business world — Morgans, Goulds, Bakers, Rockefellers, and a score of others have sought just such a retreat on nearby Jekyll Isle.

If you need what most of us need in these strenuous days, you'll slip away to this wonderful country of the "Golden Isles." The Cloister is only thirty-two hours from Detroit, with instant communication, yet there's nothing on the whole isle to remind you of business and its cares.

You will find a welcome awaiting you here.

And indeed thousands did come to find that welcome — most of them quiet upper-middle-class business and professional men and industrialists from Canada and nearly all the states, most of them little known outside their home communities. But there was also among them a goodly sprinkling of the nationally known — bank and railroad presidents, oil company chief executives, paper and soap manufacturers, and heads of large insurance companies.

With the business types there also came an amazing number of celebrities in other fields. The visit of Calvin Coolidge in 1928 was just the first of a long parade of political figures, writers, artists, actors and actresses whom Sea Island welcomed to the Cloister or the cottage colony. Among the political figures were the Hoovers, who followed the Coolidges. William Gibbs McAdoo came down wearing a high stiff collar, and Mayor Jimmy Walker and his wife were photographed holding fishing poles and a string of fish. The mayor was attired as if for a meeting of city council, in a natty double-breasted pin-striped suit with his cravat neatly knotted at the throat. Eddie Rickenbacker dropped by often, as did a young racing pilot named Jimmy Doolittle, still some years away from his famed bombing raid over Tokyo. As the years passed, the flow of celebrities increased — Hopalong Cassidy came and charmed young and old alike. Ike and Mamie Eisenhower came down, and Ike was particularly gracious toward the kitchen help who had chipped in their ration coupons to send a plank steak up to his cottage for his dinner. He put on his full dress uniform with all his medals when he went to the kitchen to thank them.

Ike's visit was cut short by an emergency in Washington. He had come down at the invitation of Charles Gowen, new president of the Georgia Bar Association, to address the assembled lawyers in Savannah. On the Friday morning before he was to speak that night, President Truman called him. A railroad strike was brewing, and Truman wanted Ike, his Chief of Staff, there to take command if he had to call out the military to run the trains. Ike went back by plane to Washington, and Gowen read his speech to the lawyers. It was, Gowen recalled, an anticlimax. The Joneses were also disappointed. Ike did not have time to plant a tree on the Cloister lawn. "Eisenhower Oak" is there in his honor, but it was planted by the landscape department.

Other notables who came were Dean Acheson, Arthur Brisbane, the Hearst columnist who was supposed to be the highest-paid newspaperman in the world, and Miss Martha Berry, of her famous mountain school. Opera singers Gladys Swarthout and Giovanni Martinelli found the Sea Island climate kind to the vocal cords. Thomas E. Dewey came in 1944 to lick his political wounds, and Vice-President and Mrs. Alben Barkley spent their honeymoon at the Cloister. This was another tribute to the romantic aura that surrounded the place for the "Veep" was many years the senior of his bride. Mr. and Mrs. Edsel Ford and their children came. Col. and Mrs. Hugh Cooper were guests, Col. Cooper being the American engineer in charge of building the $100 million Dneiper Dam in Russia, one of the greatest projects of its kind in history.

John D. Rockefeller, Jr., and Mrs. Rockefeller came down while the restoration of Williamsburg was under way. They showed much interest in the history of the area, so Bill and Kit Jones suggested they all go to Sunday services at Christ Church, Frederica. It resulted in mild embarrassment to the Joneses, for on this day the new rector, not knowing the Rockefellers were in the congregation chose as his text the passage that declares that it is easier for a camel to pass through the eye of a needle than for a rich man to enter heaven. Mr. Rockefeller did not seem to notice.

Sea Island was particularly attractive to the writing set. Ben Ames Williams, famous short-story writer, had been coming to Georgia since 1928, and he had often visited Howard Coffin at Sapelo. His work "Great Oaks" was laid there, and he followed Coffin to Sea Island, where he rented Chip Robert's cottage. At Coffin's request he wrote the charter for the Pirates Club of pretty girls, which Coffin founded to welcome *Old Ironsides* to Brunswick and which still exists.

In 1931 the nation's most famous playwright, Eugene O'Neill, arrived seeking the peace that actress Ilka Chase had assured him he would find there. Weary and tense after a number of busy and productive years in France, where he produced his great trilogy, *Mourning Becomes Electra,* he and his wife, actress Carlotta Monterey, built a spacious twenty-two-room house of Spanish peasant style, which they called Casa Genotta, a blending of the names Gene and Carlotta. The blending of the names was perhaps significant, for O'Neill's obsession with his work in France had brought about a tension between them which he had hoped a change of scene and climate would repair. On April 7, 1931, just before they left France for the United States and the opening of *Mourning Becomes Electra* in New York, he had poured out his heart to Carlotta in a poignant apology, a brief typed note that somehow found its way into the Sea Island Company files. Addressed simply "To Carlotta," it read,

> In memory of the interminable days of rain in which you bravely suffered in silence that this trilogy might be born—days when I had my work, but you had nothing but household frets, and a blank vista through the salon windows of the gray land of Le Plessis, with the wet black trees still dripping, and the mist wraiths mourning over the drowned fields. Days

when you have the self-forgetting love to greet my lunchtime, depressing, sunk preoccupation with a courageous, cheering banter, days which for you were utterly lonely, when I seemed far away and lost to you in a grim, savage, gloomy country of my own, days which were for you like hateful, boring, inseparable enemies nagging at nerves and spirit, until an intolerable ennui and life-sickness poisoned your spirit!

In short, days in which you collaborated, as only deep love can, in the writing of this trilogy of the damned! These scripts are rightly yours and my presenting them is a gift of what is half yours already. So in hope what the trilogy may have in it will repay the travail we have gone through for its sake! I want these scripts to remind you, that I have known your love, with my love, even when I have seemed not to know: that I have seen it even when I have appeared most blind — that I have felt it warmly around me always — (even in my study in the closing pages of an act!) sustaining and comforting, as warm, secure, sanctuary for the man, after the author's despairing solitudes, and inevitable defeats, a victory of love-in-life — mother and wife and mistress and friend — and collaborator.

Collaborator, I love you!

Gene
La Plessis — April 23, 1931

And indeed their sojourn on Sea Island did seem to work its spell. Here he wrote his only comedy, *Ah Wilderness,* and here, for a while at least, he and Carlotta seemed content. The house, which cost $40,000, a considerable amount in those days, was located on a six-lot spread along the ocean at Agramont (Nineteenth) Street, had been designed by Francis Abreu, and reflected the taste and moods of both O'Neill and his former actress wife. It was designed as a workshop, not a place for social gatherings, though it was described by the press as being "livable, lovely and a world all its own." O'Neill's study, reached by a narrow spiral stair, was suggestive of a ship captain's cabin, with a fine view of the sea. O'Neill, who had chosen Sea Island as a refuge from the public adulation that came upon him following the success of *Mourning Becomes Electra*, spent most of his time in his study. Here, standing at a high captain's desk, he would work, Bill Jones remembers, for as many as twenty-four hours without stopping. Occasionally, weary of his mental labors, he would row a one-man scull, or fish in the Hampton River with Sea Island land salesman George Boll. Now and then he would be seen walking alone into the gentle surf and swimming, sometimes dangerously far out. Now and then, too, he would spend a long evening with Boll, his closest friend on the island, drinking corn whiskey they had produced in a small still set up in a room of O'Neill's house. Prohibition was still upon the land, and although few people had stills of their own, nearly every cottage had a charred keg for aging and mellowing bootleg corn. Charred kegs, with contents, were much in favor as wedding presents and were the central feature at any party. The Joneses, for example, though moderate drinkers themselves, kept a number of kegs for the benefit of their many visitors. They were kept filled with Camden County corn, provided by Ed Messick of the Cabin Bluff Hunt Club, and they were rotated periodically to hasten the mellowing process.

O'Neill, of course, was a genius, and his presence at Sea Island attracted visitors, if not stayers, of equal talents; Somerset Maugham and Sherwood Anderson came to Casa Genotta, as did Lillian Gish, George Jean Nathan, and Bennet Cerf. The other islanders saw little of these distinguished wayfarers, for O'Neill kept them hidden away behind Genotta's walls. More widely known to the general public even than O'Neill, Ben Ames Williams was cranking out his novels and short stories a few blocks away from O'Neill's cottage, but neither showed any interest in the other's presence.

The O'Neills sold their house in 1936, the year he won the

Nobel Prize, and moved away to California, trying to find again the peace of mind he was forever seeking. Ten years later, Bummy Baumgardner remembers, O'Neill decided to come back to this place that once he had called his "blessed isle, this island paradise." Baumgardner had begun to landscape another beach lot for him when O'Neill fell ill, canceling his plans to come back to Georgia. He died in 1953 at a hotel in Boston. His marriage to Carlotta, a woman of theatrical presence who strode into the Sea Island Company office to pay her monthly bills as if she were making a grand entrance on stage, had long since disintegrated. And on the island, all that remained in memory of America's greatest playwright was the pitiful memo to Carlotta and a faded picture or two. One shows O'Neill and Carlotta in bathing suits, sitting face-to-face on the beach, peering warmly into each other's eyes. Another, taken by Carlotta, shows O'Neill in a beach robe and beach chair, scratching a large white dog behind the ears. And, of course, the house, Casa Genotta, cottage number fifty-seven on the company list, still remains. When it went on the market in 1936, it was immediately snapped up by Alfred Cluett, the shirt manufacturer, who still remembered how the Cloister bought his railroad ticket for him when Roosevelt closed the banks. He kept the house until 1953, when he passed it on to a friend, H.W. (Bud) Gasque, who is the present owner.

The O'Neills added color to the Sea Island scene, but there are two other guests whom Bill and Kit Jones remember even more vividly. The first of these was Sarah Churchill, daughter of Sir Winston, an actress of some renown and a highly regarded photographer's model. In June 1949 the slender auburn-haired Miss Churchill made her debut on the American stage in a stock company playing *The Philadelphia Story* throughout the eastern states. The play had closed its sixteen-week run in Atlanta, and Miss Churchill, needing some rest, relaxation, and sunshine before starting a western tour, had come to Sea Island. With her came a tall, lanky, quick-smiling young Englishman named Anthony Beauchamp, a British society photographer specializing in portraits. Some eighteen months before, he had photographed Miss Churchill and in the process had fallen in love with her. Thus there was created a situation in real life reminiscent of the role she now was playing on the stage. In the play, the heroine, Tracy Lord, tries to make up her mind whether to wed a second time. So was Miss Churchill, who in 1945 had been divorced from the British actor Vic Oliver. Beauchamp had much going for him. Miss Churchill greatly admired his art. He had taken a picture of her she liked very much, which *Life* magazine had used on its cover. He also had the blessing of Sir Winston Churchill, a painter in oils, as were Beauchamp's father and mother, the Ernest Entwistles.

Just when and where Beauchamp popped the question and was accepted, the records do not show. But as soon as she had come down from Atlanta to check in at the Cloister, bellboys began scampering back and forth between their rooms, bearing notes. And on October 17 they announced their engagement. The setting, from the romantic as well as the publicity standpoint, could not have been more appropriate. With the tabby walls of Oglethorpe's old Fort Frederica behind them, they told reporters and photographers of their plans. They would be married the next afternoon at Runnymede Light, the Joneses' cottage. (The choice of Frederica as the place to announce the engagement was suggested by Sig Kaufmann, Brunswick newspaperman, and Miss Churchill was so delighted when she first saw the place that she climbed one of the ancient oaks so that Kaufmann's photographer, Ben Caples, could picture her perched in its branches.)

Preparing so quickly for a wedding had taken some doing, of course, on the part of Bill and Kit Jones. Their first thought was of a marriage at Christ Church, with its memories of colonial Georgia. But both Miss Churchill and Beauchamp had been divorced, and to be married there would have required a special dispensation that might never be granted. So Bill Jones's answer was simple: he would ask Glynn County Ordinary Edwin W. Dart to pronounce them man and wife in a civil ceremony, the vows any rural Georgia couple might take. First though, blood samples had to be taken and tested. Dr. M.E. Winchester, Glynn County's public health officer, performed this service in his office a few hours before the wedding. He then jumped in his car and went scurrying fifty miles to the state laboratory at Waycross. Both samples were clear of taint, and the license was issued.

There still remained the last minute details—what the bride should wear, the cake, where the bride and groom should flee for privacy after the reception. The cake was easy. The Cloister chefs put together a magnificent five-layered confection topped with a purple orchid. The bridal dress was a little more of a problem. The bride had no hat, so Stella Harned, wife of Irving Harned, the Cloister manager, gathered some white flowers and pinned them onto the tiara from her own wedding gown. The bride's dress was too loose, for after 140 performances of *The Philadelphia Story*, Miss Churchill was down to 115 pounds. Mrs. Harned's dressmaker, Mrs. Alcott, took a stitch here and there until it fitted smoothly. From somewhere, Kit Jones had produced a prie-dieu, covered in white satin, and white flowers in tall vases. Standing in full uniform as an unofficial representative of the United States Government was General Edwin Hull, vice-chief of staff. Beauchamp's best man was Cleveland industrialist J.A. MacMillan, who was vacationing at the Cloister with Mrs. MacMillan. (Beauchamp had arrived at the Cloister a few days earlier than Miss Churchill, and most of the twenty-seven guests at the wedding were people he had met there.) Stella Harned served as matron of honor to Miss Churchill, and at precisely 4:00 p.m., as the hotel orchestra struck up the wedding march, Miss Churchill came in on the arm of Anthony Beauchamp. Kneeling at the prie-dieu, placed in the bay window of the Jones's living room, facing toward England as Miss Churchill had requested, they repeated after Judge Dart their brief and simple vows. After the reception and buffet in the dining room, they slipped away with a car and driver provided by Bill Jones, driving the winding island roads as darkness fell, until they came at last to their honeymoon cottage. The next morning, to their surprise, they discovered that they were in cottage number seventy-five, next door to the Jones's Runnymede, where they had been married.

The marriage of Sir Winston Churchill's daughter naturally caused a great flurry in the press, and the story made front pages all over the nation. More than 2000 clippings fluttered in from the Cloister's clipping service within the next few days, and the story was on all the networks. In far-off England, Sir Winston and Mrs. Churchill saw these reports, and in gracious notes they expressed their gratitude to Kit and Bill Jones. They also sent pictures of themselves, personally inscribed, which are now displayed in the Joneses' living room.

Miss Churchill and her photographer spouse were not the only newlyweds to focus attention on Sea Island in that busy winter. Sea Island by now had established a reputation for being a happy place for honeymooners, and in November, Vice-President Alben Barkley and his thirty-eight-year-old bride, the former Jane Ruckes Hadley, came to the place that Barkley promptly named "this Shangri-la." They were back again for Christmas, and again a picture of a happy couple cutting a cake made front pages all over the country. This time it was no wedding cake, but one literally glowing with tiny candles celebrating the "Veep's" seventy-second birthday. This picture, the Cloister's public-relations director Louise Ferguson announced ecstatically, made even more front pages than the Churchill wedding had. So did Mr. Barkley's equally ecstatic statement that, "This place was preordained since the beginning of the world as the perfect spot for a honeymoon." The Barkleys were the 5,738th couple to honeymoon at the

Cloister since the hotel began keeping count in 1940. The figure on January 1, 1978 stood at 23,921. Records are meticulously kept, and each 1,000th couple, to their surprise and delight, are given seven days at the Cloister free.

Instant weddings and the entertainment of honeymooners could be taken in stride by the Joneses and their staff. A visitation by royalty took a great deal more planning. In December 1951 word came down from the State Department in Washington that Her Majesty Queen Juliana of the Netherlands and her consort, Prince Bernhard, would be pleased to spend the Easter weekend, April 10-13, 1952, at Sea Island if that could be arranged. Naturally it could, and in late January, after an inspection by William B. Huskey, a State Department security officer, John F. Simmons, chief of protocol, was writing Irving Harned to make the final arrangements. The Queen and His Royal Highness would occupy the top floor of Ashantilly House, giving them a good view of the sea stretching away toward Holland. With them would be Prince Bernhard's brother and his wife, the Prince and Princess Aschwen de Lippe; the Prince's valet; and William Huskey and Charles Bowles, the security officers. Tucked away at the Cloister would be various other aides, secretaries, and ladies-in-waiting, including Mr. Simmons, the chief of protocol; Admiral Forrestal, the American aide to Her Majesty; and the State Department press officer, Joseph Reaf, whose duties consisted mainly of telling the American press that Her Majesty must neither be approached nor questioned.

The employees, too, had to be thoroughly briefed on how to behave in the presence of royalty. A letter from hotel manager Irving Harned to all the help spelled it out.

> During the coming visit of Queen Juliana of the Netherlands, and her husband, Prince Bernhard, Prince of the Netherlands, it is not unlikely that some of you may, on occasion, engage in conversation with one or both of them. The following simple rules of etiquette should govern your remarks.

1. Never speak to the Queen or Prince until you are spoken to.
2. Make no attempt to prolong or change the conversation.
3. If given a hand, shake it; it is not necessary to bow or curtsy.
4. Address and/or refer to the Queen as "Your Majesty."
5. Address and/or refer to the Prince as "Your Highness."
6. In conversations of more than one exchange, end your remarks to the Queen with "Ma'am"; your remarks to the Prince with "Sir."
7. The brother of Prince Bernhard and his wife, Prince and Princess Aschwen de Lippe, are also of royal blood and they should be addressed as "Your Royal Highness." The Queen herself is the only one who is referred to as "Your Majesty."

As an example of these rules, if the Queen and Prince on leaving the Beach House, should have the following conversation with Roy Sims, Roy should make replies of a similar nature as shown:

Queen: "Good morning."
Prince: "Good morning."
Roy: "Good morning, Your Majesty. Good morning, Your Royal Highness."
Queen: "Isn't this a nice morning?"
Roy: "It certainly is, Ma'am."
Prince: "How long have you been here at Sea Island?"
Roy: "About five years, Sir."
Queen: "And do you live nearby?"
Roy: "Yes Ma'am. On St. Simons, just across the river."

If an occasion should arise when you are in doubt as to what to say or do, act with the normal good breeding and politeness you would show toward any guest in the hotel.

All went very well, though the press, of course, were not particularly charmed that they had to keep their distance while the Queen followed in the footsteps of Calvin Coolidge and planted a tree, or slipped away on Easter morning with her lady-in-waiting to the services at a little community church in a cottage on Saint Simons. She also wandered through the shops in the Cloister lobby. Celestine Sibley of the *Atlanta Constitution*, tired of practicing curtsies she would have no opportunity to use, went off on her own, seeking some little feature that would make a story. She first spoke to a security man who had been close enough to hear what the Queen was saying to those around her. He had been too occupied with his own problems to listen, he said. "What problems?" she asked. "Well," he said, "all the government allows me for a room and meals is $9 per diem. And my room here is costing me $45." Clucking sympathetically, Miss Sibley moved on. And what, she asked a clerk in the Davison's Shop, had the Queen found that pleased her? Well, the clerk said, the Queen had bought two bathing suits, size forty-eight. Miss Sibley conveyed this news of the Queen's dimensions to an anxiously waiting world.

The Queen was indeed a woman of matronly girth and manner, and Bill and Kit Jones soon discovered that neither she nor the Prince were nearly so stuffy as the protocol and press restrictions had indicated. They wanted no formal entertainment of any kind, but they were happy to join the Joneses and some of their friends at cocktails one evening at Runnymede Light. The Jones youngsters were teenagers then, and a Ping-Pong table sat in the front hall. As soon as Prince Bernhard and his brother, Prince Aschwen, came in the door they spotted the table, shed their coats, and started playing Ping-Pong. The Queen, for her part, sat and chatted easily like any amiable housefrau among friends.

The Queen also expressed a desire to see an alligator, which she referred to as a "crocodile," and Irving Harned, knowing that a 'gator was sometimes seen basking in the sun at the golf course, took her there. Luck was with him. There was not one, but two alligators, in full view. The event that the Queen and her party seemed to remember most vividly, though, was the oyster roast that the Joneses put on for them at Altama, the great plantation on the Altamaha River on the mainland across from Sapelo. Here had stood Hopeton, owned by James Hamilton Couper, who in 1825 went to Holland to study water control, learning from Queen Juliana's ancestors how to drain and dike his rice fields. The Civil War had left the fields lying waste, and in 1914, after various ownerships, the plantation was bought by William Du Pont to be used as a winter home, hunting preserve, and a training track for racehorses. In 1933 it was bought by Bill Jones's good friend and mentor Cator Woolford. Woolford, neither a hunter nor a horseman, built a handsome "playhouse" to add to the ancient tabby big house that was falling into decay, and under the spreading arms of a moss-hung oak, he added a swimming pool. In 1944 Woolford died, and Bill Jones bought the property and turned it into a tree farm and a family retreat.

He also used it for informal entertaining, particularly oyster roasts, held under the great trees, with the oysters steaming over beds of coals in the old plantation way, flares lighting the night with a flickering glow, and black descendants of the Couper slaves singing the old songs of their ancestors—the stamping, clapping, arm-waving "shouts" with which they had trod the rice with shuffling feet, mixing it with clay for planting.

All of this was laid on for the Queen, and Kit Jones was determined to keep it in the same simple picnic-in-the-open-air type of get-together that hundreds of other guests had enjoyed. This caused much anguish to Dick Everett, the hotel's assistant manager, a historian and unofficial authority on protocol. Mrs. Jones, he insisted, should get out her best china and silver. It would be unheard of, he argued, to serve a Queen on paper plates with wooden forks and paper cups. Unheard of or not, it would be done that way, picnic style, she told him. And it was. She also used the same oyster-roast finger bowl that she always laid out for her friends. This was a big old-style basin and pitcher, placed on a wooden bench under a tree with a bath towel hanging nearby.

"We had the communal finger bowl and Her Majesty loved it," Kit Jones recalled. She also seemed to love the special attention that young Bill Jones provided. He taught her how to pry open her oyster, pick it up with her fingers, dip it in sauce, and put it in her mouth. Kit, noting the Queen looking a bit puzzled as Bill, Jr., explained the process, came up with a wooden fork. Young Jones protested. "No, no," he said, "if you can't eat them with your fingers, Your Majesty, there is no way I can teach you."

Toward the end of the evening, Her Majesty sent an aide over to tell the Joneses that she would like to meet the cooks. So the workmen and the singers all filed by and shook hands. One of them, making a curtsy, said "Evenin' Miss Queen." And another announced for all to hear, "I never thought I'd be shakin' hands with a real live Queen, but here I is!" Juliana herself long remembered her visit to Sea Island. Years later, when Governor Ernest Vandiver and his wife, Betty, were in Holland they called on the Queen. She told them she was happy to receive anyone from Georgia. "There," she said, smiling, "they call me 'Miss Queen'."

The Queen's quiet Easter at Sea Island went off without a hitch and marked the beginning of a friendship between the Joneses and some of the Queen's retainers which continued for years. In writing to express Her Majesty's appreciation, her lady-in-waiting, Madame C.E.B. Roell, issued an invitation to the Joneses to visit Holland, and years later when Marianna and Katharine, the Joneses' daughters, were traveling in Europe, they were asked to stay in Madame Roell's apartment in Amsterdam.

The flurry of excitement growing out of the visit of a Queen was merely a warmup so far as Sea Island and its employees were concerned, for the far more complex planning that went on when Jimmy Carter paid his first visit to Sea Island as a presidential nominee. Carter, who loved to fish and to play tennis, had been coming to the coast for years. As a candidate for governor, he had come to Sea Island, staying in the beach cottage of his good friend Philip H. Alston, who later was to be his ambassador to Australia. At Carter's request, his presence was not publicized then, for a Georgia politician was well aware that his cause could be severely damaged by having his picture taken playing tennis in this vacation spot patronized largely by well-to-do Yankees. As the Democratic presidential nominee, however, these restrictions were off, for many affluent voters throughout the country would be impressed. If Jimmy Carter chose Sea Island as his hideaway, he obviously could not be the simple rustic peanut farmer he appeared to be. So, as nominee, he made no attempt to keep a low profile. On one afternoon he and Rosalynn mounted bicycles to ride to the Joneses for a chat. They were led, flanked, and trailed by a phalanx of Secret Service men, also on bicycles. The guards made it well enough so long as the route lay along Sea Island drive with its paved bicycle path, but when Carter insisted on riding home along the beach, spots of soft sand baffled them. Now, as president, with an air armada overhead watching for hostile planes, a naval squadron afloat watching for dangers from the sea, an army of Secret Service men guarding him on land, and a throng of journalists from all over the world following his every move, there was no concealing where he was and what he was doing.

The Cloister, of course, was happy to bask in the publicity when it was asked to put up Mr. Carter's cabinet, and when the president, in informal attire, held a nationally televised press conference in the sunlit solarium. All hands, though, were relieved when Mr. Carter chose for his vacation residence the retreat of Musgrove Plantation, owned by Nancy Reynolds, (sister of Dick Reynolds), whose son, Smith Bagley, was one of Mr. Carter's earliest supporters. Designed in the early days of Sea Island by

Francis Abreu and James Robeson, Musgrove lay across the causeway from Sea Island on Saint Simons. This meant that the Carter presence would be far enough away that the Cloister could continue to function normally in looking after its guests, but it would be close enough for the hotel quietly to provide those household services that the president would need. As a result of an agreement between Bill Jones and Smith Bagley, the Cloister's assistant manager Mike Derkacz took over the food supplies. (The Secret Service ran a knife through a cake to make sure nothing lethal was concealed in it even though the cake was being delivered by Irv Harned, the manager, in person.) Two retired Cloister chefs, Herman Yursich and Carl Outlaw, took charge in the Musgrove kitchen. To Outlaw, a black man and a leader in Glynn County community affairs, highly respected by both blacks and whites, it was a fascinating assignment. The president would rise early, Outlaw would take him his coffee, and the two would sit for a while together, talking about the NAACP, in which Outlaw had a vital interest. By coincidence, while the president of the United States and a black cook could talk face-to-face about race problems, a few miles away, on the north end of Sea Island, black men and women not long before had been crowded into cages and loaded aboard ships, illustrating vividly the beginning of the problem. There, on the Hampton River, ABC photographers had found the foliage and beaches they needed to film Alex Haley's *Roots*.

Not all the Cloister's guests were queens or presidents, and occasionally there was a guest whose presence the company did not care to publicize. One evening in 1943, for example, a Chicago business executive complained that he had been clipped for $1,400 by two men and woman he had invited to his room for what he thought would be a friendly game of poker. One of the men, whom the Cloister security people seized and held for Glynn County police, turned out to be Jack Lance, a notorious

Atlanta gambler, once indicted for the murder of an Atlanta police investigator.

Such incidents were extremely rare, for in the fifty years of the hotel's existence the more colorful comers and goers have been folk of the utmost probity. Among them were Perry Como, Carol Burnett, Jimmy Stewart, Gene Tunney, Amy Vanderbilt, Senator and Mrs. Walter George, Margaret Mitchell, and McKenzie King and Sir Robert Borden, both former premiers of Canada. Frank Buck of *Bring Them Back Alive* fame stopped off for a visit with Bill Jones while en route to a circus performance of his famed animal act at Jacksonville. Jones took the kids down to see the show. They had paid little attention to Buck in their living room at home, but when they saw him working the great beasts in the circus ring, their eyes popped out. They held their father in greater esteem thereafter for being the friend of such a man.

Sometimes it was an event, as well as an individual, that left its mark on Sea Island's memory. In 1931 Sir Esme Howard brought down from Washington and planted on the Cloister grounds a sapling grown from an oak tree at General Oglethorpe's ancestral seat, Godalming, in Sussex. The tree may be seen today on the walk from the hotel to the Beach Club. The golf course and its surrounding area also was the scene of a number of highly publicized events in the early days. When Bobby Jones first played the course in October 1930, huge crowds followed the play, and to Cap Lewis's great delight, heard him say that Sea Island was one of the finest courses he had ever played.

In that same year another event full of sentiment and all-is-forgiven-brotherhood between Yankees and Rebels took place at the golf clubhouse. Early in the year, the *Brunswick News* got word from a paper in Attleboro, Massachusetts that an old clock had been found there that had inscribed on its back in pencil the message that the clock had been "taken from the home of Hon.

Thomas B. King, St. Simons Island, Georgia, U.S.S. Ethan Allen on blockade January 10, 1863." Here indeed was the stuff of history and of sentiment. Thomas Butler King in the 1840s had been sponsor of a Naval Reorganization Act out of which this blockade squadron had sprung, and he was, therefore, greatly popular with young naval officers. When the fleet cruised South in the late 1840s, the officers entertained him at dinner in Savannah. And in the 1860s, he had sent two sons to war, and one of them had been killed.

The Attleboro paper said that if any descendants of the King family could be found, the possessors of the clock would be glad to return it to them. The Brunswick paper went into action immediately. Three of King's granddaughters were still living in Brunswick, and amid great rejoicing the clock was returned in a ceremony held on May 3, 1930 at the golf clubhouse. The place was overrun with notables. Howard Coffin made the address of welcome, the clock was presented by Representative Joseph Martin of Massachusetts, and Senator Walter F. George delivered the closing address. It was a deeply emotional moment, and the only light note was introduced by Mr. Coffin. Representative Martin, speaking at incredible length, said that he was deeply honored to give the clock back to the South, and his only regret was that the North had left nothing here that he could return to Massachusetts. At this, according to historian Richard Everett, Mr. Coffin got up, quietly left the platform, and walked over to the clubhouse terrace, where a pyramid of rusty cannon balls was lying. He picked up one, and grinning broadly put it on the rostrum squarely in front of the speaker. Mr. Martin, carried away by the sound of his own voice, took no notice. It is just as well, for history's sake, that he didn't. The cannon ball was much older than the Civil War. It had been fired against Saint Simons by the British in the War of 1812. The clock was placed on display at the golf clubhouse, where it remained a conversation piece until the clubhouse burned in 1935. The clubhouse could be and was restored and expanded; the clock was completely destroyed.

Another relic of an earlier day did not fare as badly in its return to the island. In 1931 Howard Coffin offered prizes and cash and a visit to Sea Island to Georgia high school students for the best essay on *Old Ironsides* the *U.S.S. Constitution,* whose sternpost and many of whose timbers had been cut at Cannon's Point and shipped from Gascoigne Bluff. Ten thousand essays were submitted, and from these the judges, Mrs. Cate, Clarence Leavy of the *Brunswick News,* and Joe Lambright of the *Pilot,* picked the winner. Floyd Newton, age thirteen of Madison, Georgia, won first prize, and the runnerup was Albert R. Menard, Jr., also thirteen of Lanier High School in Macon. On December 12 the old ship dropped anchor at Brunswick, and with the crew drawn up in full review, the prizes were awarded on the *Constitution* deck. The millionth visitor to step aboard *Old Ironsides* at a port of call since it had left Boston on July 1 was also recognized. She was Miss Ruth Whittle, age seventeen, daughter of former Mayor John T. Whittle of Brunswick. More than 26,000 people boarded the ship before she turned for home.

In the long run though, an essay that did not win a prize attracted more attention than did all the fanfare. Eight-year-old Walker Hamilton of Augusta came up with an idea that caught fire with editors and politicans all over Georgia. He urged that *Old Ironsides* be kept permanently at anchor in Brunswick, since her early history was so closely linked with the Georgia coast. Nothing came of this, of course, for nearly every port city on the eastern seaboard could lay some claim to *Old Ironsides,* and the Bostonians were particularly upset that Georgia should attempt to shanghai the nation's most famous warship. One ongoing social good did come out of the *Old Ironsides* visit. Howard

Coffin formed a Pirates Club of pretty girls to welcome the ship, and the club exists today, its members dressing in buccaneer garb to welcome distinguished visitors.

9

CHURCHES BY THE SEA

Although Jones, Compton, Harned, and Baumgardner focused their attentions on projects serving the hotel guest or cottage owner in his quest for peace of mind and quiet pleasure, the community as a whole occupied their thoughts as well. The first land bought by Howard Coffin on Saint Simons was a seventy-five-acre tract across from Christ Church, and from the beginning Bill Jones, now a Methodist despite his Quaker ancestry, felt that a memorial to John and Charles Wesley should be erected here, perhaps a sort of Bok singing tower playing Methodist hymns. To test this idea, Jones, in 1941, invited the bishops of the Methodist church to hold their annual conclave at the Cloister as his guests. Fifty-six bishops, led by Jones's good friend Bishop Arthur Moore, came down in 1941 to look over the place.

The bishops were grateful, but after some deliberation, Bishop Moore decided that he could not approve spending church money on a project that had no immediate "good for the people" element in it. What was needed was a school, a hospital, or a conference center where preachers could come to be renewed in faith and spirit. And the location, far up Frederica Road, was too isolated for such purposes. Out of these ruminations, though, grew Epworth-by-the-Sea, a conference center, and Epworth Acres, a residential subdivision, which became a basic part of the overall development of Saint Simons as a quiet resort, appealing in the main to families.

Many seaside resorts, Jones knew, had started off quietly enough but had soon found themselves taken over by bars and night spots. A certain amount of this kind of development could be accepted on Saint Simons, but a huge church-owned and church-managed property, centrally located, would strongly inhibit this kind of growth. Thus, to Jones, Compton, and the others, it seemed a good idea for Sea Island Company to make the old Hamilton Plantation, former site of Gene Lewis's truck farm, available to the Methodist church on the most reasonable of terms. Word of this plan got out, and several people telephoned Bill Jones, protesting bitterly. To create a refuge for Methodist ministers on Saint Simons, they argued, would mean disaster to their bar, nightclub and hotel business.

Jones, undismayed, pressed on, and in 1947 the Sea Island Company sold the most valuable fifty acres on the inland waterway to the Methodist church for a minuscule $40,000. The sale included the buildings, farmhouses, old slave quarters, swimming pool, and chapel that Gene Lewis had built or restored when he owned the plantation. Ten devout Methodists — or nine strong Methodists and Bill Jones — put up $4,000 each to make the purchase; Jones, though a Methodist, never made any pretense of being motivated solely by religious feelings in this case. He wanted to help the church, but he also wanted to place a barrier between the gentlefolk he hoped to attract to Saint Simons and Sea Island, and the raucous and rowdy element who might turn them away. The first fifty acres were only the beginning. By 1963 the company had given the church an additional 100 acres of Hamilton Plantation, a tract lying west of the Sea Island Road. As an added gesture of goodwill, as the conference buildings and the motel began to go up, Sea Island Company made available at no charge the skilled services of T. Miesse Baumgardner as the landscape planner. Baumgardner, an Episcopalian, over the years had performed the same services at Christ Church and at the Catholic church in Darien.

The Epworth benefaction was only one of many by which Sea Island Company and its people sought to serve the church, whatever the denomination. The Presbyterians on Saint Simons and Sea Island, for example, for many years had no church building of their own. They worshiped first at the old Casino on the beach at Saint Simons. From there they moved to a cottage, which they shared with Baptists and Methodists as a sort of community church. The end of the war and the lifting of wartime restrictions on construction gave the faithful a chance to go their separate ways, and in the late 1940s a sudden flurry of church building began. Led by Mrs. Edwin Fendig, the Presbyterians were among the first to move, and one of those she called on for support was Jim Compton, the president of Sea Island Company. Compton, although he was the son of a Presbyterian elder and had been raised in that faith, was a cautious man about money, and he seemed curiously reluctant, Mrs. Fendig recalls, to get involved in the process of raising money for a new church. He had started his children in Sunday school at Christ Church, and he and his wife, Dorothy, seemed well content with the little cottage church they shared with other faiths. Mrs. Fendig, though, was a woman of great persuasive powers, and finally Compton was won over.

Once converted to the cause, he was indefatigable in his efforts. With Dorothy, he set off by car, headed north, visiting churches along the way and making sketches of architectural details they hoped to see incorporated in their own church. One of the churches that particularly impressed them was a little community church at Quaker Hill, near Pawling, New York, and many of its simple details were incorporated in the church that architect Montgomery Anderson designed for the Presbyterians of Saint Simons. To prepare for the assignment, Anderson himself traveled widely, studying church architecture, and in California he got the idea for the design of the sanctuary. He was talking to a Presbyterian minister in San Diego, who told him that Christ Church on Saint Simons Island was the first church in America which had been designed to make the altar instead of the preacher the focus of attention. In it, the pulpit and lectern were placed on opposite sides of the sanctuary instead of in the center. Back home, Anderson followed the same design for the little Presbyterian church.

Compton, once involved, became a pillar of the church, serving faithfully until he died. At his urging, and with Bill Jones's full agreement, he persuaded the Sea Island directors that the company sell, for a token $2,000, the property on Kings Way on which the church was to be built, and he headed the building committee. He served as elder and as trustee, and later he became a founding father of the Presbyterian Home for the Elderly at Quitman.

The Sea Island Company's desire to help churches "purely for our own selfish interest," as Bill Jones modestly insists, goes back to Howard Coffin's day. In the 1920s, ancient Christ Church, for all its aura of history and romance, was still a mission church of the Episcopal diocese of Georgia. Three Sundays of the month, a lay reader conducted the service. On the fourth Sunday, an ordained clergyman filled the pulpit. This was disappointing to some Cloister guests, many of whom were Episcopalians, and the company, at Bill Jones's urging, put up the money to bring in a full-time rector. This continued through the lean years until the church itself could afford to pay their preacher. The Catholics, too, were beneficiaries of a Cloister guest and, indirectly, of the Cloister management. A lady from New York, a deeply religious woman, gave $5,000 for the erection of a small Catholic church. Francis Abreu, Cloister architect, designed it, and the company provided the services of its landscaping staff.

The effort to be of service to all the churches has continued over the years. The company, through a gift and a land swap, made it possible for the Episcopal Church of the Holy Nativity to be constructed on Mallery Street on Saint Simons. Recently when Strangers Cemetery, a burial place under the watchcare of members of black churches since the sawmilling boom of the 1880s, needed to expand, the company came through with a gift of additional acreage. For practical reasons the company rarely gives land outright, but they have sold to church groups at rates so low that it constitutes a gift.

The contributions of Jones and the Sea Island Company to the beauty and serenity of Saint Simons and Sea Island went much further, of course, than merely encouraging the building of churches. Jones had Coffin's feeling for history and the preservation of the environment. Under these compulsions he closed off Cannon's Point at the north end of Saint Simons while an archaeological group from the University of Florida studied and analyzed evidence of cultures dating from 2000 B.C. to the period when Aaron Burr took refuge there. It was indicative of Jones's resources, and typical of his attitude toward the land, that he would let the Sea Island Company pay $1.6 million for Cannon's Point and Lawrence Plantation in 1971, and then immediately put it under archaeological observation that might go on for years before the property could finally be placed on the market. This was the third such long-range handling of a property to preserve its historic meaning, and it was an action that the speculative developers today would look upon as an unconscionable expense. It is an action, too, that modern day tax commissioners in Georgia counties make almost impossible to support financially. They insist on taxing vacant land at its presumed "highest and best use," a policy that stimulates

Jerry-building-get-rich-quick developments that mar the land. Other efforts to save as much as possible of the vestiges of a historic past were the Retreat Plantation studies and restoration, where old buildings and the ancient Avenue of Oaks were saved, and those carried out at Hamilton Plantation.

In the late 1930s, before the land that Howard Coffin presented to the county for McKinnon Airport went under the bulldozer blade, a thorough study of aboriginal people was made there, and bones and artifacts thousands of years old were found and preserved at the Smithsonian Institution. Some bones and tools were placed on display at the Brunswick Chamber of Commerce, where they remained for a dozen years or thereabout. Then a new young secretary of the chamber was hired, and he immediately threw them out. Jones, naturally, was distressed by this. Preservation, combined with orderly development, was Jones's watchword. He agreed that certain small areas of tidal marshland could be filled in without damage, but he was quick to do battle with anybody who in any way would encroach upon the vast expanse of Sidney Lanier's fabled Marshes of Glynn, knowing that encroachment would destroy a delicate ecological balance that once lost could never be restored. He strongly backed Charley Gowen when he introduced a scenic bill in the legislature making the marshes between Brunswick, Saint Simons, and Sea Island historical sites off limits to any sort of development, including signs of any size or shape.

Schools, in Jones's view, also were a stabilizing influence, and both he and Jim Compton, as their youngsters came along toward school age, became deeply interested in setting up a school on Sea Island. In the depths of the depression, when the company coffers were almost bare, they hired an erudite headmaster named Frank Plunkett to open a private school for all ages, from kindergarten through high school, in cottage thirty-three, where the Sea Island River Club condominiums now stand. There were two advantages to this: it spared the island youngsters the hurried and possibly hazardous bus ride across the causeway over rickety wooden bridges, and it enabled the hotel to offer a service few other resorts could provide. When the weather turned cold in the North, parents with school age youngsters could bring them down to Sea Island with their books and lesson plans, and here they could keep up with, and even surpass, their classes at home.

Now and then, of course, there was the question of whether school could open for another term. One year, when Headmaster Plunkett needed an extra $1,700 to hire a French teacher, Compton and Jones canceled the company's tornado insurance, using the $1,747.53 premium to support the school. Miss Alma Harris, sister of A.M. Harris, of the First National Bank of Brunswick, took over the school after Plunkett retired and operated it for several years. After her death, no educator of equal caliber could easily be found, and the school was closed. By 1950, too, the wooden bridges across the marshes had been replaced with solid structures of concrete and steel, and the Sea Island youngsters could ride safely to their classes in the Brunswick schools.

Thus in the natural course of events, the interest of Sea Island parents in providing good education for their children shifted across the marshes to Brunswick. And there it was focused for more than two decades, with Bill Jones, Sr., Jim Compton, and Bummy Baumgardner serving successive ten-year terms on the Glynn County school board. There was, though, an increasing conviction by a number of parents on Sea Island and Saint Simons that an expanded version of the old Sea Island private school must inevitably be set up again. Nothing much happened, though, except talk, until one hot night in June 1969, when "Tiggie" Benefield, wife of Dewey Benefield, vice-president of the company, roused her husband from a sound sleep to tell him that she had made up her mind. The time for talk was over; the time for action had come. Their son, Jim, was ready for the first grade, and their daughter, Helen, was approaching kindergarten age. They, and all the area children, must be given the opportunity to go to a school where they could get the best education available, taught by the finest teachers that could be found.

For all that summer Tiggie and Dewey Benefield talked to parents like themselves, wrote letters, and held meetings. The school facility, they decided, was not the important thing. First a course of studies must be laid out, a topflight faculty hired. This was done over a period of months, and the building to house the school was found. It was the old Brunswick Hospital building, long standing empty, and it could be leased at a minimum charge per pupil. The parents themselves cleaned and patched and painted, restoring the old structure. So in September 1970 Frederica Academy, a private coeducational college preparatory school, opened its doors in Brunswick. The academy was dedicated to the idea that an able faculty, working with an intellectually select student body (though with no racial or religious restrictions) could turn out productive, sensitive, and responsible citizens. The school opened with 93 students in grades one through eight, and a grade was added each year. By 1973 the enrollment had tripled.

It soon became obvious that the old hospital building would no longer be adequate, and Dewey Benefield, chairman of Frederica Academy Trustees, turned to the Sea Island Company for help. As usual, the company came through. A plan was worked out whereby the school would be given twenty-five acres of land on Saint Simons Island, in increments over a period of five years. A building program was begun, and in September 1974 the move was made. The trustees had borrowed more than $500,000 to get the building started, and in the spring of 1977 a drive for funds raised more than $400,000 in cash and pledges. The original gift of land, valued at $250,000, made the whole project possible, but Benefield would be the first to admit that it was the work of many people that got the school under way so quickly. On the twenty-five acres of wooded campus, more than a million dollars worth of buildings now stand, and 386 students pay an average annual tuition of $1,300 in a school now fully accredited by all the proper agencies.

Thus a second generation of Sea Island executives, represented by Dewey Benefield, took up the cause of education along the Georgia coast. Bill Jones, however, by no means was turning his interest in school support over to the younger generation alone. Along with James D. Gould, he established the Brunswick Junior College Foundation from money raised in the main from friends and neighbors on Saint Simons and Sea Island. The revolving fund, which now stands at $100,000, provides student loans and scholarships to any needy youngster who has the ability and the desire to get an education. A strong and highly articulate advocate of the free enterprise system, Jones also established the James D. Compton Chair of Free Enterprise at the college.

Jones's interest in education was not confined to economics. In 1955 Bill Hendrix, a young artist, became fired with zeal to start an art school and gallery on a small lot he owned on Saint Simons. He mentioned his dream to Sig Kaufmann, a Brunswick journalist who later became Sea Island Company's advertising and public relations man. Kaufmann, impressed, wrote to Bill Jones that Bill Hendrix was "a tenacious and stable young man" and his art school was the type of undertaking that Sea Island Company could well support in its effort to keep life on Saint Simons on a high aesthetic level. Jones agreed. He endorsed notes at the bank for funds with which Hendrix built the building to house his Island Art Center, and Jones backed him solidly thereafter. Out of this project grew the Island Art Association, a nonprofit organization to promote art exhibits and general interest in arts and artists. As the years passed, Saint Simons became known as an art center with several other galleries in competition with Hendrix. By this time, though, his project was well under way and prospering—so much so, in fact, that he recently was able to buy a residential lot on Sea Island.

Jones, in the matter of supporting good causes, was like Browning's Duchess—"who liked what e'er she looked on, and her looks went everywhere." Soon after his purchase in 1945 of Altama Plantation on the Altamaha River, some twenty-five miles from Sea Island, he gave a tract of adjoining land to round out the holdings of Boys Estate, a refuge and training area for boys made homeless by death, desertion, or divorce. The project has had its vicissitudes, but now, under a new director, it holds out renewed hope to the youngster from a broken home.

For all his interest in the Georgia coast and its progress, Jones's concern for youth and their welfare ranged far afield—as far as central Ontario, in fact. In the early 1900s, Kit Jones's father, an engineering contractor building a railroad in the Ontario wilderness, had set up a camp for his family some forty miles north of Sault Sainte Marie. Years later, when needing a brief change from the palms and pines and lazy surf of Sea Island, Bill and Kit Jones would take their youngsters on vacation there. And in this wild and lonely place the whole family became fond of the rough-hewn wilderness life, of the portage and the backpack, and the tumpline, and the long days' journey by canoe. There was no travel during the war years, of course, and when they went back again after the war, the place was empty, the guides and cooks gone.

The Jones youngsters were in their teens by now, and more eager than ever for camp life, so the Joneses set out to find another place not quite so isolated. Marnie Talbott Thomas, Kit's sister, and her husband, Charles Thomas, head of the Monsanto Chemical Company, came to the rescue. There was another camp, they said, all the way across Ontario, on Devil's Island, in an arm of starfish-shaped Lake Timagami. It was called Keewaydin — from Hiawatha's name for the northwest wind, "the invisible hand that sways the pines." The Thomas's son had been there as a camper and had liked it. There also was a parents camp, called Ojibway, named for the Indian tribe, near the canoe camp where the youngsters stayed.

This sounded promising, so in 1946 the two families went together, taking their eight children and two guests. It was a happy vacation for all marked by long canoe trips and camping overnight. But the elders noticed one thing: the camp had been in operation since 1893, run primarily by prep-school teachers who used the camp to augment their income. The teachers in charge this year were getting old; the camp, during the war years, had become shabby and rundown. With only twenty-five boys enrolled, besides the Jones-Thomas group, it was clear that this would be the last year for the old place. To Jones and Thomas, this seemed a shame. There were camps in plenty for under-privileged boys, and they were crowded every summer with youngsters from the slums. But a camp like this, set up to serve the overprivileged, so to speak, the youngsters whose parents were able to pay, was difficult to find. Yet the children of the well-to-do also needed the learning experience such a camp could give, the camaraderie of the trail, the self-reliance, the stern discipline, the sense of high adventure that comes to a boy as he learns to live in the wilderness like the "voyageurs" of old.

To Jones and Thomas, there was one answer. They would buy the camp and open it as the finest boys camp in the country, not for profit, but as a strictly educational project. To accomplish this, they established, with the blessing of the federal government, the tax exempt Thomas-Jones Educational Foundation, and with funds contributed to the Foundation by Jones and Thomas, they did buy the camp and hired a topflight director and staff under the Foundation's sponsorship. The camp's enrollment grew to 130 youngsters, with girls coming to Ojibway, the camp for grownups. Soon the camp was showing a profit of some $20,000 a year, all of which the Foundation plowed back into improvements. This kept up for fifteen years. By 1960, the Keewaydin Boys Camp and the nearby Ojibway Camp for families were on a firm foundation for the future. The Foundation sold the camp to its director, Howard Chivers, his note to be paid off from the camp income at $7,000 a year for ten years. When the final payment came in, the Foundation gave away all its assets and was dissolved.

To the Joneses, it was a great experience, for the effect Keeway-din had on their youngsters—the self-reliance, the love for the outdoors—endured thereafter. Bill Jones's feelings are best expressed, perhaps, in a foreword prepared for the Keewaydin brochure:

> The life of a boy is a mosaic—a year by year composite of people, events and experiences. A boy's personality grows piecemeal, until the whole of it—like a coral reef at ebb tide—emerges long after childhood and adolescence have passed. Each year is a new becoming and another ending. His far-off tomorrows will always be a product of his past and the things to come. The boy is never lost in the man. Bit by bit, from his coaster wagon days through his teens, the man-to-be accumulates the furniture of his mind, his ideals, his aims. He is in part each of many things: imitations of the people he admires, the attitudes of his parents, the training of his schools. His character will chart the course of his life; like a ship under taut sails, filled with a steady wind. Boyhood dreams are found or forgotten, but each experience that flowers in the green years—lives on.

10

SETTIN' ON JECKLE

There is an ancient jest which says that the missionaries who went out to Hawaii to do good for the natives remained to do well for themselves. In a sense, the same thing might be said of the development of Sea Island by Howard Coffin and his associates of the Sea Island Company. Coffin's project in the beginning—at least so far as he was concerned—was not planned as a money-making business. It was a rich man's toy. Profit making was incidental to his larger vision, of creating here beside Highway 17, the blacktop road pushing south from New York, a new heaven on a new earth, opened up by the automobile. But when the crash came and he was no longer able to build the roads and dig the wells and set up the light plants and the telephone companies, he lost interest. He turned over to Bill Jones the task of keeping Sea Island alive, or letting it go under. Nearly a decade was to pass before the first profit showed on the books and the company could lay its plans for pushing on toward the fulfillment of Howard Coffin's dream. By now, though, the war had started, causing a five-year hiatus in the building program.

Even so, Sea Island was luckier than most resorts in the use that was made of its facilities during the war. The King and Prince Hotel on Saint Simons was taken over by the Navy to house students and staff of the Combat Information Center School, established at McKinnon Airport. The Homestead in Hot Springs was used to house Japanese-Americans taken into custody on the West Coast. Eight different war agencies, military and others, took a look at the Cloister and Sea Island as a possible headquarters, and all decided to go elsewhere. The hotel was too small—it could hold only 250 people—and that narrow causeway leading across the marshes could be too easily sabotaged. The Cloister, therefore, was permitted to function as it had from the beginning—as a small hotel—and it did well enough to more than break even throughout the war. Many of the guests were servicemen on their honeymoons, or military people on rest and recreation leave, and there were a few old Cloister fans who continued to come down, war or no war. Finding guests was no great problem, but finding trained manpower was another matter. Dick Everett went in as a buck private and came out as a captain, running PXs in England. Irving Harned went into the Army Air Corps and came out a major in the separated Air Force. His hotel experience shaped his military career. A fine shot on the Cloister skeet range, he became first an aerial gunnery instructor, and then a hotel manager in Shanghai. Lewis Beers, Harned's reservation manager, was ineligible for military service and he took over and ran the hotel during the war years.

One wartime contribution made by Sea Island Company paid off handsomely in the long run. Until the war, all sewage disposal on Saint Simons and Sea Island, including that at the Cloister, was taken care of by septic tanks. As the Navy moved onto Saint Simons, they realized they must have a sewerage system to serve the King and Prince Hotel and the expanded facilities at McKinnon Airport. H.J. Friedman, the county manager, was a good friend of Bill Jones and the Sea Island Company, as well as a dedicated county servant. His solution to the sewage problem served everybody's best interests. The Sea Island Company gave the Navy the best site on Saint Simons for a sewage disposal plant. On the land the Navy built a $600,000 facility, serving a sewer system that covered most of the inhabited area of Saint Simons and reached across the marshes to Sea Island and the Cloister and to the cottages as far north as Sixth Street. After the war the Navy turned the whole facility over to the county for a token $5,000. This did away with the old septic tanks that had been giving trouble for years.

This friendly gesture on the part of the county confirmed what Alfred Jones had learned much earlier—that anything done for the good of the community would in turn prove to be good for the company and its operations. He strongly indoctrinated Bill Jones, Jr., and Dewey Benefield in this belief, and as a result, they and their assistants have habitually spent about as much time working for the general good as they have in pushing the Sea Island Company on to higher levels.

The efforts of all of them, from the beginning, have gone far beyond the efforts that have been described. Bill Jones, Sr., for example, almost single-handedly held the Brunswick Rotary Club together during the deepest depression years of 1931-32, and Bill Jones, Jr., and Dewey Benefield have been as active in their support of the thriving modern clubs on Saint Simons and in Brunswick. The camaraderie of the luncheon and the inspiration provided by a speaker have always been at the heart of Rotary everywhere. In the depths of the depression, the Brunswick club was down to fewer than twenty-five members and speakers were hard to come by. Jones, Sr., as president, saved the club by persuading the Oglethorpe Hotel that it should serve a luncheon consisting of a sandwich and a glass of milk for twenty-five cents. For some members, even this was too much, so those who wished could bring their own sandwich.

Jones was also able to provide a speaker nearly every week

from among his Cloister guests. Three of them he remembers particularly well. One was a distinguished industrialist, George Houston, president of the Baldwin Locomotive Works of Philadelphia. He surprised his audience by reciting Sidney Lanier's *Marshes of Glynn* in its entirety, all 105 lines of it from "Glooms of the live oaks, beautiful braided and woven," past the "emerald twilights" and "virginal shy lights," all the way to the sonorous closing line, "When the tide comes in on the length and breadth of the marvelous Marshes of Glynn." Jones, years after, remembered this as the moment when he first became aware of the wonder and beauty of the marshes and of the absolute necessity of their being preserved. Another speaker was remembered for quite different reasons. He was a Sikh, an Indian official of some sort. Wearing a turban and a magnificent beard, which he carried in a hair net, what he said might have been interesting, but Jones remembered little about it. He was too intent on watching a gray woodtick that kept crawling in and out of the speaker's whiskers. A third speaker, in 1932, was a lieutenant colonel from the garrison at Savannah. His name was George C. Marshall.

The Rotary Club also became a sounding board for Jones and his firmly held idea that the Georgia coast could become one of the great resort areas of the world. It could do this, he argued, while at the same time developing to the fullest an industry which could utilize the region's most productive crop, the slim, fast-growing pine from which paper could be produced. This was strange talk to hear from a resort hotel owner. To most of these men, industry was a competitor for labor and its entry into a resort area should be discouraged. To Jones, this was shortsighted. Clean industry that did not unduly befoul the air or the waters was a highly desirable addition to any community, and he earnestly propounded the idea not only to the Rotary Club, but with equal earnestness in the Brunswick-Golden Isles Chamber of Commerce and to anybody else who would listen.

Here, he argued, were three great resources: climate and playgrounds for the tourist; water routes for local or worldwide shipping, commercial fishing and shrimping; and the raw materials for a great paper, naval stores, and lumber industry based on the pine. And all should be developed together. He also included military and semimilitary installations as valuable additions to a community. Long before the war, at his urging, the secretary of the treasury, Henry Morgenthau, agreed that a Coast Guard station, the only one in Georgia, should be established on Saint Simons. The Sea Island Company gave the land on which the boat station was to be built on the inland waterway, and the owners of East Beach gave the beach site. When the lighter-than-air base came to Glynco on the mainland, Jones and the Sea Island Company helped to organize a chapter of the Navy League, which immediately became a point of friendly contact between the military installation and the surrounding community. Even though Glynco and the admirals for whom the Cloister held open house are long since gone, the Navy League still exists, with Howard Jones as its president. And now, it seems, the Navy will be coming back. Jones and those around him see no harm to the coastal area, and a great deal of economic good, in the plan to bring a nuclear submarine base home from Spain to new quarters at Kings Bay near Saint Marys. He and the Sea Island Company as a whole also strongly support the state's current plan to set up an industrial park on Colonel's Island for those operations that need to be on deep water.

Just as Jones believes that the coastal area should be open to any use that does not interfere with the health, happiness, and well-being of the community, he believes that the special qualities of the Golden Isles for rest and recreation should be shared by all. The Sea Island Company, admittedly, caters to an affluent clientele, both in its cottage colony and the hotel. Relatively few American couples can pay from $85 to $150 a day for a hotel room, even when three gourmet meals are included, nor can many afford $1600 to $6000 a month to rent a cottage. To Jones, though, and to his associates at Sea Island, every Glynn Countian, every Georgian—in truth, every American—whether he arrived by yacht, private plane, bus, or camper-trailer, should have access to a place where he and his family can enjoy the sea and sand and the sunsets and the play places that are the special glory of the coastal islands.

Bringing about this happy situation took some delicate maneuvering on the part of Jones and his friends in county government, a process that went on for years. When Howard Coffin bought Sea Island in 1926, the beach, the swimming pool, and the Casino there had been semipublic for a number of years. All the facilities could be used by the local people as well as the Cloister guests and the Sea Island cottagers, and this policy continued throughout the 1930s. To Bill Jones, Jim Compton, and Irving Harned, it was clear that this had to change. If the hotel was to be successful, and Sea Island was to become the happy retreat Jones, Compton, and Harned had in mind, the Casino, pool, and at least a good portion of the beach would have to be reserved for hotel and cottage guests. The problem was how to turn away the local folk without destroying all the goodwill the company had built up in the community over the years. The answer, as Jones saw it, was to build a far better facility, for public use, on the south end of Saint Simons. Once this was done, the Sea Island Company could get on with its plan to shut down and then rebuild the Casino and the pool, close the beach to automobiles and local picnickers, and set up the Beach Club on a membership basis. County officials agreed that such a facility in time would be of more value to the county than a shaky dance hall standing beside a public pool and beach.

Since the county obviously did not have the money to develop an outstanding public park on Saint Simons, Bill Jones called on his friend Governor Ellis Arnall, who had appointed Jones to the first Georgia Ports Authority. Arnall agreed with Jones and Harold Friedman that an adequate state park was needed and promised to put up $250,000 from his emergency fund to build it. To provide a site, Jones for $50,000 bought from the Massengale family a tract of land north of the King and Prince Hotel which contained 1100 feet of beach frontage. To this he added, for $10,000 more, some 50 acres of adjoining marshland—the idea being that this marsh would be filled in to provide a large recreational area behind the beach park. And both tracts would be turned over to the county at cost so that the state park project could go forward. By this, several things would be accomplished. Residents of Saint Simons would have a fine beach park close by without having to travel all the way across the causeway to Sea Island, and on Sea Island the beach area could be reserved for hotel guests and cottagers.

It turned out to be a naive assumption on the part of Jones and the county officials. Saint Simons residents, it seemed, did not want a public park in their midst. A town meeting was held to oppose the plan, and Governor Arnall, sensitive to the faintest murmur of political opposition, withdrew his promise of funds. Jones suggested that the Governor sit tight until some missionary work could be done that might change this attitude. Before anything could happen, though, Arnall was out of office and the great two-governor squabble was underway between Herman Talmadge and Melvin Thompson. Thompson prevailed, and as tempers cooled, Jones took up with him the matter of the state park at Saint Simons. Thompson agreed, in principle, but he suggested that a state project should be larger than anything Saint Simons had room for. In search for another, bigger site, Thompson sent Glynn County attorney Charles Gowen traveling the coast from Savannah to the Florida line.

And this brought Jekyll into the picture, an island in which Bill Jones had long been deeply interested. First, in the late 1920s and early 1930s, he and Howard Coffin had used Jekyll as a selling point for Sea Island. The nation's richest men, who could vacation anywhere they pleased, had sent scouts across the world seeking the most pleasant and secluded spot and had settled upon Jekyll. Obviously, therefore, little Sea Island, lying on the horizon just five miles north of Jekyll, would be equally salubrious, a point deftly made in all Sea Island's advertising. But as the years passed, many of the old Jekyll clubmen had died, and their descendants were less interested in spending money or time in such a quiet stuffy hideaway. Once, around 1930, Jones remembers, Howard Coffin sent him on the yacht *Zapala* to bring twenty-five members of the Jekyll group to visit Sapelo. The Jekyll guests had a business meeting en route, which Jones could not help overhearing. The Jekyll Golf Club Committee, all millionaires, argued for an hour over whether to spend $250 to build a new shower house for the golf caddies. This discussion of high finance much surprised Jones, who was spending thousands of dollars a month on Sea Island with no more discussion than a casual comment by Mr. Coffin.

During the 1930s, with J.P. Morgan still serving as president, Jekyll continued to decline in popularity, the younger Jekyll Club members feeling less and less attracted to the isolated place with its inadequate golf course and its musty Victorian atmosphere. The Sea Island Company, at Jekyll's request, did what it could to help revitalize the old place. Bummy Baumgardner went over on weekends, carrying a Sea Island crew to work on landscaping and golf course maintenance. Then the war came along, gas rationing put boats in drydock, and in April 1942 the old Jekyll Club closed its doors forever. In Jones's words, Jekyll was "a dead duck."

All that winter, with Nazi subs sinking ships almost in sight of land, marines patrolled Jekyll's shoreline by night, and Compton and Baumgardner, with their Sea Island crews, provided basic maintenance by day. Bernon Prentice, a Rockefeller connection, had succeeded J.P. Morgan as president of the Jekyll Club, and often during that time he and Bill Jones talked about what might be done with Jekyll after the war. Prentice felt that he might be able to persuade the older members to come back, bringing their friends, for winter vacations as in the past. Jones believed that under his and Jim Compton's guidance, Sea Island Company would be able to bring in enough guests to keep the facilities in use all summer. And the Sea Island Company, under Compton, would manage the island the year round. Both knew, of course, that in the age of the motorcar, no island resort could flower without a causeway leading to it — and neither Jones nor Prentice had the million dollars such a project would cost. They talked to Frank Gould, a member of the Jekyll Club and a homeowner there, about financing the causeway and an understanding was reached. Prentice went to the club members, most of whom were willing enough to sell their Jekyll bonds to Jones, Prentice, and Gould at a considerable discount in the belief that by this arrangement the club would continue to operate in the winter after the war.

Unfortunately, Frank Gould died of a heart attack, at age forty-five, in the last year of the war. His first wife and his children inherited most of his assets, but his second wife inherited his Jekyll bonds — which she used to pay the lawyer who represented her in the settlement of the estate. This left Jones and Prentice in partnership in the Jekyll deal with Lawrence R. Condon, a New York lawyer. Condon, during the depression, had been able to reorganize several famous old New York clubs including the River Club and Maidstone at East Hampton. He insisted that he could also reorganize the Jekyll Club on its prewar basis, though Jones and Prentice were positive this could not be done.

Thus the partners reached an impasse — which eventually was

broken by Melvin Thompson. With Charley Gowen, Governor Thompson had visited the barrier islands, looking for one on which to create the kind of state park he had in mind. When they went to Jekyll, Jim Compton went with them, and here Thompson found what he wanted—unspoiled beaches and dunelands, forests, marshes—an ideal vacation spot for Georgians of all ages and all economic levels. Jones, of course, was delighted at Thompson's decision. He had the vision to see the state's ownership of Jekyll would be the best thing that could happen to Sea Island and Saint Simons. Sea Island would no longer be pressured to provide public recreational facilities, and Saint Simons would become a more desirable place, slanted toward the retiree who wanted a year-round residence rather than to the casual visitor looking for a place to picnic on the beach.

Larry Condon, the lawyer, seemed reluctant to sell his bonds, clinging to the idea that he could restore the old Jekyll Club to its past glories. Bill Jones and Charley Gowen went to New York to see him, and there the point was made that Governor Thompson was proposing to bring condemnation proceedings against the island property in the name of the state. The sale went through. The state now owned Jekyll, and upcountry Georgians could see themselves at last "settin' on Jeckle," their own descriptive phrase for the equivalent of dwelling just this side of heaven.

The Jekyll bonds owned by Jones, Prentice, and Condon had a face value of $687,000, and this is what Thompson paid for them. Their cost to Jones, Prentice, and Gould had been something less than half that figure. Thus the current partners made a profit of roughly $80,000 each, after Sea Island Company had been paid for its caretaker service during the war. To Herman Talmadge, preparing to run against Thompson for governor, this was a colossal boondoggle—three rich men unloading a white elephant on the state. To most Georgians, though, it was a handsome gift by Governor Thompson to all of the people. Talmadge's political antennae quickly sensed that he was on the wrong track. After a year as governor, he sponsored the building of the causeway across to Jekyll and came up with the idea of setting up a Jekyll Island Authority. Charles Gowen blocked this in the legislature, figuring that a Talmadge appointed "authority" would sell the island to the first speculator who came along. Talmadge, though, persuaded Gowen that he was sincere, and he told Gowen if he would let the Jekyll bill pass in the legislature, he in turn would let Gowen appoint one member of the authority. Gowen agreed, and he suggested that Talmadge appoint Bill Jones, as a man who knew more than anyone else about the Georgia coast and how to operate a resort there. Talmadge demurred, saying that this would require Jones to work for Jekyll, in competition with his own resort at Sea Island. Gowen argued that this would be like Woolworth competing with Tiffany. But when Gowen called Jones and told him that Talmadge would like to appoint him to the Jekyll Island Authority, Jones turned the appointment down. What was needed, he suggested, was a man with Jim Compton's detailed knowledge of how a resort should be run.

So, Jim Compton, president of Sea Island Company, went on loan to the Jekyll Island Authority, and for some two years thereafter he gave half his time to Jekyll. He would go over with Mrs. Compton, stay in a cottage there, and prowl the island from one end to the other, laying out in his mind where the roads should run, where the picnic spots should be located, the motels, the camping areas and trailer parks, the sport fields and convention centers. He then called in Robert and Company to lay out the master plan—and this plan is in great degree the one under which Jekyll operates today. The planning was a pleasure for Compton, but when the time came to carry out the plans, to choose concessionaires and builders, the human and political element crept in. This was not Compton's forte. He knew how to handle money, but when money got mixed up with politics, he wanted no part of it, so he went back to Sea Island.

True enough, as Jones expected, Jekyll proved to be highly popular with Georgians of all ages and economic levels, reaching its optimum potential in recreational facilities and accommodations without taking anything away from Sea Island. Even after Jekyll was open and operating, the growing interest of Georgians in their offshore islands made more beach areas necessary. Saint Simons, for example, needed swimming and recreational facilities, for there was no surf at the public areas at the south end of the island. As a result, people still were swimming and picnicking, sometimes raucously, at the end of streets leading down to the beach, to the vast annoyance of those living nearby. Though nothing had happened since 1945, when the gift of the Massengale property had fallen through, Bill Jones had been working quietly but actively to remedy the situation. His reasons were still the same — partially selfish, partially eleemosynary. If Saint Simons had additional public beach frontage, the value of the property the Sea Island Company owned there would be enhanced, and Saint Simons would be more of an attraction on its own. So, in 1955 the Sea Island Company gave 600 feet of beach front property to Glynn County through an exchange, and after nearly a decade of delay Massengale Park was finally built.

Thus a handsome public beach front park, centrally located on Saint Simons, came into being and quickly became an important and popular place for public enjoyment. And, carefully maintained and protected by the Sea Island Company, the Sea Island beach grew in distinction as a well used but completely unspoiled and delightful bit of American shoreline where the great Atlantic, undisturbed dunes and man enjoyed one another's company in peace. Through Bill Jones's untiring and lifelong efforts Glynn County now could offer a variety of beach enjoyment including the state-owned Jekyll Island, the county administered Saint

Simons Island, and Sea Island. Each, he felt, had its merits and society had need of each. Happily, the public flocked to Jekyll and Massengale, and Sea Island went back to its quiet dreaming in the sun.

11

FROM SAINT CATHERINES
TO CUMBERLAND

The transfer of Jekyll to the state to be used as a public play-ground was only one of many transactions by which owners of private islands, under pressure of fantastic county tax increases during the 1960s and the 1970s, began to turn over their family holdings to the state for cultural or educational purposes.

This meant that resort development, in which Bill Jones and Howard Coffin had been pioneers, would focus on other accessible islands—Saint Simons in Georgia, Amelia Island in Florida, Hilton Head in South Carolina and others. All of these developments, Jones felt, were of great value to the region for they called national attention to the whole mid-south coastal section. One of his great handicaps in getting Sea Island started in the early days was the fact that many people up North did not know that Georgia had a coast, and those who had read of it in books written by northern "scholars" thought it was a miasmic swamp. Thus, the more development that came into the area, Jones felt, the better for all concerned. Even resorts next door to him were welcome—Sea Palms was a few miles away on Saint Simons, and he sold the land on which another developer built the Island Club and golf

131

course. This one cost Jones money, but not through competition. The company went bankrupt, leaving C&S Bank holding the land and the Sea Island Company holding the bag. Come Hilton Head or high water, though, Jones and his associates were confident that Sea Island and the Cloister would continue to attract in great number the distinctive clientele they had built up over the years. He was pleased when his friends and neighbors on other islands sold their family holdings to the state. This meant that Georgia's coast could now reach fulfillment in what he considered its highest and best use, as a resort area, as an industrial area, and as a center for specialized education.

He had long held the idea that certain of the islands should be used as great outdoor classrooms and conservation areas where scientists in all fields of biology could study the complex life patterns of the area, the interdependence of marsh, highland and seashore. In all such projects, from Tybee to Cumberland, he had an interest, and in some of them he was deeply and personally involved. His first interest away from Sapelo was in Saint Catherines. In 1927 Howard Coffin, along with two of his wealthy friends from New York—C.M. Keys and Jim Willson—bought the island from the three Savannah families who owned it. Remote, beautiful, rich in such ecological wonders as tidal marshes, creeks, and miles of unspoiled beach, Saint Catherines was also rich in history. In earliest time it had been a hunting ground of the Guale Indians. Later it became the site of an important Spanish mission. In fact, the Spanish, bloodily harassed in Florida by Indians and colonists alike, had once considered abandoning Saint Augustine and moving their seat of government in the new world to the quieter reaches of Santa Catalina.

After the founding of Georgia by Oglethorpe in 1733, Saint Catherines, along with Ossabaw and Sapelo, had been given to halfbreed Mary Musgrove, as her fee for serving Oglethorpe as his translator with the Creeks. She had turned it over, as part of her dowry, when she married Oglethorpe's chaplain, Thomas

Bosomworth in 1775, and Bosomworth sold the island to Button Gwinnett.

The ruins of the Gwinnett house and the slave cabins nearby were still clearly visible when Coffin and his friends bought the island. They left the renovation to Coffin, who immediately brought Arthur Wilson from Sapeló and put him to work. The Button Gwinnett house, a small cottage, was restored exactly as it had been, and to it was added a living room with high windows and a huge stone fireplace. Behind the house, the double row of slave quarters was partially restored. Every other cabin was converted into a comfortable guest house, with one or two bedrooms and a bath, and each of the new structures was separated by the ruins of a fallen cabin. Before the new owners had time to enjoy their hideaway, however, the crash came. Coffin and Willson turned over their interests to C.M. Keys to get rid of the expense of keeping the place up. Keys held on until 1943, when he sold out to Edward J. Noble, Life Saver and Beechnut millionaire, who was also at one time head of ABC. On his death, the island became part of the Noble Foundation. Since Howard Coffin's day, Jones has had no connection with Saint Catherines, except to approve warmly what was being done there by Ed Noble's daughter, Mrs. Frank Y. Larkin of Greenwich, Connecticut.

The island's 7200 acres of upland and beaches, surrounded by 15,000 acres of tidal marsh, would have been an ideal place for commercial development. Mrs. Larkin, instead, preferred to use it as a site for long-range environmental studies. First, the University of Georgia was invited in to make an archaeological study of the island, with its many Indian mounds and remnants of the Spanish missions. When the university was unable to continue on a long-term basis, the American Museum of Natural History in New York took over the study of all aspects of the island's history and ecology.

It was discovered that wild pigs and cattle had caused drastic changes in the forest undergrowth, and to restore the natural conditions a vigorous pig-hunt was carried on until at last only two pigs still roamed free. Wrote Mrs. Larkin, "It is too much to expect that we will capture the last two pigs, but the removal of most of them has resulted in the recovery of the grasses, small bushes, and seedling trees, in addition to ground-nesting birds, small mammals, and to the delight of the scientists—if not to me—snakes."

Digs at forty-four archeological sites turned up fascinating mementos of Saint Catherine's prehistory. Shadow boxes prepared by Dr. David Hurst Thomas, chairman of the Department of Anthropology at the American Museum of Natural History, summarized nearly 4000 years of human habitation on the island. Up until the findings on Saint Catherines, the oldest burial sites in North America were believed to be located in Ohio and to date back to roughly 1000 B.C. The oldest in the southeast were dated A.D. 500. All the Saint Catherine mounds were created before A.D. 1, and one of them apparently was built around 1350 B.C. If this is true, then the Saint Catherines mounds are the oldest known burial sites in North America. Thus, on Saint Catherines, as perhaps on the other barrier islands, the whole history of Georgia can be seen in microcosm, beginning with the Indians in 1350 B.C., through Spanish times, the colonial days, the era of the slave plantations, and to the modern day when islands such as this became the hideaway of the ultra-rich.

The Noble Foundation Trustees since 1973 have joined with the New York Zoological Society to create on Saint Catherines a a survival center for endangered species, which, under pressure from encroaching civilization, as well as from such predators as poachers, could not survive in their original environment. The experiment began when a handsome African antelope called the gemsbok was enclosed within eight acres of eight-foot, plastic-coated fence. The gemsbok took to the environment very well and more land was fenced. To the gemsbok population were added a male and two female sable antelope, and six addaxes. All went well, and in 1976, gemsbok, addax, and sable antelope all had calves. Twenty more acres went under fence, and kangaroos and another variety of antelope were added to the animal population. In 1977 crowned cranes and rare parrots were brought in, and to Mrs. Larkin's delight, the delicate crowned cranes and the addaxes seem to have a particular affinity for each other.

Sapelo, of course, was Jones's first venture into converting an island into something more than a rich man's playground. Though he had had nothing to do with the island since 1933, when he sold it to Dick Reynolds for enough money to save Sea Island from the Detroit banks, he was pleased to know that Reynolds shared his views that Sapelo's archaeological sites and its natural environment should be preserved. In 1952, at the urging of Eugene Odum, the University of Georgia's famed ecologist, Reynolds had established the Sapelo Island Research Foundation, and working with the University of Georgia, he had set up the Marine Research Institute to study the marshes and their complex relationship to the land and seas that feed them. The Reynolds Foundation supported the project at a cost of some $100,000 a year and contributed some $100,000 more for the upkeep of grounds and buildings. A great deal was learned from those studies. From them, says Jones, the state was able to develop the basic legislation that would save the marshes, based on a new understanding of the delicate ecological balance on which not only the beauty of the marshes, but much of Georgia's shrimp, fish, and oyster industry depends.

Within a decade, though, the program was in trouble. Taxes were soaring, and to raise the $200,000 needed, the Foundation was having to dig into capital every year. In 1964 Reynolds died in Switzerland, and in 1969 his widow, Annamarie, sold the north end of Sapelo to the state of Georgia, to be placed under the Department of Natural Resources as a game preserve and propagation area. Knowing that Bill Jones had a special flair for handling complicated financial matters, she and Reynolds's sister, Nancy, asked him to serve on the board of trustees of the Foundation which managed the South end of the island. The next year, in 1971, he was made president of the board. His first concern was to find out what to do with the great white elephant of a house at south end. Since Reynolds had walked out in 1963, the house had been maintained exactly as it was when he was in residence, which cost the foundation a great deal of money. For sentimental reasons, Jones could not bear to see the handsome place abandoned, for it had been his home when he first came to Georgia. Nor could it be used as a hunting lodge as it once had been, for hunting was now prohibited on the island.

Fortunately for his own desires, and for the Foundation's finances, forces were soon at work which in due time would bring about a happy solution to the problem. In 1972 the United States Congress had passed the Coastal Zone Management Act—one part of which provided for estuarine sanctuaries to be established in coastal waters all around the United States. On the east coast they were to be established in the Cape Cod area, along the Hatteras Banks, and in what was called the Carolina area between Virginia and Cape Canaveral. Other areas were in competition for more federal funds in the Carolina area, but Sapelo had two great advantages. First, the island lay halfway between Savannah and Brunswick, in a so-far-virgin territory unpolluted by industrial wastes, and in all likelihood it would remain that way. Second, by the time the estuarine sanctuary gained force, the University of Georgia's Marine Institute had invested twenty years of basic research in these marshlands and tidal rivers.

So in 1976, Jones, as president of Sapelo Island Research

Foundation, sold the south end of Sapelo Island to the State of Georgia for $4 million—though it was valued at $9 million. At the same time, the Foundation agreed to support the Marine Institute by making a contribution of $150,000 a year to the University of Georgia for fourteen years. The span of years was significant; the scientists by that time would have been at work on Sapelo for thirty-five years, and they would have completed the first cycle of their studies. In this way, the grand old house was saved. To Governor George Busbee, and to his fellows in the high echelon of government, here was a place that could be used not only for scientific seminars but for entertaining high-ranking official visitors in a place of elegance and quiet beauty.

Thus, without disservice to the university's scientific purpose, the south end of Sapelo became one of the showplaces of the Georgia coast. While the scientists labor over their test tubes in the old carriage houses and barns which have been converted into laboratories, parties come over by boat to see the lab exhibits, hear lectures, and view movies describing the work of the Institute. By bus the visitors travel over the island, seeing the deer and the Indian mounds at the north end, the beautiful marble fountains in the gardens of the big house at the south end, and the exterior, at least, of the house itself. Jones still serves as the Foundation head, his main concern now the protection of the little village at Hog Hammock, owned by people whose parents worked this land as slaves.

Jones also had a deep personal interest in Ossabaw, owned by a friend of his and Kit's, Eleanor (Sandy) Torrey West, and operated by her for several years as a haven for intellectuals in many fields of study. Still one of the wildest, loveliest, and least changed of the barrier islands, Ossabaw, like Sapelo, was one of the hunting islands claimed by Mary Musgrove. Ancient records show that on May 17, 1760, it was sold by the colonial government to one Gray Elliott for 1325 pounds. More than 200 years later

Howard Coffin learned that his friend, Dr. H.N. Torrey, a wealthy Detroit surgeon, inspired by Coffin's love for the area, had begun looking for a place on the Georgia coast similar to Coffin's Sapelo. Soon Coffin learned that Ossabaw was for sale, and at his urging Dr. Torrey bought it for $225,000 along with its animal population, estimated in 1924 as being 5,000 deer, 2,000 wild cattle, and 10,000 wild hogs.

The island has been in the Torrey family since, and Dr. Torrey's daughter, Sandy, for years stubbornly resisted any impulse to permit any development there that would destroy or even infringe upon its still unspoiled beauty. Determined that the island should remain a wild and lonely place and knowing that when she died, her own and her brother's children would be forced to sell it, she began looking about for a landlord who would guarantee that her beloved island would remain a uniquely beautiful place forever. Many agencies, including the federal government, were interested, but the one she trusted most to carry out her wishes — the Georgia Heritage Trust — did not have the resources to buy 25,000 acres of marsh and highland. The island was appraised at $15 million, but Mrs. West and her family were willing to sell it to the Heritage Trust for $8 million, thus, in effect, making a gift to the state of property worth $7 million, of which roughly half would be tax deductible. Governor Busbee could raise $4 million, and if another $4 million could be found, all would be well. The money soon was forthcoming. Robert Woodruff, of Ichauway Plantation and Atlanta, quietly let it be known that he would match the state's $4 million. So in May 1978, thanks to Sandy West, Bob Woodruff, George Busbee, and Joe Tanner, Georgia's commissioner of natural resources, Ossabaw was under new ownership.

The state will keep it and protect it as Mrs. West and her family have protected it for the past half century. It will be used as a wildlife refuge and for research and study in many fields. Artists, writers, painters, poets, philosophers, economists, serious students in every field of the humanities as well as the sciences will be welcome as they have been welcomed by Sandy West in recent years. But mainly it is Joe Tanner's purpose as commissioner of natural resources to keep the island wild and beautiful and unchanged except as God's own winds and waters change it, so that Georgia will always have, now and forever, one of the unique sea-washed islands in the world. Jones's interests in Saint Catherines and Ossabaw was expressed mainly in observing, with an appraising eye, and in general approving what was happening there.

He was also pleased, though he had nothing to do with their decision, when the Berolzheimers, a California family who owned Little Saint Simons Island, sought to change that beautiful wild land from a hunting and fishing club to a game preserve where photographers and bird-watchers could come to look and marvel and take pictures.

In the preservation of Cumberland as a national seashore recreation area under the direction of the National Park Service, however, he played an active and a vital role. Here was another island rich in history and still virtually unspoiled, though for generations it had been a barony of the Carnegie clan, and of the Candlers, whose members built great houses there as manorial as those on Jekyll.

As on other islands in the golden chain there was evidence that a prehistoric folk had lived on Cumberland as long as 4000 years ago. The Spaniards of Saint Augustine built missions there and stayed for awhile, plagued by Indians, spied on by colonists, and harassed by pirates. Oglethorpe built Fort Frederica on Saint Simons and then moved on to Cumberland in 1736, his purpose "to see where His Majesties and the Spaniards dominions joyn." He found bark huts built by wandering Indian hunters, but no Spaniards, and on high bluffs that commanded the water approach to the south, he had Captain Hugh MacKay's Highlanders build a little fort, which he called Fort Saint Andrews. He named the island Cumberland. This was done at the request of a young Indian, Toonahawi, son of Tomochichi, who had gone on a trip to England with Oglethorpe and while there had been given a watch by his friend the young Duke of Cumberland. Southward, down what is now the Intracoastal Waterway, Oglethorpe built another fort, Fort William, defended by high log walls and eight cannons. Fort Saint Andrews was not a peaceful place. Though they had their wives and children with them, the soldiers, many of whom had come from the easy life of the Gibraltar garrison, did not like this wild and lonely land. Mutiny, duels, and court-martials were frequent.

After the Battle of Bloody Marsh had ended the Spanish threat forever, Cumberland's forts, like Frederica, were abandoned. Planters moved in with rice and Sea Island cotton, and all along the golden isles Scottish immigrants came seeking their fortune. Rivers and plantations and political units began to hear the names of McIntosh, MacKay, Cuthbert, MacDonald, and Spalding. Two wars—the Revolution and the War of 1812—left Cumberland's fields devastated, but the planters came back and with their slaves set up feudal fiefdoms that lasted until the Civil War. In 1786 Revolutionary General Nathanael Greene came down to build his house, called Dungeness, on the site of an old hunting camp that Oglethorpe had given the same name. In 1818 General Richard Henry Lee—Light Horse Harry Lee—died at Dungeness. Taken ill on a ship returning from Cuba, he had asked to be put ashore at Cumberland, so that he could go to the home of the daughter of his old friend General Greene. There he died and was buried. Robert E. Lee visited his father's grave several times in future years, and in 1913 the Virginia Legislature brought Harry Lee's body home to lie by the side of his son.

The end of slavery brought an end to the great plantations on

Cumberland and elsewhere. No substitute could be found for slave labor, and the old fields grew up in pines. Then began the era of the private island, which only now is ending. In the late 1880s, while the Morgans, Vanderbilts, Astors, Rockefellers, and Goulds were creating their legendary fiefdom on Jekyll, just on the horizon to the south Thomas Carnegie, brother of Andrew, was creating his own barony on Cumberland. He bought Dungeness, Nathanael Greene's old estate, and on it built a new Dungeness, a mansion of fifty-nine rooms, with formal gardens, stables, a gymnasium, and a village for employees. Around it his children, in time, built their own fine places—Greyfield, Plum Orchard, Sweetwater—and there they and their children lived a life of idle ease and opulence which changed but little in seventy-five years. Thomas Carnegie had specified in his will that the family holdings should remain undivided until the last of his nine children died. This happened in 1963 with the passing of the island matriarch, Florence Nightingale Carnegie Perkins. And here, in a minor role as mediator, Bill Jones entered the Cumberland picture. By now there were only five families left who were direct descendants of Thomas Carnegie. Four children had died without issue, and now two of the remaining families asked Bill Jones and Jim Stockton of Ponte Vedra if they would devise a plan for dividing the island, fairly and equally, among the five groups remaining. The solution was fairly simple. The island was first divided into two parts—the north end, where there were supposed to be deposits of valuable titanium—and the scenic south end, where the families lived. Then each of these areas was divided into five strips, with each family being assigned a strip in each section, the one in the south being the one that contained their home.

This proved satisfactory to all, and for a while nothing happened. But some Carnegie heirs, like the heirs of the Morgans and the Vanderbilts on Jekyll earlier, had gotten tired of the island life. The cost was becoming burdensome, the taxes were increasing. In the early days the revenues from the Carnegie Building, in Pittsburgh, had carried the costs of the island operation. Now the building, outmoded, had been torn down.

First a family member needing income sold his strip to Robert Davis of Saint Marys, a local developer, who immediately subdivided it and began selling lots. Then in 1969 three other Carnegies sold their holdings to Charles Fraser, who paid $1.5 million for 3,117 acres of centrally located land. Here, Fraser announced, he would build another Hilton Head, another Sea Pines. Here he would erect clusters of vacation villas and cottages, to sell to individual families, with bike and hiking trails, an air strip, a boat marina, a golf course, tennis courts, and a meeting center.

This, naturally, caused a great uproar. Citizens of Camden County immediately took sides. Some favored all the development that Fraser could cram into the place; others pushed for its use as a National Seashore Recreation Area, where anybody could come to enjoy the natural beauty of a barrier island, its air unsullied by the scent of gasoline, its terrain undisturbed, its quietness unshattered by the snarl and snort of dune buggies.

The uproar spurred the action of the officials of the National Park Service. Years earlier, in 1955, after an intensive study, the Park Service had fixed its eye upon Cumberland Island as a national asset, calling it, along with Cape Cod, the outstanding undeveloped seashore area remaining along the Atlantic and Gulf coasts. At Cape Hatteras a National Seashore had been established and was drawing thousands of people yearly to its scenic wonders. But in the plan for Cumberland, to the preservation of the scenery and the protection of such rare species as the pocket gopher had been added a new dimension—outdoor recreation—all that the island could accommodate without damage to its natural beauty. This would include all sorts of beach

activity, except dune-damaging beach buggies. Swimming, surf-
ing, surf fishing, strolling, and beachcombing would be permitted.
Fishing and boating would be encouraged; camping would be
provided for in tents and trailers; hiking, cycling, and horseback
riding would be encouraged; and a program of nature and
historical lectures would be set up. Many of the more dedicated
ecologists felt that any recreational use would destroy the pristine
beauty of Cumberland. But as word of these things got around,
more and more people began to express their support of the
National Park Service and its ideas. Charles Fraser, reorganizing
his plans to fit these concepts, announced that he felt the island
could serve a dual purpose. In one area would be his cottages and
condominiums, restaurants, tennis courts, and golf courses. In
another all the recreation areas the National Park Service proposed would be open to the public.

And so the matter stood, until Congressman Bill Stuckey,
himself a Sea Island cottage owner, offered in Congress, and
pushed through, the Cumberland Island National Seashore Bill.
There still remained the question of where the National Park
Service would get the money to buy up the land that could be
bought. And again Bill Jones played a quiet role. One night Dick
Everett, the Cloister's reservations manager, who also lectured in
history, delivered a dissertation on Cumberland. And in the
audience that night was Stoddard Stevens, a friend of Bill Jones's
and for many years one of the trustees of the Mellon Foundation.
After Everett's lecture, with its colored slides of Cumberland,
Stevens admitted to Jones the fact that the National Park Service
had hopeful plans for the island interested him very much. The
upshot was that on the next day, Bill Jones took Mr. and Mrs.
Stevens down to Cumberland to look the place over. Then he
asked Paul Mellon to come down to spend the day, knowing that
Mellon also had a deep interest in the national parks and had
helped the Park Service at other times and in other places.

All of this resulted in the Mellon Foundation's agreeing to put up $7.5 million to acquire the property. This bought about 76 percent of the land, including Fraser's 3000 acres, for which he got his investment back. But like family members who held on to their homeplaces, he held on to a small acreage to the south, which he later sold for $600,000, making a tidy profit. Two Carnegie heirs, one a Ferguson, the other a Rockefeller, held on to their property, not wishing to sell. Mrs. Lucy Ferguson, a doughty widow, in fact, turned her family mansion, Greyfield, into a hotel. Nor did the Candler family to the north of the island come under the Park Service wing. But enough land was in hand so that the Park Service could go ahead with planning for a National Seashore. And, if this is handled right, Bill Jones believes, Cumberland will still be a source of wonder, joy and peace to Georgians and all Americans a hundred years from now.

Fame and the Famous

Prominent personalities frequently visited Howard Coffin at his Sapelo Island estate and later at Sea Island. Henry Ford, right center, and his brother-in-law are flanked by Coffin, left, and Alfred W. Jones, far right, during a 1927 trip to Sapelo.

Photo left, later a younger contingent of Fords came to call at Sapelo. At left are Mr. and Mrs. Edsel Ford, with Mrs. Jones and Henry Ford II, seated. Benson Ford stands at center with Coffin, right.

Photo right, new American hero Charles A. Lindbergh leaves his plane after landing at Sapelo in 1927 en route to Mexico. There he was to meet and later marry the U.S. Ambassador's daughter, Anne Morrow.

President Calvin Coolidge plants "Coolidge oak" on the Cloister lawn in late December 1928. Looking on are his White House aides, Mr. and Mrs. Coffin, center, Mrs. Coolidge and Charles Redden.

Photo left, President and Mrs. Coolidge and Mr. and Mrs. Coffin relax before the great fireplace at Cabin Bluff, which served as Sea Island's hunting preserve in Camden County for many years. Photo right, President Coolidge and Coffin return from a Sapelo hunt.

Mrs. Herbert Hoover demonstrates the dress and camera techniques of the day during her visit to Cabin Bluff in 1932 while her husband was President.

America's leading press and radio figures came to help open Sea Island and bag turkeys at Cabin Bluff. From left: the guide, lodge manager and C.F. Redden, vice president of the Sea Island Company; then M.N. Aylesworth, president, National Broadcasting Company; Kent Cooper, general manager, the Associated Press; Roy Howard, president, Scripps-Howard Newspapers; Ben Ames Williams, author and Saturday Evening Post writer; Robert H. Davis, New York Sun; John N. Wheeler, Bell Syndicate; John Oliver LaGorce, National Geographic Society; Ray Long, president of International Magazine Corporation and publisher of Cosmopolitan; and Tom Shipp, Washington, D.C., newspaperman.

Alfred Jones displays his bag of two prized Cabin Bluff turkeys.

Bobby Jones, third from left, with a group of distinguished young Atlantans after a Cabin Bluff hunt. Left to right: William A. Parker, Clark Howell, Jr., Jones, Malon Courts, Howard Dobbs, Richard W. Courts, Jr., Harris Robinson.

Georgia's Walter F. George, long-time dean of the United States Senate, and his Cabin Bluff turkey.

The Constitution, known as Old Ironsides, returns to Saint Simons where her oak timbers were cut and is "raided" by the Pirates of the Spanish Main. This group of pretty young high school girls was established by Coffin. The group still is called upon to welcome prominent visitors to the Golden Isles. Their charter was written by Ben Ames Williams.

A representative of the British government is greeted
by Coffin during the ceremonial planting of
Oglethorpe Oak on the Cloister lawn. The oak was
grown from an acorn from Oglethorpe's estate
in England.

Eugene Lewis, Detroit banker, and his wife on a
Cloister visit. Lewis was an early partner of Coffin
and later owned Hamilton Plantation on Saint
Simons, now site of Epworth-by-the-Sea.

Sir Robert Borden, ex-premier of Canada, and Lady Laura Borden, spend their third season at the Cloister.

Another former Canadian premier, McKenzie King, tries his hand at bowling on the green at the Cloister.

Photo left, author Ben Ames Williams came to Sea Island to write and relax at golf.

Photo right, O.B. Keeler, famed golf writer for the Atlanta Journal, followed Bobby Jones to Sea Island. At left in background is James D. Compton, Sea Island Company president.

Mrs. Maxfield Parrish, wife of the famous painter, made a lasting contribution to coastal Georgia history by searching out and preserving the "Slave Songs of Plantation Days."

Jimmy Walker, colorful mayor of New York City, and Mrs. Walker display their day's catch at the Cloister's fishing dock.

Frank "Bring-'em-Back-Alive" Buck and Mrs. Buck sharpen their sights at the Sea Island Gun Club.

Mr. and Mrs. Alfred W. Jones with Bill, Jr., left, and Marianna at the Sea Island Casino pool.

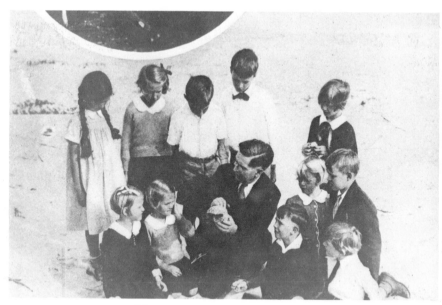

The young resort established its own school for children of cottagers and long-staying Cloister guests. The first headmaster was Frank R. Plunkett, shown here with his students.

Sea Island and the Cloister became a fashionable gathering place for Atlantans. At a house party at the Sea Island Casino: left to right, Miss Connie Adams, Miss May Latimer, Mike May, Preston Arkwright, Jr., Bernham McGeehee, Miss Mary Adair Howell, Buster Bird, Miss Louise Moore, Mrs. Preston Arkwright, Jr. Seated, front, Dan Conklin.

Louisa Robert Carroll, then national junior backstroke champion from Atlanta, today a Sea Island cottager.

Three daughters of Judge and Mrs. Shepard Bryan of Atlanta, Sea Island Cottagers: Left to right, Mary (later Mrs. Bill Benedict); Cobbie (Mrs. W. Colquitt Carter); and Poncie (Mrs. Bonneau Ansley.)

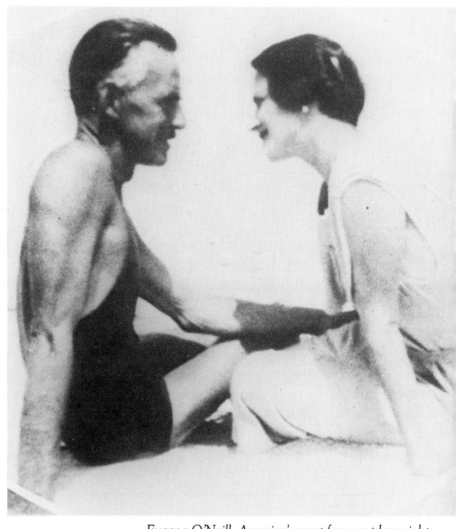

Eugene O'Neill, America's most famous playwright, and his wife, Carlotta, at their Sea Island cottage, Casa Genotta. Here he wrote "Ah Wilderness."

Richard J. Reynolds, Jr., tobacco heir, whose
purchase of Sapelo Island
helped the company survive the
depression years.

Scrip issued by the Sea Island Company during the
1933 bank holiday ordered by President Franklin
Roosevelt kept the company and virtually all of
Glynn County in business through the crisis.

During World War II, the Cloister became scene of bandage-making sessions as part of the volunteer war effort.

General and Mrs. Dwight David Eisenhower at
Sea Island after the war ended.

Photo left, World War I ace and president of Eastern
Air Lines Eddie Rickenbacker, second from left, at
McKinnon Airport with Alfred Jones, left, J.D.
Compton and Irving A. Harned of the Cloister.
Photo right, Giovanni Martinelli, opera star,
on the beach.

Photo left, singer Dorothy Kirsten with husband
Dr. J.D. French.
Photo right, Alfred Jones and Sea Island cottager
Clifford Perry with singer-TV personality Perry
Como, who became an annual Cloister visitor.

Photo left, Secretary of State Dean Acheson strolls
the beach with his daughter and son-in-law.
Photo right, Hopalong Cassidy, cowboy star, and his
wife relax at the beach club.

Photo left, Mr. and Mrs. Ralph Bellamy outside their
beach house room.
Photo right, Art Linkletter, TV-radio entertainer,
with George Scherer, maître d'.

Women's golf stars receive prize money from Alfred
Jones after one of Sea Island's annual tournaments
for the Ladies Professional Golf Association. From
left, Marlene Bauer, Mickey Wright and Mary Lena
Faulk. Bill Roach, then Sea Island's golf professional,
is at left rear, and I.A. Harned, Cloister manager,
is at far right.

Marshals for the 1953 playing of the annual Sea
Island LPGA tournament, known as the "red hats."

Sarah Churchill, daughter of Sir Winston Churchill, and Anthony Beauchamp, following their marriage in 1949 at the home of Mr. and Mrs. Jones.

Vice President and Mrs. Alben Barkley chose the Cloister for their "Shangri-la" honeymoon in 1949 and also to celebrate his 72nd birthday. They returned in 1954 for their fifth anniversary.

*Queen Juliana and Prince Bernhard of The
Netherlands plant an oak on the lawn of the Cloister
during their visit at Easter in 1952. Jones looks on.*

Texas Gov. John B. Connally addresses the Southern Governors' Conference in 1965, Georgia Governor Carl E. Sanders, now a Sea Island cottager, beside him.

Photo left, Vice President Hubert Humphrey speaking at a Cloister meeting.
Photo right, Secretary of State Dean Rusk with I.A. Harned.

Time Magazine photographed Michael Anderson of Nashville for a cover story on Sea Island in 1965.

Attorney General-designate Griffin Bell is interviewed by the Washington press corps in the Cloister's Spanish Lounge during President-elect Jimmy Carter's December 1976 visit and first gathering of his cabinet appointees.

President-elect Carter and Vice President-elect Walter
Mondale (right) with ABC's David Hartman and
Hartman's young son in the Solarium of the Cloister
after taping of Hartman's "Good Morning America"
interviews.

By 1953 the Cloister had added its first two beachfront hotel buildings, Ashantilly and Retreat Houses,
and built a new beach club.

Sea Island Company President J.D. Compton, second
from left, with former Cloister managers Norman
Pancoast, left, and Clarence Wannop and then-
manager Irving Harned.

12

WIN SOME, LOSE SOME

Jones's interest in Jekyll and Saint Simons as a public playground, and in the other islands as places dedicated to conservation, preservation, and education, were examples of the several ways he as an individual and Sea Island as a company have left their lasting mark on Glynn County and its environs. His interest in industry, from the beginning, was equally keen. His goal was to create a balanced community, a resort area providing services at all economic levels, and around it an industrial community built on the region's greatest assets—trees and waterways. When Jones and Coffin came to Saint Simons in 1926, the only industry in the Brunswick area was the Hercules Powder Company, which made naval stores out of resinous pine stumps. The process left mountains of spent pine chips which Howard Coffin believed could be used as the basis of a pulp paper industry.

One of the largest of paper manufacturers was George Mead of Dayton, president of Mead Paper Company. He was a friend of both Coffin and Jones and was married to Elsie Talbott, Kit Jones's sister. At Jones's urging, and with Coffin putting up $10,000 to cover the cost, Mead, in 1927, ordered his engineers to test the Hercules chips as a possible source of pulp for paper. Hercules, it turned out, did not produce enough chips to support a paper mill, but the test did confirm what Coffin believed — that someday Georgia pine would make paper. Out of these tests there eventually grew the huge industry that was to feed millions of dollars in payrolls into the coastal economy. In 1936 Mead invited Scott Paper Company, another huge manufacturer, which needed a bleached sulphate pulp, to join Mead fifty-fifty in forming the Brunswick Pulp and Paper Company, which in time became one of the world's biggest manufacturers of its kind. Mead also went into another partnership, with the Inland Container Company, to form a company called Georgia Kraft, which built plants in Rome, Macon, and in Alabama across the river from Columbus, Georgia.

Thus, through his interest in paper manufacturing, Bill Jones embarked on a dual career as an industrialist and a resort owner. He was a director of Mead Corporation for thirty-three years and chairman of the board of Brunswick Pulp and Paper for ten. During the period of his service, production at Brunswick rose from 150 tons to 1,800 tons a day, and Mead's total sales rose from $50 million to $1.5 billion a year. He was also a director of Georgia Kraft, as representative of Mead. His final contribution, before retiring as a director of Mead in 1972, was the so-called Jones Report, an analysis of the company's goals and organization, which is still used by Mead officials as a guide to the future.

Although the mills poured millions of dollars into the community economy, they poured other ingredients into the air and water which neither Bill Jones nor anybody else was pleased about. After years of effort, and the expenditure of many millions of dollars, the companies now meet federal environmental pollution standards. Black ashes from the smokestacks no longer fall in a thin dust on the land, and the water effluents no longer poison the streams as once they did. But one unhappy by-product still remains. The mills still smell, and to filter out the last molecule that causes these odors would cost more under the present state of the art than any company could afford. Fortunately, the tourists on the islands, or in the motels on the mainland, rarely notice this effluvia. The prevailing winds are from the southeast off the sea, carrying the odors inland. Those exposed to it every day claim that they get used to it and do not notice. When they do, they observe wryly that it smells like money. Those on Saint Simons and Sea Island, who get it only when a west wind blows on a day of low-hung clouds, feel differently. It may be the smell of money, but it is still an affront to the nostrils.

The combination of companies described above, making everything from Kraft paper boxes to paper towels, make use of both the slash pine of the Georgia uplands and the "trash hardwoods" of the Georgia swamps. With the replanting of cutover areas, Bill Jones is proud to point out, Georgia has more standing pines today than it had when the mills started operating forty-odd years ago. Jones's own family plantation, Altama, 6000 acres of marsh and upland, is being operated not only as a game preserve, but as a scientifically grown and harvested tree farm.

Not all of Jones's ventures into the wood and paper business were as successful as the paper mills. Right after the war he joined with John Houk, a cousin of Kit's, to start a plywood plant in Brunswick. Houk, a former Mead employee who had served in Air Force procurement during the war, buying all the wooden or textile products the Air Force used, was convinced that plywood was the building material of the future. An eloquent salesman, he proposed the idea to Bill Jones. Jones, who was always interested in helping any young man put a good idea into effect, went into partnership with Houk, putting some $100,000 of his own money into the company. Local investors, friends of Jones's, put up about $50,000 more. They bought an old veneer plant on Highway 17, tore it down, put up a new building, installed the best equipment they could find, and set out to become the kings of the plywood industry. But they had not done their homework well enough. There were not enough logs of plywood quality in the area. The plant failed; Jones bought out his partner and liquidated the corporation, breaking a little better than even on the deal. He sold some of the real estate to the Seaboard Construction Company, a road-building firm set up by the Sea Island Company and owned jointly with Harold Friedman, the former county manager. To the local people who had come into the venture because Jones was in it, he then made a gift of their net investment. So none of the locals lost anything.

There were a few other failures over the years. One project, for making handsome living-room furniture out of pressed paper, never got off the ground. In the main, though, Jones's confidence in a young man trying to start a business paid off handsomely. In the early 1960s, he financed Bill Portman, son-in-law of his brother, Robert Jones, in a dealership selling a highly regarded brand of forklift trucks. He guaranteed a loan of $50,000 for Portman's company at a Cincinnati bank and persuaded his brother, a more conservative man than he, to share the endorsement with him. Young Portman paid off the $50,000 loan in a few years, and Portman Equipment Company has been thriving ever since. Another project, Thompson Industries, which operated fine metal working plants in south Georgia, also did very well. And a housing project in Jesup, where Jones went into partnership with Charles Gowen, Lucian Whittle, and J.W. McSwiney of Mead, was a success.

McSwiney, it might be noted in passing, was in a sense a protégé of Jones. As a young Tennesseean with no technical education, he had come to work for Brunswick Pulp and Paper, where Jones immediately discovered that he had remarkably sound business judgment and a talent for organization. Jones persuaded his fellow Mead directors to transfer McSwiney to the home office in Dayton to give him broader responsibilities. This was done, and McSwiney rose rapidly into the top echelon of management, becoming chairman of the board and Mead's chief executive officer. It was in this capacity that he asked Bill Jones to do his classic study of Mead, its organization, and its goals.

Whether they succeeded or failed, Jones in his backing of young men invariably dealt with them in a spirit of kindness, warmth, and understanding, offering guidance and counseling when they needed it and backing them throughout if it had to be done. He was more stern and critical in dealing with his own ventures, and he readily admitted that he, too, had made a few errors in financial judgment along the way. In 1942, faced with the need to raise money for taxes and worried about what the war could do to Sea Island (which after years of struggle was just beginning to show a little profit), he sold Cabin Bluff, in Camden County. Here was one of the most historic regions along the Georgia coast. First the French and then the Spaniards had tried to establish a fort there, and after the defeat of the Spanish at Bloody Marsh the English took over. In 1800 Captain Charles Floyd, hero of the Revolution, established his family seat there, at Belleview Plantation. There also his son John built his own great house, Fairfield. From here, John Floyd went on to distinguish himself in the military as a brigadier general in the War of 1812 and as an Indian fighter. In later years, he served in the Georgia House and Senate and was a presidential elector in 1824. A son Charles, named for his grandfather, was equally distinguished as a poet, painter, and musician.

Cabin Bluff between the Revolution and the Civil War reached its greatest glory under the three generations of Floyds. It was a great plantation area; and as it remained for years thereafter, it was a hunting preserve of the Camden Hunt Club, which gave hunting parties and boat races to which invitations and challenges were sent to sportsmen as far north as New York City. The boat races were particularly famous. Prizes were as high as $10,000, slave crews were pampered like professional athletes, and a wager might be anything from a tract of land to a beaver hat or a chew of tobacco. Rivalry between coastal plantation crews was as fierce as the proverbial competition between Tech and Georgia. The boats were made of cypress logs, thirty feet long, three feet wide, hewn to a shell one inch thick. An exact replica of one of them can still be seen preserved on the Cloister lawn.

Howard Coffin knew all this history and was fascinated by it. He was possessed, too, with the idea of making paper out of Georgia pine, and on Cabin Bluff's 40,000 acres of highland, there were millions of standing pines. In 1927 and 1928, Coffin bought Cabin Bluff, 61,400 acres in all, of which 22,510 acres were marsh. The land cost him $576,000, and by the end of 1931 he had nearly $800,000 invested in the place. He had fenced a vast acreage, drilled artesian wells, built roads and fire lanes, brought in telephone lines, and set up a small naval stores operation and a forest management program. He made no real effort to turn the place into a paying proposition. Some timber was sold, a few cattle, and a little turpentine. His greatest interest was in recapturing the mood of the old days of the Camden Hunt Club. He restored and expanded the old hunting lodge, making it one of the most comfortable such places in the country. There, before a great stone fireplace, he entertained his most distinguished guests, politicians and journalists in the main, many of whom were freeloaders. The place was not an entire loss, however, for pictures of these notables, holding high a dead wild turkey or standing triumphantly over a defunct deer, made sports and society pages all over the United States.

But here it was 1942 and Bill Jones needed cash. He was faced with an Internal Revenue Service demand for a final settlement of Howard Coffin's estate, which at the time of Coffin's death had shrunk to some $432,000. So he sold Cabin Bluff to the Brunswick

Pulp and Paper Company for roughly a half million dollars. The sale, he later said, was the greatest mistake of his financial career, for a few years afterward, acreage of the size and quality of the Cabin Bluff land was selling for twenty times that figure.

Happily, the paper company is using the property in a way Coffin and Jones would both approve. They are managing the forest lands with two things in mind—to maintain a continuing yield of forest products by employing all of the methods known to forest science, while at the same time protecting the habitat where deer and turkey may still be found. Jones and his guests are still welcome to hunt there or to toast their shins before a log fire in the lodge, where the huge Jones "honeymoon alligator" still hangs.

About the time Bill Jones was liquidating his venture in the plywood business, he was going into a new business that caused him a lot of work, over a period of some thirty years, but which in the long run made him a lot of money. From the late 1930s until 1945, Glynn County was managed by Harold Friedman, a man Jones held in high regard. Friedman was a good manager, he knew how to handle money, and he also was an expert at building roads and bridges. At the end of the war, at Jones's urging, he and Friedman formed a local road-paving company which they called the Seaboard Construction Company. The Sea Island Company put up $100,000, for which it took debentures. Friedman put up his know-how in lieu of cash, and 1,000 shares of stock were issued, at one dollar a share. Sea Island held 55 percent and Friedman 45 percent. The company made a little money building roads, but in the years immediately after the war, good profits came from buying and selling surplus equipment. As a result the debentures were paid off in a few years, and the partners' positions were reversed—Sea Island holding 45 percent and Friedman 55 percent. So, Sea Island Company's total investment in Seaboard Construction was $450. It proved to be one of Bill Jones's most profitable ventures. In 1951 Seaboard Construction bought for $75,000 a ready-mix concrete plant (which included three revolving-drum trucks) and set up the Glynn Concrete Company. In 1955 Glynn Concrete expanded into concrete blocks, and in 1974 the company built a new plant costing a quarter of a million dollars. Four years later the appraised value of the company was roughly four times that figure. In 1973 the stockholders pulled Glynn Concrete Company out of the parent Seaboard Construction and set up a separate trust to hold title to undeveloped real estate that had been acquired over the years. Once this was done, Jones and Friedman sold Seaboard Construction to the Ashland Oil Company for 67,500 shares of Ashland stock, then selling at $33 a share. So, his original investment of $450 gave Jones the following assets: about 30,000 shares of Ashland Oil stock, worth nearly a million dollars; a 45 percent interest in Glynn Concrete Company, worth about $450,000; and 45 percent of the Realty Trust, worth about a million dollars. (Keeping abreast of modern trends among the young folk, the Realty Trust recently put a quarter of a million dollars into a skateboard park in Brunswick.)

Jones worked hard for Seaboard for more than a quarter century, but he is quick to point out that the real success was due to Friedman's unusual talents. He and Friedman still see each other frequently. Both like to walk the beach, and Jones can recognize his old friend coming from far away. Friedman, in his eighty-third year, strides along at a great pace, and then, without breaking stride, turns around and walks swiftly backward to develop all his leg muscles. He frequently plunges into the surf and swims out half a mile.

Now and then, out of a sense of obligation to a friend or to the community, Jones has taken on some complicated business proposition from which he could anticipate no advantage whatever, to Sea Island Company nor to himself, except perhaps a modest compensation for his time. One of these was his fifteen-year effort to put a bankrupt railroad back on its feet. When in 1946 Frank Scarlett, the Sea Island Company lawyer in Brunswick, was elevated to a federal judgeship, his court inherited the tangled problems of the Georgia and Florida Railroad, which had been in receivership for a generation. Scarlett's solution was to ask Bill Jones to take over as receiver and get it running at a profit, junk it, or sell it. Jones agreed to try it for a year and sought the advice of William Wyer, an expert in such matters. Wyer came south in 1948, rode the line, talked to its employees and to the people in the towns it served. The road ran from Greenwood, South Carolina, to Augusta, and on through Georgia by way of Vidalia and Valdosta to Madison, Florida — a total length of some 320 miles. Floods in its early days had wrecked it; the depression had further crippled it; and it had been running at a loss for years. The railroad had been kept alive by putting every penny of income back into operations, without retiring any debt, and its bonds were selling at about two cents on the dollar, with no buyers. There were about 700 employees, which were far too many, and they were on substandard wages which were coming under attack by the railroad brotherhoods. The easiest thing, Jones knew, would be to scrap the line and forget it. But this would have put 700 people out of work and would have left a dozen little Georgia towns without railroad facilities of any kind.

So, keeping the railroad in operation became a challenge, not only to Jones as a businessman but to Jones as a man with a sense of civic responsibility. With Wyer's help he began to work out a way to save the road. The first thing he did, after a tremendous struggle before the Public Service Commission, was to take off two money-losing passenger trains that made the round-trip run every day. Then he went to the Reconstruction Finance Corporation with his plan. First he would sell whatever surplus property was not actually needed to run the railroad. He would cut off all nonprofitmaking services, beginning with the two passenger trains, and would abandon two short branch lines. Then he would cut off all nonessential personnel, including the third man on the old steam locomotive. To increase income, he would replace the steam engines with more efficient and less costly diesels. The RFC listened, pondered, and loaned him a million dollars to buy the new equipment. He then went to the railroad brotherhood and outlined his plan. They, in effect, told him to go to hell.

Now he played his trump card, a profit-sharing proposal. Labor in the past had received about 50 percent of the railroad's total income. This proportion would not be changed, he told them. Personnel would be reduced from 700 employees to something more than half that number, but the 400-odd who remained would still divide half the total income. Jones went up and down the railroad, talking to the railroad employees in all the little towns. Their answer was to go on strike. The strike lasted three days. It might have lasted longer, but Jones and Judge Scarlett got on the phone to union headquarters in Cleveland. The union leader was adamant. "Very well," said the judge, "call off the strike or we start dismantling the railroad next week." There was a long pause at the other end of the line. Jones and Scarlett waited. Then the union leader spoke, without putting his hand over the mouthpiece, "That judge down south says they are going to start dismantling the railroad," he said to somebody near him, "and I believe the son-of-a-bitch means it." The strike ended the next day.

For the next fifteen years Jones, as receiver, kept the little railroad going. In the first year it lost $450,000. In 1950 the loss was down to $95,000. In 1952 the road showed a profit of $75,000, after labor was given a dividend of $55,000. In 1953, the wage dividend was $112,000. Gross business increased by a million dollars to $3,750,000 in the next three years. One reason was the employees' enthusiasm for the income-sharing plan. Every man was out beating the bushes for more business, trying to figure how to reduce personnel and increase efficiency. For the fewer there were on the payroll, the bigger would be each worker's share of the profit.

As the road began to grow in freight volume, improve its equipment, and increase the wages paid to the work force (now down to 365 employees), Jones began to look around for a buyer. First he tried the Central of Georgia, which owned many of the Georgia and Florida bonds. No dice. Next he tried the Seaboard, then about to merge with the Coast line. Nothing happened. He knew that the Southern had plans for competing with the Seaboard, and here at last he found his buyer. In 1963 the Southern bought the Georgia-Florida for $7 million, giving the bondholders about thirty cents on the dollar, instead of the two cents the bonds had been worth when Bill Jones took over in 1948. Jones had made it a going line again after fifteen years of hard work. More important to him, though, was the fact that he had done what he liked to do best. He had worked out a tangled and almost impossible human and financial problem, to the ultimate satisfaction of all.

13

BERRY, BOWDOIN, AND THE BAC

Judge Frank Scarlett was not the only one who had noticed Bill Jones's ability to manage complex financial matters with the same finesse with which he brought peace and happiness to people who came to his Sea Island resort. He was that rare combination of an articulate spokesman for the free-enterprise system and at the same time a strong advocate of a program of conservation that would make the beauties of the Georgia coast available to all who wished to share in them. This point of view, blending the caution of the ecologist with the vision of the industrialist and entrepreneur, first attracted attention among his friends and neighbors in the community. As a top officer of the pulp mill, he went on the board of the First National Bank of Brunswick. Soon businessmen far beyond the boundaries of Glynn County were asking him to expound in their boardrooms his thought that conservation and development should go hand in hand if the good of all the people was to be served. In 1953 he became a director of the First National Bank of Atlanta. (First National's president, Ed Smith, had been a member of the Cloister's Gentleman's Club in the early days—young men of good manners who were invited down to lavish attention on the northern belles who came to Sea Island with their parents in the winter time.) He also served on the board of the Georgia Power Company, finding himself surrounded there by old friends. One was Lamartine Hardman, Jr., of Commerce, whose father, the governor, once predicted with great confidence that Jones's Sea Island resort would eventually attract people from as far away as Tennessee and North Carolina. Others were Mills Lane, Jr., of Savannah, Robert J. Maddox and John Sibley of Atlanta, and D. Abbott Turner, Coca-Cola tycoon from Columbus. From the Georgia Power board, Jones went on to serve as a director of Westinghouse.

From each experience, he learned something of value, and each of his associates in turn learned something from him. And out of it all came Jones's basic philosophy: it is extremely important for a foreign-owned corporation to create a friendly and helpful personality in the community in which it operates, as Sea Island Company had tried to do from the earliest days. The corporation should provide community leaders from all levels of management. But men and women in business and industry must go much further than merely being "good citizens" by going to PTA meetings, supporting the United Fund, or giving to the Salvation Army. They must become more deeply involved in politics, become much more vocal when the basic free-enterprise system was threatened. Business, Jones knew, would always be a minority group, whose voice could easily be drowned out by other minorities speaking more loudly and more angrily. Business, though, should not try to engage in a shouting match. It should instead work quietly at the grass roots, providing from its ranks the calm, wise, civic leadership from which all progress is born.

This view that it was the duty of a businessman to serve his community and his state in any way he could was not mere talk. Jones backed his words with actions. Out of his fascination with the rich history of the islands, he was one of the many like-minded Glynn County citizens who founded the Coastal Georgia Historical Society and persuaded the federal government to turn over to the society the old lighthouse at the south end of Saint Simons. Once the lighthouse itself was in hand, money was raised to buy the lighthouse keeper's cottage and turn it into one of the most fascinating maritime museums along the eastern seaboard. In addition to his own contribution, Jones also called for, and received, financial help from Nancy Reynolds, Dick Courts, and his friends on the J. Bulow Campbell Foundation. A special interest in the subject also led him to serve on the board of directors of the Glynn County Association for Mental Health, a nongovernmental organization whose purpose was to improve the care and treatment of persons suffering from mental diseases and handicaps. Though his own higher education had been cut short by illness in his youth, his concern for the education of others never lagged. He served as a trustee of the Brunswick Junior College Foundation, which by raising money to match federal and state grants was able to offer an education to every child in a seven-county coastal area who had the ability and the desire to go to college.

He was equally interested in the education of deprived children in the more remote parts of Georgia. In 1967 he was one of the seventeen United States executives who were named to the Berry College Board of Visitors. As one who subscribed fully to Berry's creed—that every person should have the opportunity to become all he or she is capable of being, regardless of economic, ethnic, or social background—he served on Berry's board until 1973. When he resigned, he expressed agreement with Berry's president, John Bertrand, that "the private enterprise system is the greatest antipoverty program known to man."

Jones went off the Berry Board of Visitors in the same year that Trust Company banker, William Bowdoin, a good friend who shared his views about how a businessman could serve his state, replaced William McChesney Martin as chairman of Berry's Board of Trustees. Bowdoin and Jones had served together earlier on another board of broader scope. When Carl Sanders became governor in June 1963, he resolved to carry on a program originally conceived by his predecessor, Ernest Vandiver, which would seek to increase economy and efficiency in Georgia's state government. He therefore created an organization made up in the main of outstanding business and professional men who would serve for four years, without pay, on the Governor's Commission for Efficiency and Improvement in State Government, later known as the Bowdoin Commission. Bill Bowdoin, president of the Trust Company of Georgia Associates, was chairman, and the other members were men Jones knew well. Col. Robert J. Mashburn, Homer businessman, was the vice-chairman; others were William Harris, Winder banker; Julian T. Hightower, Thomaston textile executive; William P. Simmons, Macon industrialist; Dr. John B. O'Neal III, Elberton; and Dr. M.W.H. Collins, Jr., Athens, executive director.

The committee started to work in April 1963, bringing in national experts in every field of government to assist them in making their studies and recommendations. In the four years of the commission's existence, the members made more than thirty reports, covering all the major departments and programs in state government—education, highways, agriculture, mental health, the retirement system, fish and game, and the prison system. Basically the commission found that Georgia government, like any state government, suffered from the political reality that government agencies usually hired two inefficient employees instead of one competent one. It was this personnel policy of rewarding the faithful regardless of their ability, that department heads were most reluctant to change. Knowing that the system was likely to continue, the commission recommended that those hired be put through a broad program of training and education that could, in time, give some meaning to the so-called merit system. Many of the recommendations made by the Bowdoin Commission were put into effect by legislation in the years to come. Many were not. To Bill Jones, though, and to his fellow members of the commission, the years they devoted to this study proved to be one of the most significant undertakings of their lives.

Jones also was for a number of years a member of the Georgia State Chamber of Commerce, where he stressed the development of the whole state, both as an industrial and a resort area, with the two living compatibly side by side. In April 1962 the state chamber named him Man of the Month.

This was only one of many testimonials that were to be awarded him over the years. His work to convert lonely and undeveloped Fort Frederica into a National Park visited by more than 300,000 people every year, and his efforts to establish a National Seashore on Cumberland brought him two cherished citations. One was the Department of the Interior's Conservation Service Award, signed by Secretary Rogers C.B. Morton. Hanging across from it on the wall of Jones's unpretentious office at Sea Island is a gold shield bearing the picture of a buffalo. It is a badge designating Jones as an honorary Park Ranger, the highest award the National Park Service can bestow on a citizen. In his letter of presentation, Gary Everhardt, director of the National Park Service, told Jones that "in recognizing your magnificent work in conservation and continuing support of the national parks idea, this token represents the high esteem the Service holds for you and your work." Here indeed was paradox, the champion of free enterprise basking in the glow of approval from a government agency. The award was illustrative, though, of Jones's deepest belief, that the earth and its riches and its beauty could best be utilized when the businessman and industrialist, which he was, and the ecologist and conservationist, which he also was, worked together with the educator for the good of all the people.

Jones's many-faceted services did not go unnoticed on the state level. In 1974 Governor Jimmy Carter gave him a Distinguished Georgian Award. Cited were his "diligent efforts to share the bountiful treasures of Georgia's Golden Isles (which) have resulted in the creation of the Cloister Hotel, one of the world's most famous seaside resorts." Also mentioned was the vital part he played in the purchase of Jekyll Island by the State of Georgia for development as a State Park, and his role in having Cumberland developed as a National Seashore. As a result of his appreciation of Georgia history, Governor Carter pointed out, Jones was at least partially responsible for the preservation of such national historic shrines as Fort Frederica and Bloody Marsh. Also, as president of the Sapelo Island Research Foundation, he had arranged for the sale of Sapelo Island to the state for the use of the University of Georgia's Research Center.

All the people of Georgia, the citation concluded, were in Jones's debt "for his tireless efforts on behalf of the Georgia Travel Industry." This was confirmed nationally by the Society of American Travel Writers, who in 1976 gave Jones their Connie Award for his "inspiration, distinguished leadership, and significant accomplishment in the struggle against encroachment on precious public preserves, national resources, wildlife, and historic land marks." The Connie Award was presented to Jones by Governor George Busbee, who in his address at the Cloister was even more eloquent than Governor Carter had been in his tribute to Jones for "a lifetime dedicated to conservation in its highest and best sense." "Sea Island," said Governor Busbee, "stands as a monument to the unflagging effort of Alfred Jones and to his total commitment to orderly development policies that have preserved the character and the natural beauty of the island." "It is no exaggeration," said the governor, "that this truly remarkable man has been the guiding influence in achieving the balanced use and preservation of fully two-thirds of the Georgia coast. Within this sixty-mile stretch of islands, marsh, and water, can be found the true genius and foresight of Alfred Jones."

Jones's own neighbors felt the same way about him. Also on the wall of his office is a parchment, in illuminated lettering like the book of Kells, which announces that the Brunswick-Golden Isles Chamber of Commerce was establishing an annual award in the name of Alfred W. Jones, to be presented to outstanding leaders who contributed unselfishly of their time and talent to improve the quality of life in Brunswick and the Golden Isles. Tucked away in a box are a number of citations less mellifluous in tone but equally deserved. Inscribed in bronze on polished wood, they express Governor Carl Sanders's appreciation to Jones for his service on the Bowdoin Commission; the gratitude of the Navy League of the United States for his "outstanding service as president of the local chapter"; the appreciation of the Saint Simons Jaycees for his "outstanding guidance"; and, from Ohio, the Outstanding Service Award of the Bicentennial Committee of the West Milton-Union Township, home and final resting place of many of Jones's Quaker ancestors. And tucked away in the back of an office closet is the longhandled shovel used by his Methodist friends at the groundbreaking for the Alfred W. Jones Auditorium at Epworth-by-the-Sea.

Most of the personal honors bestowed upon Jones were for activities peripheral to his main profession as an innkeeper and resort operator. But under the skilled management of his aides Jim Compton, Irv Harned, and Dick Everett, in the first years, and Bill Jones, Jr., Howard Jones, Dewey Benefield, Dennie McCrary, and Ted Wright in more recent times, the Cloister, year after year, has reflected the quietly effective touch of Jones as dedicated innkeeper. In 1960 the *Plymouth Traveler* gave space to colored pictures of Sea Island and the Cloister, to Bill Jones and "the modern miracle" he had wrought, and to Mrs. Cate and Charles Fairbanks, National Park Service archaeologist, for the history they had preserved. In 1971 *Carte Blanche* magazine told the story of the "Unique Sea Island Community," describing how the company "runs things, but in the role of benevolent godfather, country southern gentlemen style . . . No blight here, natural or manmade, no ugly sights, no night clubs, nothing to detract from the great private estate atmosphere you feel once you cross the causeway." In 1975 *Town and Country* magazine called Sea Island "one of the 100 greatest resorts in the world"; *Diversion Magazine* in 1977 listed it as one of the ten best resorts in North America; in that same year *Harpers Bazaar* called the Cloister one of the ten best hotels in the world, the only American resort so honored by the *Bazaar*. In his book *A Different World* English writer Christopher Matthews named the Cloister among the fifty hotels he considered to be "the very greatest in the world"; and again in 1977 and 1978 the respected *Mobil Travel Guide* gave the Cloister its Five-Star Award, naming it as one of America's nine top resorts. Twice, in 1977 and 1978, leading authorities confirmed what Bobby Jones had said when he first played the Sea Island Golf Course. In 1977 a ten-page section on the Cloister and the Sea Island Golf Course was listed by Dick Miller in the book *America's Greatest Golfing Resorts*, and in 1978, *Esquire* magazine called Sea Island one of the twenty best courses in the United States.

Though Jones is a modest man, unpretentious almost to the point of shyness, he is naturally pleased at the recognition that has come from his efforts. He is happy to respond when some agency, government or otherwise, asks him for advice in matters of business.

The deep-held belief that people in business should willingly offer free and fair-minded guidance to people in government has found full expression in the prestigious Business Advisory Council (BAC) of the Department of Commerce, of which Jones was a member for more than a quarter century. This organization was founded in the early days of the Roosevelt administration, when Daniel C. Roper, FDR's first Secretary of Commerce, called on the country's top industrialists to serve as advisors to his department on how to pull the country out of depression. And later, when war came on, it served as a great reserve of top industrial talent supporting the military effort.

Six times a year since the 1930s the council has met to listen to, and to advise, top federal officials. Four of these meetings were held in Washington, the other two at some quietly elegant resort, such as the Homestead at Hot Springs, leading irreverent journalists to refer to the council as "America's Most Powerful Private Club" — and probably its most exclusive. In 1945 Bill Jones was asked to become a member of the council, one of the few relatively small businessmen so honored, and in 1947 the council accepted his invitation to hold the 1950 meeting at Sea Island.

Jones since 1945 had participated in many meetings, but this was his first chance to serve the council in his own special field — as innkeeper. Along with Jones, there were three other members of the council from Georgia — Harrison Jones and Robert Woodruff of Atlanta and Will Vereen of Moultrie — who asked to share with him the role as host for the November meeting. All went well at this first meeting — so well in fact, that in 1951, Jones got the word that the BAC would like to meet at the Cloister again in 1952. Naturally, the hotel was happy to play host again to the top industrialists of the nation.

Dwight D. Eisenhower had just been elected president as the 1952 meeting started, and he was relaxing at Augusta, playing golf, and going over in his mind his choices for his cabinet. There was a great scurrying back and forth of dignitaries between Sea Island and Augusta, and three of the BAC members were chosen. Charles E. Wilson of General Motors was named Secretary of Defense, George M. Humphrey of the A.M. Hanna Company was named Secretary of the Treasury, and Robert T. Stevens, of J.P. Stevens and Company, was made Secretary of the Army.

Not for half a century had such important political decisions been made on a remote Georgia island, with business exerting such a compelling influence on government. In 1899 the nation's multimillionaires had invited President McKinley and the powerful "president-maker," Mark Hanna, to their Jekyll Island retreat to discuss the upcoming elections. The question: should McKinley offer to run for a second term, or should the nation's wealthy support Speaker of the House, Thomas B. Reed, who wanted to run. McKinley got the nod; Reed, bitter and disillusioned, resigned as Speaker.

The BAC meetings were in many ways the most prestigious ever held at Sea Island, for here the highest government officials got together with the nation's top industrialists to discuss their mutual interests in sessions made up of equal parts of work and play. The last one to be held at the Cloister was in 1956, when the speakers were the Secretary of Commerce, the Attorney General, the Secretary of Health, Education and Welfare, an Assistant Secretary of Defense, and Arthur F. Burns, Chairman of the President's Council of Economic Advisors. Not until Jimmy Carter came down with his cabinet twenty years later was there such an array of top level politicos on Sea Island.

Jones in these BAC sessions learned much that was to be helpful to him in later years in meeting the challenge of shifting political, economic, and social patterns. From his association with the BAC group, he learned first hand how the upper echelons of business and government—the most powerful men in America— worked together to get things done.

From the glowing thank-you notes that Bill Jones received after the 1956 meeting, it was not the solemn speeches that the BAC remembered. It was the oyster roast at Altama, lit by the flare of torches—where Jones's plantation singers sang the work songs, the spirituals, and the shouts preserved years earlier by Mrs. Max-field Parrish. The speeches of the working sessions were what the meeting was all about, of course, but it was the spiritual, "When the Saints Go Marching In" and the shout, "Oh Eve, Where Is Adam," and the work song, "Pay Me My Money Down," that lingered in the memory. One of the work songs was "I Wish I Was Mr. Jones's Son." This brought a laugh from the company, but the fact is, to be related to Bill Jones and Kit Talbott Jones, in any way, by blood, marriage, or through friendship, is a very good thing indeed . . . as three generations of Talbotts and Joneses, each in their time, would discover.

14

ONE MAN'S FAMILIES

Alfred William Jones and Katharine Houk Talbott were married on September 6, 1928, in her mother's house in Dayton. The "friendly little hotel" called the Cloister was opened October 12 at Sea Island, Georgia, with the young couple welcoming the first guests. Thus in this autumn of 1978, the Joneses and the Cloister are celebrating their golden anniversary. It is a long time for a marriage to last, a long time for a resort hotel to keep its personality and survive.

In fact, it might not have survived its earliest troubled years if it had not been for a certain stubborn quality in Kit Jones. Not only Howard Coffin's fortune, her husband's vision, Jim Compton's close-to-the-chest money management, but her own determination went into carrying the Sea Island Company through its first days. Many times she and Bill Jones talked over the idea of chucking the whole thing and going back to Dayton, where they had family and friends, or to Detroit, where the name of Howard Coffin would open all doors to them. Each time her decision was to stay, to learn to love this wild green island lying between the marshes and the sea, and to make the little hotel on which all their hopes depended into a place to be remembered. To that end, she and Jim Compton's wife, Dorothy, took over the task of decorating the rooms, choosing the colors for walls and drapes, the type of furniture, seeking always to create the ambience of a happy sunlit room in a private home. And this they continued to do as the Cloister Apartments were built, until finally the ex-panding hotel, all fear of bankruptcy past, required the services of a professional decorator. But their touch remained, the comfort-able and restrained elegance, with never a trace of the garish, the gaudy, or the strident.

For a bride from a well-to-do family, brought up in a northern city, several things required some getting used to. There was little refrigeration then in the stores in Brunswick or Saint Simons. Fresh beef, newly killed, was brought around on wagons, and pork was quickly salted and put on sale at Everett's store near the Saint Simons pier. The Cloister did have iceboxes, and the hotel ordered the best meats that could be had from the North, but Kit and Bill Jones decided not to make use of the Cloister supplies, for if they did they would have to turn the Cloister into a commissary for all Sea Island residents. Once a week, therefore, Kit Jones and Dottie Compton made the five-hour roundtrip to Jacksonville, buying supplies for their families. Frequently, Bill Jones remembers, when things were tight it was Kit's money that bought their groceries. Prices, by today's standards, were incredi-bly low. Fresh-caught shrimp, for example, sold from door to door at two pounds for a quarter.

One small incident early in her Georgia stay almost persuaded Kit Jones to pick up and go back North. One morning in her cottage on Sea Island she heard a strange clanking sound and looked out the window to see a dozen men amble past the house. Their legs were in chains, tied ankle to waist, and men with shot-guns walked beside them. It was her first encounter with a Georgia chain gang and it frightened her.

In addition to helping Bill Jones keep his courage up as he traveled back and forth between Sea Island and the Detroit banks, Kit Jones had to comfort and care for Howard Coffin, sinking ever deeper into despair after the death of his wife. She also had her hands full with a rambunctious and rapidly growing family. Friends who saw her in those days remember her calmly rising at 6:00 a.m., getting four children washed, dressed, and off to school, spending a busy day at the hotel on matters having to do with rugs and drapes, and then in the evening, serene and poised and seemingly without a care in the world, she would play hostess to a party of fifty or more guests from the hotel and the cottages. These parties were important. They gave people from different parts of the country the chance to look each other over and make friends. The hotel guests remembered the Joneses and their hospitality, and the other Sea Islanders they had met, and many of them decided to come back and build their own cottages in this serene and happy enclave so seemingly remote from all the worries of the world.

One thing that gave Kit Jones poise and confidence and a sense of direction was the memory of what her mother, Katharine Houk Talbott, had endured as a young wife. Her father, Harry Elstner Talbott, was a young construction engineer in 1890, when he was commissioned by the Algoma Steel Company to build a railroad through twenty miles of hilly, stream-cut Canadian wilderness, from an iron mine in the interior to Lake Superior. His pay was $500 a month plus expenses, and the job was admittedly a gamble. If he brought the line in on time, he would get more, and richer, contracts. If he failed, he might as well seek some other line of work. He left his wife and six children at home, and moved into the wilderness, working at fifteen degrees below zero, growing more and more tired in mind and body, and with every check he sent home, he sent word to put as much as possible on their debts.

Though lonely and worried and almost desperate, Mrs. Talbott's replies were cheerful and warm and confident. Finally the weather, too, turned cheerful and warm, and the work gangs moved over thawing ground. And Harry Talbott fulfilled his contract on time, and went on to become very well off indeed, with one big house in Dayton and another in Miami. But he never was without financial worries, and his wife never forgot that fearful winter. She was always able to stretch a dollar nine different ways, even when entertaining with great flair at Runnymede, her house near Dayton, or at Fieldstone at Miami, on behalf of some favorite project in music or the arts. A pianist and singer of concert quality, her deepest interest was in music, and one of her most successful sponsorships was of the Westminister Choir School, near Princeton, New Jersey, for the training of ministers of music.

Unlike her mother, Kit Jones never had a reason to be too concerned about her husband's financial management, for Bill Jones had an uncanny instinct for making his investments turn out well. Over the years, he was to display that talent on behalf of the entire Talbott family. In 1932 Katharine Houk Talbott had given to her nine children, share and share alike, property in the Dayton area plus other holdings in Florida worth almost $3 million. The company, known first as the Talbott Realty Company and later as the Talbott Corporation, was from the beginning a family-owned and family-managed enterprise. Bill Jones, as a son-in-law, went on the board in 1936, serving as a back-bencher representing Kit's interest as the elders of the clan, Bud and Harold Talbott and George Mead, made the decisions involving investment properties. In 1956 Jones was named chairman of the board, and eight years later, in September 1964, the Talbott family, after much soul-searching and debate, reluctantly decided to liquidate the corporation. Each of the nine family groups received just under a million dollars as their share, and if the dividends paid out over the years were added, each would have received well over a million. This, said Bill Jones in his final report to the directors, meant that "Grandmother Talbott's great foresight in setting up the corporation thirty-two years ago has certainly proved of great benefit to her descendants." The way Jones, along with Jack Greene, Charles Thomas, and Bud Talbott, Jr., handled the liquidation also attracted some approving attention. On September 12, 1963, E.L. Ostendorf, who had appraised the properties before they were sold to realtor John Galbreath, wrote to Jones, "I think your handling of the deal was unusually good. You have had a difficult spot to fill. In a large family where many complaints can develop and where you all are involved, I certainly feel you should have praise for your decisions. It is difficult to dispose of properties that have a large individual interest and handling it the way you did I can see nothing but praise from the participants of ownership."

In passing on the corporation to her children in 1932, Mrs. Talbott had expressed the hope that the joint ownership would bind the families together in mutual affection, a rare thing indeed when families, including in-laws, share an inheritance. She wrote of her keen sense of joy and gratitude in being able to pass on the company to her children.

> I do not presume to dictate to you all in minor matters of your affairs. If the years in which your father and I strove to inculcate in you all that blessed "spirit of the hive" have not made a lasting impression upon your lives, no word of mine could avail. But I am sure that now, and in all the years to come, you will all feel that beautiful spirit of love which means all for one and one for all.
>
> That I have been and am able to give you material things gives me great happiness, but the real desire of my heart is that you shall all have a heritage far more worthwhile – of a perpet-

ual spirit of love, tolerance, understanding, generosity, loyalty, and a fidelity to the clan spirit which nothing may disturb and which you may pass on to your children and your children's children.

And indeed, for forty-five years, the spirit of the hive did prevail. Every five years the clan gathered—at Runnymede or Lake Placid or at Keewaydin in the Canadian woods. When the corporation was sold in 1964, the fun and games did not cease. A sum of $150,000 was set aside in a Reunion Trust, so that the meetings could continue. In 1972 the reunion was held at Sea Island, where the forerunner of the gatherings, a three-day surprise party for Mrs. Talbott on her seventieth birthday, had been held in 1934. And in 1977, with the clan grown to 267 members, the final meeting was held there. To be sure that the members, now living all over the United States, would recognize each other on the beach or on the tennis courts, all wore T-shirts bearing the inscriptions "Talls" or "Butts."

A poignant summing up of what the members of the Talbott clan had meant to each other, and of their relationship to the rest of the universe, was given at the 1972 meeting in a Sunday morning sermon delivered by the Reverend Nelson Thayer, son of Eliza Talbott and Frederick M. Thayer. Before the group assembled on the front lawn of the Joneses' house at Sea Island, he began quietly:

I'd like you all to close your eyes and remain silent for a moment. Take a few deep breaths. Listen to the ocean behind, think of the lush island. These are the Lord's. Think of the cities and the mountains, these are the Lord's; think of the people of this land: the poor, the rich, the white, the black, these are the Lord's. And think of the sky and the galaxy in which we are a speck. These are the Lord's, and the galaxies beyond them. In our celebration this weekend, let us celebrate the deep unsearchable mystery at the heart of creation; the mystery which also gives each of us our own particular life. The center of the universe, the center of our spirit, the strength of our life: God our Lord.

After the Lord's Prayer, he continued:

This is a time for celebration and thanksgiving and remembering. We celebrate, and we give thanks and we remember: Grandfather and Grandmother Talbott; Harold and Peggy Talbott; Daisy and George and Harry Greene, and Dud Brown; Lill, and Abe and Sonny Hilton, and Squee Church; Bud Talbott; George Mead and George Jr., and Loulie Walker; Marianna and Tom Hilliard; Ted Thayer. We're thankful for the life we shared with them. We are all here because they were here. In our love for each other we love them still.

We celebrate and give thanks and remember: all the good times together: Runnymede; shared Christmases; reunions; the visits from aunts and uncles, cousins, brothers and sisters, grandparents and grandchildren; the hours spent with family members who care; sadness borne by sharing, and happiness so multiplied; all those weddings perpetrated on non-Talbotts; for Talbott-to-Talbott toasts; and for those who from time to time prick the bubble of our Talbott pride. In days of desperate self-reliance, of competition and conflict, of temporary friendships quickly established and soon forgotten, we give thanks for bonds which stretch across miles and strengthen with age.

We give thanks and we celebrate the rich diversity among us. For different points of view, and various interests. For long hair and short; for old values long-proven and for new ways which will preserve and express them better.

We give thanks and we celebrate, and we remember. We also look forward with hope: to future meetings made buoyant with the pleasure of this reunion; to future friendships, to new faces brought by marriage, to new children and grandchildren who, we hope, will share with each other and pass on to theirs the spirit of love and affection which God has permitted us these decades past.

And now may the Lord bless us and keep us. May the Lord

lift up the light of His countenance upon us and give us and the world peace, this day and forever. Amen.

It was a deeply moving moment for all who heard him. Bill Jones, with his sense of history, particularly shared the hope that the family name, and the family united, could be perpetuated. Earlier, in 1960, he had entered wholeheartedly into a plan to raise $50,000 with which to build a properly marked memorial gateway honoring his late brother-in-law, Harold Talbott, at the new stadium under construction at the Air Force Academy at Colorado Springs. Congress would not appropriate money to build a stadium, so the Air Force, like the Army and the Navy before it, had to raise the $3 million construction money from friends. To Robert Stevens, president of J.P. Stevens, Harold Talbott, who died in 1957, had been literally the father of the Air Force Academy while Secretary of the Air Force, and Stevens urged his friends to help him raise the money for a memorial gate, the Talbott Portal through which Air Cadet teams would go on the field. Bill Jones himself raised the $50,000 from Talbott family connections and their friends. The Falcon Stadium was dedicated on October 20, 1962, with Bill Jones flying to Colorado Springs with Bob Stevens in his company plane. They were highly pleased with the Talbott Portal and the plaque, which they found to be "a huge success, everything in perfect taste."

Jones's feelings for the past applied equally to his own family, whose roots went deep into American history. His father, Samuel Rufus Jones, Dayton banker and building and loan executive, died in 1931. His attributes, as described in his obituary, could be applied with equal aptitude to his son in his mature years. "Far-sighted, possessed of a keen financial mind," the paper said, "he was frequently consulted by bankers living in many parts of the state and his judgment was usually found to be right. Though a natural conservative he was forward looking and progressive and was a man of unusual acumen."

There were other qualities in Samuel Rufus Jones which he passed on to his son. "He was progressive and modern in his business activities, and yet he possessed a certain old-school friendliness. . . . He liked to meet the people and to make personal contact." To illustrate the character, friendliness, and bigness of the man, the paper reported that once when a small boy came into his bank with a nickel to open a savings account, Rufus Jones, not wishing to disappoint the little fellow, accepted the nickel, added $9.95 to it, and opened the account.

When Roosevelt closed the banks two years after Rufus Jones's death, Bill Jones's mother went downtown, stalked into the bank where her husband's picture hung, took it off the wall and took it home. She said she would not permit her late husband's picture to hang in a bank that had been closed through no fault of his own.

When his father died in 1931, Bill Jones was in the midst of his desperate struggle to keep the Sea Island Company from going bankrupt. Ten years later, when the battle had been won and the company had shown its first slim profit, he turned his attention to another matter that deeply interested him. Naturally, he wanted to pass on to his children a prospering business. He wanted to pass on to them, too, a knowledge of who they were, and from what manner of folk they had sprung. Who was his father, and his father's father, and all the long line of Joneses going back into the mists of time? He engaged that superb historian Mrs. Margaret Davis Cate to trace the genealogy of the Joneses and all the collateral lines whose records could be found. To most people, tracing one family named Jones back to its beginnings would seem much like tracing the lineage of one seagull back to the original egg. Fortunately though, the first Joneses were Quakers, and the Quakers, like the Mormons, were great keepers of family records. Mrs. Cate rose to the challenge. The surname Jones, she discovered, was known and spelled the same in England, Scotland, Ireland, and Wales, which was evidence that Bill Jones's ancestors had lived in each of these places. The name was derived from the word *John,* which early Britons insisted on pronouncing *Jone,* without the *s,* and it was originally a Hebrew word, meaning "Jehovah Hath Been Gracious," an appellation that no modern-day Sea Island Jones would deny.

The first of Bill Jones's line to come to America was Francis, who brought his family to Pennsylvania from Ireland by way of Wales. They were devout Quakers, bringing with them to their friends in America papers from the Welsh Quakers, testifying that they had "all along lived in love and peace with friends and neighbors and behaved themselves orderly and civil in all respects," and that they "do depart out of our country in love and charity with the Council of Friends who truly wisheth and desireth that the Lord may bless and prosper them." This was written in September 1711 in Wales. Three months later this certificate was recorded at a Friends meeting in Philadelphia and Chester, Pennsylvania. In England, Francis Jones had married Rachel Newton, sister of Sir Isaac Newton, and an element of Sir Isaac's sagacity was to manifest itself in the generations to come.

The Joneses who came to Pennsylvania in 1711 were relative newcomers to the country compared to the Coffins. Peter Coffin had arrived in Nantucket in 1642, bringing with him his wife and his children and his mother and her sisters. One of his granddaughters, Mary Coffin Starbuck, became the first Quaker convert on Nantucket, and she opened her home to members preaching the doctrine of the Friends. One preacher remembered that when those who came to hear him overflowed the house, she had the glass windows removed, so those seated in the yard could hear. She stoutly refused, though, to let him stand on one of her cane-bottom chairs for fear he would break it.

When he came to Georgia in the 1920s, Bill Jones was only vaguely aware that his family roots went deep into Georgia soil. Jones's ancestor, the third Francis Jones, arrived in Georgia on a wintry day in January 1774, bringing with him his wife, six sons, and six daughters, ranging from one to twenty years old. He was given a tract of 200 acres on the south side of a fork in Little River, near Wrightsborough, in what was then Columbia, and is now McDuffie, County. They were one of many Quaker families moving south through Virginia and the Carolinas into Tennessee and Georgia. Evidently they sought to escape the Revolution that was brewing in the northern colonies against the king, and for a while they did find peace, except for an occasional murderous foray by the Creeks. When war did come to Georgia, true to their peaceful Quaker faith, they took no part in it. Some, in fact, were Tory in their sympathies, but to both Tory and Patriot they were suspect, and they found it necessary to pack their silver and all their valuables in boxes and bury them, to save them from the soldiers on both sides. The end of the war brought a testing of their beliefs as severe as the Revolution had been. Slavery in the years after the war became deeply imbedded in the Georgia economy, and the Quakers were surrounded by slaveowning planters. They found themselves morally unable to accept what their neighbors looked upon as a God-given right. Thus, when Ohio was admitted as a free state, forty families of Quakers from Georgia headed north. Among them were Samuel Jones, his seven sons and four daughters, and his father, Francis, who now was eighty years old.

They left behind some unhappy memories. Samuel's wife had died in Georgia. His brother had been killed by Indians shortly after they had arrived there, and another relative, Mary Kirk Mendenhall, and her twelve-year-old son, Abiah, had been killed when she went to the woods to milk a cow. Joseph Mendenhall, another son, had been captured by the Indians at the same time, and when his father tried to ransom him some six months later, he had become so well adapted to the life of the wandering Creeks that he did not want to leave them. The Cherokees, by contrast, were more civilized, and when Samuel Jones, headed for Ohio, started moving through their territory with his family and all his goods loaded on two wagons, they gave him safe passage. They even hand-carried his father, the aged Francis Jones, recognizing him from his Quaker dress as one of "William Penn's men." (Quakers in the North had served as peacemakers between the Indians and the whites.)

Samuel Jones and his family crossed the Ohio River at Cincinnati in early June 1805. The town then consisted of one brick store, one frame building, and a few log cabins. The Joneses moved on to their destination, a piece of land beside a wooded glen, near a place called West Milton in what was to become Union township in Miami County. Before night came they had felled a white oak, sawed it into boards, and cut forked poles for the tent frame. Soon they had a snug shell, weatherboarded shoulder high, with a canvas cover over it.

And here began the story of the Jones family in Ohio, a story that was to last for more than a hundred years, until Bill Jones moved back to Georgia. Samuel Jones and his wife, Mary Mote, begat John Jones; and John and his wife, Sarah McGhee, whose grandmother had been Mary Kirk Mendenhall, gave life to Samuel Jones, who married Anna Jay; and Samuel and Anna were parents of Samuel Rufus, who married Mary Adele Yost. And from this union, in 1902, came Alfred William Jones, known as Bill, who had two older brothers, Rufus and Robert. Their mother had been a Pennsylvanian by birth, but their father, Samuel Rufus Jones, had been born at West Milton, Ohio, where the family had made its home since the first Samuel Jones had set up his board-and-canvas shelter there in 1805.

Samuel Rufus Jones as a young man left the farm, moving to

Dayton to go into the banking, building, and loan business. And in leaving the farm, he also left the Society of Friends, the Quaker sect to which the Joneses had been loyal since its founding. Dayton had no Quaker meetinghouse at the time, so he and his wife joined the Methodist church. Thus, Bill Jones was brought up in the Methodist faith, but there was in him some atavistic memory of his Quaker ancestors, and as he prospered with the years, he felt the urge to honor them. As early as 1941 he had begun to seek some means of doing this. Often in his childhood, his father had taken him back to his own birthplace, West Milton, Ohio, where in a little burying ground called the West Branch Cemetery, generations of Jones ancestors had been buried.

When Samuel Jones and his family arrived in West Milton in 1805, a small but active group of Friends, gathered from all over the East and South, were already there, including the great-great-grandparents of future president Herbert Hoover. The first little log meetinghouse had been constructed in 1804, and the first burial had taken place in the little cemetery.

In 1941 Bill Jones and his brothers, Rufus and Robert (the latter the innkeeper of Ohio's oldest hotel, the famous Golden Lamb at Lebanon), began to think of constructing a memorial to their Quaker ancestors. By this time the first little log church had long since disappeared, as had a second and larger log structure built in 1807. The third meetinghouse, a brick church built in 1818, remained, but when the Quaker colony at West Milton moved on to Iowa and points west, it fell into ruin. For many years after its last use, around the turn of the century, it had been a corn barn, its bricks slowly crumbling.

To Bill Jones this was an opportunity to honor the memory of his grandparents, Samuel and Anna Jay Jones. He would buy the old structure from the family who now owned it and use its bricks to construct a beautiful memorial wall around the cemetery where they were buried. It took five years to build, for only a few hundred of the crumbling old bricks could still be used. But in 1948 the wall at last was completed. It ran for 300 feet along the front of the cemetery, was 18 inches thick, with cupolas at each end and an impressive entrance gate of decorative iron on which was placed a bronze plaque honoring those members of the West Milton Society of Friends who were buried there. It was Jones's feeling that the township would in time want to expand the cemetery, but this was never done. In the 1950s, Jones visited the old burial ground and found that vandals had desecrated many of the graves, including those of his family. He immediately began a campaign to finance the extension of the wall around all four sides, but he could arouse no interest in the township nor among the few remaining Friends.

In 1973, though, a brilliant and dedicated young woman named Arlene Clifton, a journalist and history buff, wrote to him to say that she would like his help. She had persuaded the Ohio Historical Society, for the bicentennial, to reconstruct the first little log meetinghouse the Friends had built. The Union Township Trustees agreed, and they bought the land beside the cemetery on which the little church would stand. The 20 by 30 foot structure was quickly built, out of logs taken from an old barn dating back to before the Civil War. Alfred Jones bought the cedar "shakes" for the roof, the hand-hewn shingles that were replicas of those that had covered the original structure. And around the three open sides of the old cemetery, where no further burials would be held, he erected a vandal-proof chain-link fence. Now, at last, his Quaker ancestors could sleep in peace, beside a little meetinghouse exactly like the one where they had worshiped 175 years before.

15

A NEW JONES MAKES THE SCENE

For all his doughty Quaker ancestry it is hard to imagine the urbane and soigné Alfred William (Bill) Jones, Sr., driving a team of horses pulling a covered wagon from Georgia through Indian country to new lands in Ohio. By contrast, his oldest son would fit perfectly into such a role. From some pioneer ancestor or ancestors, Bill Jones, Jr., inherited the instincts of a farmer, a hunter, and a woodsman, a man who finds himself happier at at coon-hunt than at a cocktail party. At the same time, though, he seems to have inherited a great deal of his father's and his grandfather's talents for making his money work for him — and for those dependent on him. A thousand-acre pecan farm near Albany is a going concern, and under his watch-care the Sea Island Company so far has survived the growing threat of rising taxes and inflation. Primarily, though, his main concerns are with the natural world around him.

His interest in all things having to do with the outdoors began early. When he was a little fellow, riding his scooter down the driveway, he would see a leaf turned differently than it had been the day before and quit his play to see what kind of bug was on the leaf. He kept the house full of small creatures he picked up in the yard and in the woods, among them, snakes and terrapins. When he was in his subteens, going to school in Brunswick, he would take his hunting clothes to school with him on Friday and go down by bus to Cabin Bluff in Camden County to spend the weekend there with Ed Messick. Messick, who was Jim Compton's right-hand man, ran the hunting preserve, but Bill didn't do a lot of shooting. He loved to be in the woods, watching the guides, finding where the turkeys roosted and the deer walked. He did, however, kill his first turkey when he was eleven, and his first deer at age twelve. In the summer he spent his weekends on the marshes and the rivers, fishing and camping and coon-hunting with like-minded friends from Saint Simons. Other friends thought he was crazy, sleeping in the woods every Friday and Saturday night when he could be going to dances and proms. He still prefers the outdoor life to the social ramble, though, and knows that in his service to the Sea Island Company, he will never enjoy going to parties, and giving parties, as do his mother and father. This feeling does not apply to membership and service in civic clubs. In this respect he is a true son of Bill Jones, Sr., working hard in Saint Simons Rotary, in United Fund drives, and in other campaigns for funds to support good causes.

He is involved in everything having to do with the civic welfare, and at present he is director of three chambers of commerce — Saint Simons, Brunswick-Golden Isles, and the Georgia State Chamber. Though Sea Island cottage residents make up only about 1 percent of the county population, Bill Jones, Jr., like his father before him, is highly pleased when the cottagers contribute up to 15 percent of the total raised for every good cause they are called upon to help.

For a man with an innate instinct for learning by doing, seeing, feeling, testing, he has had a considerable amount of classroom education. Starting in the little school his parents and the

Comptons opened on Sea Island, he went to grammar school in Brunswick until the ninth grade. After Brunswick, his parents sent him to Millbrook, in New York, for four years. This he detested, for he missed his weekends in the woods and on the rivers. He came back south and earned his degree in agricultural economics and forestry at the University of Georgia. In Athens he always lived in his own apartment instead of a fraternity house or dormitory, and he always chose one that had a plot of ground nearby where he could keep a garden, raising beans and corn, peas and peppers.

He didn't particularly like the rah-rah aspects of college life. The uproar of the big football weekends and the dances seemed a waste of time to him, and he pushed through in three years, taking a lot of wildlife courses to make the duller subjects bearable.

One good thing did come out of the university, however. There he met a fraternity brother, a fellow Pi KA named Dewey Benefield, who in the years ahead was to become one of Bill Jones's closest friends and most trusted business associates. Trained both in journalism and the law, Benefield, executive vice-president of Sea Island Properties, in charge of property sales, now serves Bill Jones, Jr., president of the company, in the same capacity that Bill Jones, Sr., served Howard Coffin, and that Jim Compton served the senior Jones.

Fortunately, as in the case of their predecessors, their wives also were good friends. When young Jones finished at the University of Georgia he joined the Navy, and while in Officer's Candidate School he met a pretty young girl from Savannah, a schoolteacher newly come to Brunswick. Her name was Betty Macdonald and they were married in 1955. Not long thereafter, a classmate of Betty's from Coker College, South Carolina, visited her in Brunswick. And there, Miriam Hooks, known as "Tiggie," met Dewey Benefield. In 1960, they too were married.

Jones came out of OCS an ensign, assigned to minesweeper

school. There he took special training as a supply officer, and for a while his duties required him to remain ashore, getting new minesweepers ready for the sea by supplying them with every item that a crew of seventy men would need. Transferred to sea duty, he soon discovered that despite the fact that he had been brought up beside the ocean he was extremely susceptible to seasickness. No matter how he tried to overcome it, he never got his sea legs. On a four day trip from Charleston to Key West, he would lose up to twenty-five pounds. The Navy finally transferred him to courier service, and he finished out his tour carrying classified messages to Navy Commands all over the Southeast. He also got airsick, but it was over as soon as the plane rose up into smooth air.

Coming out of the Navy as a lieutenant (jg.) in December 1955, he and Betty lived at Altama Plantation, while he worked with the Seaboard Construction Company, the highly successful road-building outfit his father and Harold Friedman had founded. Bill Jones, Sr., naturally would have been happy if his oldest son and namesake had elected to come into the Sea Island Company to take over from him, in the fullness of time, the operation of the hotel and Sea Island Company's real estate holdings on Saint Simons. He did not pressure him however, knowing that young Bill's interests were different from his own, and knowing too that any man, to be a success, must be allowed to choose his own profession. Bill's father and mother both anticipated that when he did go into business for himself it would be in some way connected with the land — as a farmer, a forester, a rancher raising cattle and horses. They were delighted, therefore, when Jones, Jr., after some six months with Seaboard, came to his father and told him that he had been thinking things over and would like to come into the company. The elder Jones was so deeply moved that his eyes filled with tears as he told Kit Jones about it.

This, of course, did not mean that young Bill would move immediately into the presidency—or even into the lower echelons of managment. Since the Cloister was at the heart of the company's operation, and the heart of the Cloister was its famed kitchen and dining room, he started there as a trainee.

A booklet given to him by a longtime food supervisor, steward, and Cloister maître d' named John Chalfa became his guide. It started off on a high note:

> As a new employee you have been carefully selected to help further the Sea Island tradition of fine food, properly served in elegantly appointed dining rooms to a well traveled and sophisticated clientele . . . Your employment at Sea Island brings you into a new world—A world of quiet and refined dignity, of elegant and expensive working materials; of courteous and fine service; of concern and personal interest in each and every guest. We hope this booklet will help you get the feel and feelings of Sea Island."

Whereupon young Bill found himself getting the feel and feelings of several jobs. He became the dishwasher, the garbage-disposal operator, the busboy who brings the heavily loaded trays of food from the kitchen to the dining room and takes the equally heavily loaded trays of dirty dishes back to the kitchen, being careful not to spill or break anything. He worked as a passer, offering butter, rolls, vegetables, and relishes; and as a waiter, taking orders and serving salads, soups, and entrees. He moved up to captain, supervising a section of the dining room, seeing to it that at every table the silver and glassware were clean and gleaming, the flowers fresh, the plates placed exactly one-half inch from the table's edge. Finally he served a stint as that authoritarian figure, the maître d', overseeing the dining room in all its aspects, keeping the service flowing smoothly, quietly, swiftly, while seeing to it that the guests were seated when and where they wished to be at every meal.

From this uplifting experience, he went on to spend four months working with the engineers, learning the separate tasks of the many people who kept the great engines running, heating, cooling, lighting the far-flung hotel complex, and keeping it clean and painted and in good repair. Security, landscaping, golf-club maintenance, bell service, laundry, cottage rentals, accounting, housekeeping, personnel — the nursery and the flower shop and the liquor store — for eighteen months he moved from one to the other, looking, listening, making notes, then reporting to Jim Compton, who would question him minutely on what he had seen, and heard, and felt.

In looking into every detail of the operation, he came to have a profound respect for the people behind the scenes, doing their daily jobs quietly and effectively. He was especially impressed by the women on the staff, notably Miss Catharine Clark, executive secretary to Bill Jones, Sr., and Jim Compton. She came to the Sea Island Company from Jekyll, when both she and the company were young, and in her more than forty years here she became as indispensable to Jones and Compton as Lena Carle had been to Howard Coffin. Dewey Benefield, too, in his training period soon learned that no executive could function effectively unless he were backed by the tact and competence of a top-flight secretary. His choice was Madeline Dozier, who smoothed his path in his first days. Young Jones was also particularly impressed by Mrs. Ethel Camp. She was in the engineering department when first they met, and she later became, at his recommendation, the highly competent executive housekeeper, in charge of keeping all the cottages clean and rentable — an extremely important job, for in a year the changing seasons brought as many different people to the cottages as it did to the hotel.

Jones, Jr., in his training, watched the seasons change and studied the life patterns of the changing clientele both in the cottages and in the hotel. The summer people were southerners mainly, young couples coming down with their children to swim and walk the beach in family groups and play golf and tennis, giving their kids the same happiness their parents had given them when they were young. Then came September and the opening of school, and the sudden disappearance of the young-sters of school age. Now the guests were older folk, and in the hotel many were convention people, doing everything in groups. Then came the colder months, again bringing older folks, these mainly from the North and Midwest. Many of them had been coming to the Cloister for Thanksgiving, Christmas, and New Years for many seasons past, and they had come to expect certain things: venison, oyster potpie, roast goose and leg of veal at the hunt-style Thanksgiving feast; the bringing in of the Yule log, and a little child's stocking stuffed with goodies, hung on the doorknob of every guest at Christmas; the "raid the kitchen party" for Auld Lang Syne at New Years Eve.

Spring brought the big months—March, April, and May. Many groups came in May, and there were many youngsters again, coming with their parents for the Easter holiday. Spring visitors were mainly northerners and midwesterners, well-to-do and social folk who overflowed the hotel and filled up the beach cottages. They crowded the golf courses, the tennis courts, and champion Fred Missildine's skeet range, and they kept Percy Walters, the Beach Club swimming teacher-masseur, busy knead-ing and rubbing the spring back into winter-stiffened muscles.

How the cottagers and the company worked together to keep cottages rented was among the things Bill Jones, Jr., learned as he watched the cottage housekeepers, and the landscape people, and the security patrols, and the accounting office all joining hands to keep the cottages clean, their yards and gardens neat, their taxes paid, and their possessions safe—for which, of course, the company received a fee. All of this was part of the paternalistic relationship that had existed from the beginning, when there was no other source of service to which the cottagers could turn. But, with the company's strong encouragement, this relationship would change as the cottage colony grew and more and more members chose to manage for themselves.

The cottagers' relationship to the company and to each other, often brought about problems that needed deft and careful handling. Where so many people from so many parts of the country were involved, there were bound to be small crises. Some cottagers just didn't fit into the Sea Island pattern, and these required special handling. Some wanted to drill wells down to the aquifer, which was against the rules, or to put up gazebos or some other obstruction on the marsh, or in the dunes, between their property line and the high-tide mark. Both marsh and dunes are company owned and can be protected against trespass by a stranger or an adjacent property owner. And Bill Jones, Jr., learned from Jim Compton and Irv Harned how to deal with these things without unseemly uproar. The cottage colony, of some 300 houses owned by folks from everywhere, was like any little community. It had its little cliques, and claques, and social clusterings which formed, and dispersed, and merged again. It had its full quota of joys and sorrows, too, of triumphs and tragedies, of love and loneliness, and now and then small scandals surfaced involving alcohol, adultery, and divorce. Some are still remembered along Sea Island Drive, but most enlivened cocktail party chit-chat for awhile and were then forgotten as the season changed and one group departed and another came in.

The Sea Island Company, of course, has never made any effort to control the private lives of its cottage owners. It can control what a house looks like on the outside. If a study of the architect's plans indicates that a structure would not be in keeping with its surroundings, the design may be rejected. But what goes on inside the house is the owner's own concern—and indirectly, the concern of the other cottage owners. This group is made up of congenial folk in the main, similar in background, and homogeneous in their outlook no matter where they come from, and they are as concerned as are quiet people everywhere that they have no rude and boisterous neighbors to disturb their peaceful days. The company, therefore, makes every effort to discover, before a sale is made, whether the prospective buyer would fit in. If there is some doubt, they suggest that he lease a cottage for a year instead of buying outright. If the sale goes through, though, and the buyer does turn out to be a mover and shaker who disturbs the island's tranquil ways, there is not much the company can do about it so long as the unseemly conduct does not merit calling out the security patrol. The cottagers have developed their own quiet way of handling those whom they find offensive. They extend no invitations to the newcomer and they accept none from him. Life at Sea Island revolves around golf, tennis, and the Beach Club by day, bridge and the cocktail party by night. When the new cottagers find themselves walking the beach alone or watching television while parties go on around them, they soon get the message and move on. The company also has to be aware of the fact that the new cottage owner who proves completely acceptable to all, himself automatically becomes the sternest critic of the next person who wants into the colony. Each new buyer wants his house to be the last one built—with all the woods and trees around him remaining ever thereafter unspoiled.

Eccentricity, of course, bears no stigma, and over the years Sea Island has attracted a number of individuals who seemed slightly fey. One old gentleman, for example, kept the list of friends he wanted to serve as his pallbearers in the office safe—which required two men to open it. Every week or so he would decide that he wanted to add a new name to the list or take off the name of one who had offended him, causing a flurry in the office until somebody could be found to open the safe. One old lady, when she felt the service in the dining room was slow, would put her fingers in her mouth and whistle shrilly through her teeth. And a number of elderly ladies, when they discovered a leak in their cottage roof, or the sign of termites, insisted on reporting this disaster personally to Bill Jones, Sr. Since Mr. Jones might be anywhere from Tanganyika to Timbuctoo at the time, this occasionally created difficulties.

It was only boorish conduct which the colony found offensive, however. The quiet loner would never find his privacy invaded. If he wanted to read a book or snooze in the sun, or paint the seagulls swirling above the dunes, or search for sand dollars, or roam the woods to catch a glimpse of a deer, or block traffic on Sea Island Drive while staring upward through binoculars at a dozing owl, he was free to do these things to his heart's content.

Bill Jones, Jr., came out of his training program to be made assistant to Jim Compton, handling many different jobs under Compton's watchful eye. Compton, of course, was well aware that his good friend, Bill Jones, Sr., was using him to train his own successor, but if this disturbed him he gave no sign of it. One of young Jones's first acts, and, as time would prove, one of his smartest, was to persuade Jim Compton, and his father, that his old college chum and Pi Kappa Alpha brother, Dewey Benefield, would make a fine addition to the company roster. Compton agreed, and in the spring of 1958 Benefield arrived, to embark on a shortened version of the training program that Bill Jones, Jr., had just finished. One of their first joint activities was a continuation of training on a larger scale. In 1964 the two set off with their wives on a tour of other great resort hotels, studying how things were done at the Greenbrier, the Homestead, and at Williamsburg. Particularly they wanted to know how these places handled their maintenance facilities, which at Sea Island were scattered from the old falling down workcamp at Thirty-sixth street to the hotel itself. They came back to put into effect many things they had learned which they felt would be useful at Sea Island. One thing they discovered, but which they did not adopt, was that the Homestead saved thousands of dollars a year by operating a hog farm, feeding the hogs on kitchen scraps. The money did not come from selling the pigs, or serving them as bacon and ham, though this was a source of income, but by recovering from their feeding troughs many pieces of valuable silver that had been thrown into the garbage by the kitchen help.

As Benefield and Jones, Jr., began to work their way into management, subtle changes were taking place in the relationship of the Sea Island Company to its cottagers. The lady who called Bill Jones, Sr., to report her leaky roof, the gentleman who kept his list of pallbearers in the company safe, reflected the old paternalism which was rapidly changing. The company was once the sole spokesman for the cottagers with the county officials. It made the individual cottagers' tax returns, paid their taxes for them, and then billed them for the service. The company, not the cottagers called on the county to help keep Sea Island's streets in repair, to pick up trash after a windstorm, to provide extra police patrols when there was an occasional outbreak of pilfering from the cottages. The company was a big frog in a small pond in the early hungry years, when there was little progress going on in all Glynn County except that set in motion by Mr. Jones and his Sea Island Company.

During this time projects emanating from Sea Island, sponsored by the company and supported by its cottagers, ranged across the whole spectrum of community interest. In addition to the gifts of land already mentioned, Sea Islanders gave the cobalt radiother-apy machine to Glynn-Brunswick Memorial Hospital and equip-ped the intensive-care facility there. Jones himself had a leading part in founding the United Way, and the Sea Island cottagers contributed to it far out of proportion to their numbers. The Humane Society and Animal Shelter, brought into being by Mr. and Mrs. Charles Moeser, had the full support of the company and all the cottagers, and so did the Mozart Society, founded by Mrs. Artiss deVolt Zacharias.

As years passed, and the Sea Island Company became a smaller frog in a larger puddle, more political clout was needed. The Joneses and the Sea Island Company deliberately began to play a less dominant part in the affairs of the cottage community. As cottages began to approach 300 in number, the company could foresee the day when all of Sea Island's lots would have houses on them owned by individuals. The island as a real estate development would have reached its climax growth. The company would be reduced to the role of a rental agent or to that of an agency providing such housekeeping services as mosquito control, trash removal, street repair, police, fire, and ambulance service. To deal with such matters as the use of Sea Island's beaches, and the ever increasing tax assessments that the county had begun to impose, a stronger voice was needed. To Bill Jones, Sr., as well as to his associates, the time was swiftly approaching when the cottage colony should cut the apron strings and stand forth in its own right, speaking for itself as a social, political, and economic entity.

When he began to drop these ideas into his cocktail party talk (the cocktail party is the informal forum where most of Sea Island's ideas, large and small, first find utterance), he found many a listening and approving ear. Many cottagers, he discovered, long had felt a need to speak out for themselves as a community of taxpaying citizens strongly aware of their relationship to the county and its government. So, in order to make their collective voice heard, they formed the Sea Island Property Owners Association, and their spokesmen began to be listened to with respect in Brunswick and Glynn County. It was the Property Owners Association, not the company, in fact, which finally was able to persuade the county to put a county police substation at the causeway entrance to Sea Island, and it quickly became a strong deterrent to the wandering housebreaker and petty thief.

Benefield and Jones, Jr., were willing enough for the cottagers to begin speaking out for themselves, for Jim Compton was finding enough for them to do elsewhere. For twenty-five years, until 1960, the real estate operation had been more or less a hit-or-miss operation, supervised by George Boll, one-time architect. If somebody came down and wanted to buy a lot and build a house, or buy a house already built, the company would do what it could to help, and by this method Boll had sold several million dollars worth of real estate over the years. But most of the attention was concentrated on the resort operation, the Beach Club, the Golf Club, the tennis courts, the skeet range, etc. In 1960 Boll retired, and Dewey Benefield was given complete charge of the real estate operation. From there on it would be his duty actively to push real estate sales—concentrating on lots and houses owned by others, with the company taking a fee. He would also work with the engineering and landscaping departments, putting in new streets toward the marsh and toward the ocean, laying off lots and landscaping them, and building speculative houses on them. In this year, too, Potter Gould, member of a famous old Glynn County family, retired after many years of outstanding service as Sea Island's secretary-treasurer. After he stepped down, in fact, two men were needed to take over his jobs. Benefield became secretary, and J. Elliott Brown was named treasurer.

Benefield, young and enthusiastic, was determined to make real estate development far more important to the company than it had been up to now—to make it more than just an appendage to the resort operation. In 1961, the first year after he took over, sales totaled $9,225. By 1968 sales of Sea Island Company property, combined with that of lots owned by others, for the first time reached a million dollars. They were just over six million in

1977, highest in the company's history, and by mid-1978 were pushing toward an even higher total.

Young Jones, under Compton's watch-care, was making his own progress in many areas of management—sometimes working hand-in-hand with Benefield, sometimes on his own. He spent some ten years under Compton's direct tutelage as his assistant, and in 1966, when Compton retired and Bill, Jr., became president of the company, he continued to look to Compton for counsel and guidance. Out of this experience, some of Compton's conservatism rubbed off on him—a tendency to read the fine print carefully, to consider all the angles, to make no impulsive decisions. This tendency toward conservatism, though, did not stop progress. Under Compton's direction, young Jones played a leading role in many long-range improvements. He had overall supervision of the construction, at a cost of $300,000, of the third nine of the Sea Island Golf Course, and it was a proud occasion when on January 14, 1960 his mother christened the new links. Assisted by her grandchildren, David Kuntz and Ann Jones, she cut the ribbon to open the new Retreat Nine. Charlie Yates acted as master of ceremonies, and Daniel Pomeroy, age 91, swatted the first ball. (Pomeroy's lasting contribution to St. Simons' history was the brick fence around Christ Church yard and cemetery.) After the ceremony, Yates and Eddie Thompson, just beginning his fine career as Sea Island's pro, played an exhibition round with two lady pros, Louise Suggs and Marilyn Smith.

Later in the same year, Bill, Jr., turned his attention to another $300,000 project—the enlargement and redecoration of eighteen rooms in the main hotel and the addition of two deluxe rooms to the River House (formerly the Cloister Apartments) across the street from the hotel. Decisions, large and small, were thrust upon him. Should dial telephones be placed in all the hotel rooms? The answer was yes. Should cable television be brought to the Cloister? Again, yes, but no television sets would be placed in individual rooms. The reason? The Cloister was a place, the management hoped, where guests would get to know and like each other, make friends, and look forward to coming back each year to see each other. Television in the rooms would defeat this purpose. But high-quality television in the public rooms, in the Colonial Lounge, the Solarium, the Clubrooms, would bring them all together in happy family groups. Those who wanted to watch football could gather in one lounge, those who wanted to listen to the symphony in another. Those whose devotion to their favorite soap opera is such that they would be lost without it, now may indulge their habit by taking rooms in the new guest houses. Standing between the hotel and the older apartments on the beach, these new quarters now have television sets in their parlors.

The problem of how to make improvements without going into long-term debt was of constant concern to Bill Jones, Jr. On Compton's orders he worked with Irving Harned, the Cloister's manager, on a plan to remodel the kitchen — at a cost of some half million dollars — without inconveniencing the guests. Personnel decisions also came his way. Rita Van Pelt resigned as publicity director and Nancy Beyer replaced her. Beach erosion was a problem, and Jones, Jr., and Dewey Benefield were told to work with the Corps of Engineers in an effort to control it. It is an effort which still continues, for as Jones was to discover, one year the ocean giveth, the next it taketh away. How to handle the Beach Club area was a problem. Here, romping youngsters in wet bathing suits were thrown in close proximity to oldsters wanting only to lie back in their beach chairs, reading and sunning until they fell asleep. John Lucas, an urbane and witty man who helped Harned in the management of the Cloister, was chosen for this job. Now it is handled with brusque but friendly discipline by Howard Jones, who has a special way with youngsters.

In September 1964 hurricane Dora came along, and young Bill

Jones was named to supervise the engineering department in picking up debris and making repairs to damaged seawalls in front of the Beach Club. Smaller jobs also were his responsibility. A year earlier he reported to Compton that the dishwasher at the Beach Club was at last installed and working and that the sunshade by the baby pool was in place.

Golf carts were much on young Jones's mind for a year or so. President Eisenhower vacationing at Augusta had made the golf cart popular, and a number of Sea Island Golf Club's more venerable members bought their own. This caused complications, with carts trundling around the course along with the caddies. If the club could buy its own carts, and rent them, this would be a source of income to the company as well as a favor to the golfers who needed transportation around the course. A compromise was worked out. The club would permit the cart owner to use his own cart until it wore out, then he would be expected to rent one. This worked very well, except in the case of one stubborn old gentleman who kept rebuilding his cart until all that was left of the original vehicle, according to Eddie Thompson, was the air in the tires.

Thompson's Golf Club activities included a myriad of things — from teaching golf and selling merchandise to telling wide-eyed visitors that the ancient knobbed shaft on display in the clubhouse, a rhododendron with the root forming the club head and the branch forming the shaft, might — or might not — have been a primeval golf club used by the Scottish Highlanders who had manned Fort King George for Oglethorpe at Darien.

More expansion was underway in 1965, with Bill Jones, Jr., playing an important part as a new dining room, the South Georgian Room, was added to the old Georgian Room, with six guest rooms going in above it. This was done in an effort to make more space for conventions, which the company did not actively seek, except in the dull time between the summer and winter seasons. The new dining facilities would permit "conference groups" — a title which the Cloister management prefers — to come together in a separate space, where, if they got a little boisterous, they would not disturb the other diners. The hotel soon discovered that the groups were happy enough to be set apart, for some of them found the presence of the regular guests somewhat inhibiting. The Cloister has always tried to attract only the more sedate professional groups, but even these sometimes make noises more joyful than other guests think necessary. The construction of the new wing also proved a little more flexible than was expected. One startled guest reported that in her bedroom above the new dining area she stared transfixed as a bottle of expensive perfume, set in motion by the heavy beat of a band in the dining room below, jiggled across her dressing table and fell on the floor.

The Cloister, trusting its clients implicitly, has always been happy to accept personal checks from a departing guest, or if he preferred, they would bill him at his home address. Amazingly few deadbeats showed up under this system, but now and then one did fail to pay up within a reasonable grace period, and the hotel was forced to take action. This consisted in the main of a firm but friendly telephone call from J. Elliott Brown, head of accounting and treasurer for many years. This usually worked. Under certain circumstances, too, it was necessary to notify a Cloister guest that henceforth he would be on a strictly cash basis.

All these matters, simple and complex, had been on the shoulders of Jim Compton, until in December 1966, as had long been planned by him and Bill Jones, Sr. in their Sunday morning confabs at the offices, Compton laid down the burdens of the presidency. He turned them over — hotel, Beach Club, Golf Club, cottages, everything — to Bill Jones, Jr., and to the man who was to serve as his good right hand. At the meeting in which Bill,

Jr., was named president, Dewey Benefield, keeping his job as secretary, moved up to vice-president.

In August 1967, by mutual agreement, James Compton and his family sold their Sea Island stock to the Joneses for roughly a million dollars. This was considerably more than its market value, but the extra, it was felt, was well deserved, for Compton's service to the company had been invaluable, his money management superb. So much so that it sometimes worked against what he was trying to do. At one time Compton felt it would be to the benefit of the company to put Sea Island's nursery, which provided flowers for the tables and flowering plants for the gardens of the cottages, under a concession arrangement. He offered the nursery to a young employee named Dyson Flanders, who examined the proposal from all angles, decided he could make money on it, and hurried down to a Brunswick bank to borrow the purchase money. The banker listened and shook his head, "No, Dyson," he said, "if Jim Compton is willing to sell it, you don't want it." Flanders still works with horticulturist Ralph Graham, growing beautiful flowers and plants from a nursery still owned and operated by the company.

Compton continued to serve as director, and as unofficial consultant to young Bill Jones. He could look about him with pride at what had been accomplished since he first came with the Sea Island Company in 1929, and had taken the job of president in 1944. Nothing spectacular, but a steady growth: in his time the hotel had grown from 46 rooms to 187; the employees from 40 to 500; the Sea Island cottage colony had risen from 46 houses in 1929 to 200 in 1966, with more abuilding. Thus, Jones, Jr., took over a prospering business that was still ably led despite Compton's retirement. Bill Jones, Sr., still chaired stockholders meetings, giving sound advice—though he frequently was heard to murmur that he was happy to lay his burden down. And Irving Harned, vice-president of the company and manager of the hotel, was still showing the same high talent that had made the Cloister one of the great resort hotels in the nation. And backing up Harned was Dick Everett, noted for the amiable acerbity with which he handled guests, and Terry Thomas, indefatigable director of a myriad of activities.

Their combined talents showed up in the hotel records. In 1967, 65 percent of the Cloister's patrons were people who had been there before; and that year it had one of the world's highest resort hotel occupancy rates—90 percent full for ten months of the year. More than 100 of the 500 employees on the staff had worked for the company for ten years or more. They knew their jobs and carried them out well, and the company was protected against the wanderlust which affects many hotel employees by the fact that a retirement program, started in 1955 and thought to be the first in the resort hotel business, served to keep them at Sea Island.

The hotel still welcomes honeymooners, and makes a big fuss over them—the 24,000th couple since the count began in 1940 was registered in 1978. It is also a favorite spot of families with young children and of the elderly. Many of the older folk come to Sea Island to spend their last years in an atmosphere of quiet elegance, to die there, and to be buried in Christ Church cemetery. Among those long known to Sea Island and deeply missed are Mrs. Cate—postmistress, lecturer on history, and author of the fascinating book *Early Days of Coastal Georgia*—who died in 1961, and Dr. Orrin S. Wightman—Bill Jones's friend, an outstanding surgeon, and noted amateur photographer—who passed on at his home in New York in 1965.

Dewey Benefield, faced with wide responsibilities as a company vice-president soon discovered that even though he held degrees in journalism and law, and was trained in accounting, he still needed to sharpen his management skills. In the spring of 1966, he went off to the University of Georgia to take a crash course in management. Back at Sea Island, he helped to establish the Credit Union (which had taken place of the old paternal system by which the staff, when needing money, would line up every Friday in front of Jim Compton's door to borrow what was needed or to pay back what had been borrowed). Taxes were Benefield's main concern. He was convinced that Glynn County's tax assessors were placing valuations on Sea Island properties in excess of valuation placed on other comparable properties in the county, and he wanted an arbitration hearing. He got it, and in time taxes were moderately reduced. He also needed help in his sale of Sea Island properties, while he laid off streets and built houses that he hoped would sell. To handle the sales department he first called in Captain John T. (Jigger) Lowe, retired naval aviator, Annapolis graduate, and former commander of Glynco Naval Air Station and the Naval Air Technical Training Center. As sales climbed, more help was needed, and Benefield brought in an energetic young Atlantan named William C. (Bill) Smith, an MBA with wide experience in many aspects of sales and management. The job required varied talents, for it had many facets, from taking a couple out to look at a brand new house, to trying to settle a squabble between a divorcing couple over who would get the house after the breakup. In one situation, both did. The lure of the island was too strong and the couple happily stayed on, in separate quarters. An equal talent for settling problems is required of the cottage rental managers, in succession, Bill Summers, Gordon Craighead, Tom Davis, B.B. Griffin, Frances Hill and Suzanne Engel, who are called upon for every type service, from hiring servants to tracking down a lost poodle.

The first years were busy ones for Bill Jones, Jr. A fourth nine, Marshside, was being laid out at the Golf Course, food prices were jumping at the rate of 6 to 7 percent a year, and the Cloister considered for a while buying its meats from the meat department of a local grocery chain. A comparison of price and quality ruled against it. Charles Willis was closing his beautiful shop in the Cloister and a number of replacements were considered, with Davison's getting the nod. There was the matter of finding a new maître d', to replace Harry Welch, retiring after twenty years, a man so fondly remembered that the cottagers gave him $2000 for a trip to Europe and the staff gave him a set of golf clubs and a membership in the Sea Island Golf Club. Something, as always, had to be done about the Yacht Club restaurant, which, unlike the Cloister dining rooms and the Golf Club restaurant, had never had the warm and friendly atmosphere that Irv Harned desired. Bummy Baumgardner, moving on in years but still brisk and busy, reported that his topographic survey indicated that the Marshside Nine would have some of the flora of the old Scottish moors, and Dewey Benefield reported that he would check on the cost of installing lightning rods on the golf course rain shelters.

So Bill Jones, Jr., worked, slowly but steadily, listening, thinking, making decisions every day which might cost the company one dollar or a hundred thousand dollars. Often, though, his thoughts roamed over the marshes, and up the highway to Altama—the place that since he was a little boy had been close to his heart. There he had fished and hunted, trapped wild hogs, fattened them on acorns that gave the meat its flavor, and when the time came, killed them quickly and without pain with a rifle shot between the eyes; then he skinned them, not scalding and scraping in the old country way, and cut them up to hang in the smokehouse as winter meat. For five years, from 1955 to 1960, he had lived at Altama, commuting to Sea Island and his little office in the bell-towered administration building at the end of the causeway. Now he had his own house on Sea Island, and he went there every night. But Altama called to the hunter in him, the farmer and woodsman, and he went back there every weekend that he could.

The newspapers, in announcing Bill Jones's accession to the

presidency of Sea Island, made much of his accomplishments—as a director of the Brunswick-Glynn County Chamber of Commerce, trustee of the Glynn-Brunswick Memorial Hospital Authority, director and vice-president of the Saint Simons Rotary Club, officer of the Navy League, and director and past-president of the United Community Fund. They named his business connections, with McKinnon Oil Company, Seaboard Construction, Glynn Concrete, and his posts as director of the First National Bank of Brunswick and trustee of the Southeastern Investment Trust.

These showed his capacity for accepting responsibility, for working hard and effectively with other people. They did not particularly stress one quality in Bill, Jr. that was obvious then, and would become more important to him, and his company, over the years. This was his ability to recognize, and bring in to counsel and advise him, top people in all fields touching on his business. In the decade of the 1970s this was to prove crucially important, for running a hotel and resort operation which tries to take a personal interest in the desires and needs, the whims and crochets, of a clientele representing all ages, drawn from every corner of the nation, can be a grueling business. And in the span of a few years, the men who had served Bill Jones, Sr., so well— Jim Compton, Dick Everett, Irving Harned—all had died.

A Record of Service

Loyalty and long service of staff members are a large part of Sea Island's appeal to guests. Cloister orchestra leader Frank LaVine here plays for a hotel patio dance in the Fifties, as he does in the clubrooms of today.

Tom and Nancy Gallagher arrived to perform and teach Cloister guests to dance in 1956 and are still at it today.

During two generations of instructing at Sea Island
Fred Missildine became world's champion
professional in skeet shooting. Here in the Fifties he
teaches Cloister manager I.A. Harned, watched by
social hostess Rosalie Hull and beach club manager
John Lucas (center).

Photographer-philanthropist Dr. Orrin S. Wightman
made this picture in 1961 of company executives J.D.
Compton, left, president; Dewey Benefield, then
secretary; and A.W. Jones, Jr., T.M. Baumgardner
and I.A. Harned, then vice presidents.

Sea Island's late postmaster, historian and lecturer,
Mrs. Margaret Davis Cate, at Fort Frederica, a national
monument largely as a result of her research.

Landscape architect T.M. Baumgardner joined the company in 1927 and continues as consultant after 51 years. He checks a Cloister planting with his successor as director of landscape operations, Ralph Graham.

Cloister landscape superintendent Dyson Flanders has 25 years with the company, groundsmen Charlie Shedd, center, and Dave Pinckney, 31 and 33 years.

Photo left, Norris "45" Sheppard's Sea Island career began with the golf course construction and spanned 47 years. I.A. Harned congratulates him on retirement. Photo right, Oakley Booth retired as bell service captain after 24 years on the job. With him is A.W. Jones, Jr.

Mrs. Frances Hill, cottage rentals manager, retired after 18 years with the company. Here she is thanked for her service by Alfred Jones.

Brunswick Junior College established the James D.
Compton chair of Free Enterprise in honor
of the late Sea Island Company president. His
portrait was presented to the college and beside it are
Mrs. Compton and their daughter, Mrs. Patricia
Compton Euler.

Because of his great love of the game, the golf club
was chosen for the hanging of this portrait of
I.A. Harned, who died in 1977. His widow is beside
the portrait.

Photo left, R.G. (Sam) Hawley handled advance reservations for 30 years. This photograph and many others in these pages were made by his brother-in-law, Gil Tharp, who began at the Cloister as a member of the orchestra.

Photo right, Harry Welch, maître d' from 1947 until retirement in 1967, with one of his regular guests, L.B. Shapleigh, right, of Cincinnati.

Long time Cloister chef Herman Yursich and beach club chef Carl Outlaw were called from retirement to cook for President Jimmy Carter during visits to Musgrove Plantation.

Cloister resident manager Richard A. Everett spent a lifetime on the staff, distinguishing himself as a hotel executive and historical lecturer during 41 years service.

Returning guests count on reservations and reception desk personnel remembering their room preferences. Reservation manager Julian Cason, right, has been with the staff 29 years. Assistants Beverly Gardner, left, and Jerry Rowland, next to Cason, have had 11 and 17 years on the job. Cashier Vi Wells, second from left, had 15 years before her death in 1978.

A crew of veterans anticipates guest needs at the beach club. From left, Herman Coleman, 12 years on the job, Howard Jones, manager, 23 years, Tobe Tyson, 32 years, Percy Walters, assistant manager, 28 years, George Drayton, 10 years.

Emma Murphy aided generations of swimmers at the beach club during her 25 years on the staff.

Leroy "Stretch" Livingston spent 37 years on the
Cloister staff and still returns from retirement to assist
at plantation suppers and family beach parties.

Stables manager Marvin Long has been on the job 30
years. Daughter Amy, left rear, assists.

Each of these staff members had more than 30 years service when this picture was made in 1977. From left are James E. Jones, Curley Thompson, Margaret Wilson, Dave Pinckney, Ethel Camp, Charles Wynn, Tobe Tyson and Leroy Cooper.

Forty-one years in the clubrooms — almost the lifetime of the company president — rates a handshake for Vance Shaffer, right, from A.W. Jones, Jr. The occasion is a periodic recognition ceremony for long-time staffers.

Golf club service records read like this among key
personnel here: from left, Gerald Atkinson, caddy
master, 17 years; Jim Hildebrand, superintendent, 5
years; Marion McKendree, retired greens keeper, 46
years; Eddie Thompson, director, 19 years; Harry
Peterson, clubhouse manager, 42 years; Tommy
Kukoly, professional, 19 years.

Gus Peeples has directed the Cloister's tennis
program for 18 years.

Reviewing 1978 building plans: A.W. Jones, Jr., company president, with Dewey Benefield, left, and Dennie McCrary, center, vice presidents. Together they represent 45 years of service.

Ted Wright, left, became the Cloister's managing director in 1977 but had worked one year with the hotel 24 years earlier. With him are M.A. Derkacz, assistant manager, and Helmut Reher, executive chef.

Experience in greeting Cloister guests: bell staff veterans, from left, Superintendent of Service Bill Miller, 5 years, Jerry Fox, 22 years, Tommy Pickels, 19 years, Marshall West, 28 years, Richard Law, 8 years and Earl Wiggins, 5 years.

Jack Grant, second from left, became maître d' in 1978, succeeding George Scherer, whose service dated from 1967. They stand with three generations of one family on their staff: Juanita Goldman, captain, right, with 16 years, her daughter Barbara Plunkett, captain, 20 years, and Mrs. Plunkett's son, Chuck Strickland, waiter, four years.

Directors of the Sea Island Company after their mid-1978 meeting: seated, from left, Howard C. Jones, Mrs. Marianna Kuntz, Alfred W. Jones, chairman, Mrs. Katharine O'Connor, A.W. Jones, Jr., president. Standing from left, J.D. Benefield, vice president, J.W. McSwiney, John Gilbert, Ted Wright, vice president and managing director of the Cloister, T.M. Baumgardner, A.M. Harris, and D.L. McCrary, vice president.

The Society of American Travel Writers honored Alfred W. Jones, right, in 1976 as one of America's outstanding conservationists to the benefit of the traveling public. Georgia Governor George Busbee, left, and the national president of the society, Carolyn Patterson of the National Geographic Magazine, presented Jones the writers' "Connie" award.

16

WHERE CARE EBBS OUT WITH EVERY TIDE

There are two worlds at Sea Island that merge and meld and still are separate. One is made up of the hotel guests, the transients who come, for a little while, year after year. Their lives revolve around the Cloister and the many pleasant things it offers. The other is the world of the cottage people, renters and owners, many of whom were hotel people once themselves. As cottagers they share in all the hotel and Beach Club amenities, the golf and tennis and swimming, the dancing in the clubrooms, the art shows and the concerts in the Spanish Lounge, the bird and history lectures in the Solarium. At the same time, they move in other circles—in the small, interlocking, and ongoing social-cultural, church, and good-works groups around which cottage life revolves and in which the hotel guests have little part.

Both guests and cottagers, however, share the one element that gives Sea Island its ambience, that lies at the heart of its charm—the special quality that brought all of them here in the first place and that makes of every day spent here a treasured memory. This is the sense of peace, of silence deep as time; the sleeping majesty of old oaks drowsing under a golden sun, of palm leaves rustling in a gentle wind, of deer drifing like shadows beside a traveled road, of sea gulls crying and surf curling in muted music along miles of uncrowded beach.

These are not manmade things, of course. But a handful of men have protected and preserved them for fifty years, and their successors, in the new generation coming on, are determined that this policy shall not change. There have been many resorts established along this sundrenched littoral in the half century since Howard Coffin's and Bill Jones's Sea Island came into being—the first such happy place created between Pinehurst and Palm Beach. And these too have offered sun and surf and sand and a big sky, and each for a time has attracted a loyal following. But none yet has had Sea Island's sense of permanence, its feeling of stability and continuity. For this mood grows out of a family ownership still truly dedicated to the idea that no matter what may be going on in the garish and clanging world outside, here may be found a place of refuge, where care does, indeed, ebb out with every tide.

The carefree life, though, is for the guest. Care—even a deep concern for the direction Sea Island should take in the future, is as much in the thoughts of those who head the company today as it has been in the past. From Howard Coffin's time to the present day, deep thought and planning have gone into creating the life of tasteful opulence that is the cachet of Sea Island. At first this planning seemed casual, almost off hand, requiring only the approval in cut and dried executive meetings of plans worked out by men and their wives—the Joneses, the Comptons, the Baumgardners, the Harneds—who seemed to know by instinct what such a place should offer. First, it should be a resort, with all a seaside playground's social courtesies, centered around a little hotel that every guest would come to look upon as a happy combination of home and inn and country club. And this is the way it worked out, at first, with the Cloister carrying the struggling little company through the first years of the depression and then the war.

But Sea Island had been conceived as a real estate development too, a place to be shared with many owners, drawn from everywhere. And as the depression ended in the surge of war, and the war ran its course, it became clear that the time had come at last for the pattern of growth—centered in years past around the hotel, the Beach Club, and the Golf Club—to take a new direction. The hotel would remain the central jewel in this necklace, continuing to grow and expand its facilities and increase its comforts. New houses would be built on the beach, and off the beach, as adjuncts to the hotel, and all would be air conditioned, a new thing in the islands. The hotel rooms and River House were also air conditioned, first with window units, then with a central system. This raised mild protest from the older guests. No cooling would ever be needed at Sea Island, they argued, other than the sea winds blowing through an open window. Other protests came from some hotel guests. Startled folk began calling the desk at midnight to complain that their sleep was being disturbed. The wailing cry of cats, making love, was being piped into their rooms through the air conditioning ducts. Unfortunately, it is a problem that the board of directors still must ponder.

As the 1960s loomed, Sea Island's management turned its thoughts to larger matters than caterwauls in the duct work. From the mid-1950s on, there had been a steadily growing market for lots on which cottages could be built—*cottage* being the modest name by which Sea Islanders referred to the handsome houses some of Georgia's top architects designed for them. Prices reflected this interest. An oceanfront lot which was sold for $200 in 1923 by the old Saint Simon-Long Island Company was worth $12,000 by 1933 and would go for $30,500 in 1960. Nor did the rising tide show any sign of ebbing in the 1970s. The same beach lot commanded a price of $120,000 in 1971, and had soared to $205,000 in 1977. Marsh lot values increased at an even greater rate, as laws came on the books protecting the marsh lands from commercial development. As more and more people realized that the view of the marshes which inspired Sidney Lanier would remain unchanged and unspoiled, more building began on the marsh side of the island. Among these were condominiums, sixteen units, no smaller and no less expensive than the cottages, operating under the name of the River Club.

The demand for lots and the building of new cottages (very few buyers, it seemed, bought and held land purely on speculation) placed new and heavier demands on the Sea Island Company. New roads had to be built off Sea Island Drive, westward toward the marshes, eastward toward the sea. Lots had to be laid out, cleared of underbrush, and landscaped—all in such a way that fine old trees would be undisturbed. The construction of new habitations naturally meant an increase in the services that the company must provide the cottagers, services ranging from having their cottages clean for their arrival with lawns neatly barbered, to hiring servants for them and providing catering services from the Cloister kitchen when they wished to have a party. Company security officers patrolled the cottage community, keeping an eye out for fire or thieves or unauthorized picnickers, and the company would also find renters for those owners who wanted to pick up a little cash while they themselves were not in residence.

Obviously such an expanded operation could not function in the old informal way, with the elder Jones and Jim Compton sitting around on Sunday mornings making casual offhand decisions which they would call on Ed Messick, or the housekeeping or engineering staff to carry out. Something more "organized" was needed; and it was Jim Compton, in his retirement, who put together the corporate structure under which the Sea Island Company would operate in the years to come.

The form was simple enough. Two separate corporate entities, all of whose stock would be owned by the parent company, would be spun off from the Sea Island Company. One, Sea Island Properties, would be responsible for real estate sales, rentals, and all landscape activities. The other wholly owned subsidiary, Sea Island Services, would operate the water system, the bus lines, and any other company activities that might come under the Interstate Commerce Commission or the Public Service Commission. The parent Sea Island Company, for its part, would continue operating all of the resort activities—the hotel, the Beach Club, the Golf Club, the tennis courts, and the Skeet Club—and an interlocking directorate would manage all three companies. On October 1, 1971 Sea Island Properties and Sea Island Services held their organizational meeting and began their operation.

The architect of this new plan did not long survive its adoption. On January 11, 1974 James D. Compton died, in Brunswick-Glynn County Hospital, of a cardiovascular illness. At his request, he was buried with simple graveside services in Christ Church yard. He was seventy-two years old, and for forty-five years his life had been wrapped up in the Sea Island Company.

On March 20, 1974 Alfred W. Jones, Sr., chairman of the board of Sea Island Company, offered to the officers and directors an eloquent and heartfelt tribute to his friend. Compton, he told them, had come with the company in 1929, on the eve of the depression, and with an "unbreakable faith, broad vision, and sterling integrity" he had guided it through its early years. As president of Sea Island Company, Jones pointed out, Compton had directed the company through a period of orderly but substantial growth, until Sea Island had become known worldwide as a place of unsurpassed beauty and genteel elegance. Compton, Jones noted, not only had served his company, he had worked diligently as a member of the Jekyll Island Authority throughout its early years, had given years of valuable service to the Brunswick-Glynn County Planning Commission, and had been an outstanding leader in the Saint Simons Presbyterian Church, as well as a trustee of the Presbyterian Home at Quitman.

Compton, Jones concluded, had made an indelible imprint on his community, his church, and all who knew him. The board, therefore, extended to his family its deepest sympathy and its gratitude to their husband and father. This expression of the board's feelings was placed on permanent record in the minutes of that meeting.

Another eloquent tribute to Jim Compton came from his wife. "He was a cheerleader by nature, always happy, always smiling," said Dottie Compton. This caused her some small problems when some years after his death she sought to have his portrait painted to hang in the living room of their cottage. "All the pictures showed him laughing or smiling," she remembers— "meaning that his eyes were squinched almost shut and the artist could not see their size or shape or color."

Bill Jones was not a man to wear his emotions on his sleeve, but the death of Jim Compton stirred him deeply. For Compton was one of that small coterie who, by their counsel and by their faith in Jones, had insured the survival of the little company through its first struggling days. Eugene Lewis was one of them, a man whose knowledge of financial matters was such that he could find answers to problems that profoundly puzzled Jones and Compton. Dick Courts was another. He had saved the company from collapse by finding, in Dick Reynolds, a buyer for Sapelo Island, and the Sapelo money pulled Sea Island back from the brink of bankruptcy. Cator Woolford had no financial interest in Sea Island at all, but he served as ably and as earnestly on Jones's board of directors as if his own fortune were at stake. Chip Robert was a cottager as well as a counselor. And finally, Charles Wright, Jr., served Bill Jones as he had served Howard Coffin—with a consummate legal skill that guided the little company through the labyrinthine complexities of the Detroit banking system to make it stand free and clear at last. Even now, in moments of remembering, Bill Jones runs their names over in his mind – Coffin and Lewis, Woolford and Charles Wright, Courts and Compton – "Without them," he admits, "we'd never have made it. We'd have been just another little company that went under in the depression, and then was forgotten."

At the time of Jim Compton's death, many of these men were gone, and their advice was only a treasured memory. But the company at last had begun to carry out many of the plans they, and Compton, and Bill Jones had talked about over the years. To put these long-held concepts into some coherent form, the company in the early 1970s began an intensive planning process for the development of all the company's properties on both Sea Island and Saint Simons – a program that might be spread out over a quarter of a century. For expert guidance the company turned to several nationally known firms which specialized in economic forecasting, land use planning, and community development. The guidelines laid down by Bill Jones, Jr., Dewey Benefield, and their associates were similar to those under which the senior Jones and Jim Compton had operated over the years. Above all, any plans evolved should bear in mind two points: one, whatever was built, from a single structure to a planned community, should be beautiful to look at, useful in ways that would not be disturbing to others, and in no way befoul the air, the land, the surrounding waters, nor any of the creatures that dwelt therein. Second, nothing should proceed past the planning stage until the time was right. The company still remembered the struggling years and how near it had come to bankruptcy. Sea Island Company had no intention of letting itself be caught in the financial bind that even then on Saint Simons was forcing two large and handsome club, golf, and residential developments in the direction of the bankruptcy courts. This cautious attitude, however, did not mean that Sea Island should overlook any opportunity to make a sound investment or to add to the 3500-acre "land bank" of undeveloped property it already held on Saint Simons.

Therefore, when after many years the Strachan family of Savannah decided to sell Cannon's Point, a famed pre-Civil War plantation on the north end of Saint Simons, the Joneses and their associates moved fast. Here was an area wild and beautiful and rich in history. Here nearly 200 years ago a tall blue-eyed Scot named John Couper had earned worldwide fame as an experimental planter and horticulturist. Here he proved that long-stapled Persian cotton would grow well in Georgia soil, so well, in fact, that in time it became known as Sea Island Cotton and its sale brought Couper some $100,000 a year. He taught Thomas Spalding how to grow sugar cane in ditched and irrigated fields, he grew date palms from Persia, and at Thomas Jefferson's suggestion he sent to Spain for olive trees, which grew and flourished for generations, giving 200 to 300 barrels of oil in a good year.

Couper's genius as a man of science and Rebecca Maxwell Couper's charm as a hostess were not the sole qualities that brought fame to Cannon's Point. So did the talents of their cook, Sans Foix, whose skill in the great kitchen of the big house matched the reknown of his master in the field of agriculture. Thus not only horticulturists and agronomists but scholars in many fields came to share the lavish hospitality that flowed from Cannon's Point, including the romping music of Johnnie, a fiddler who also played the bagpipes. In Miss Bessie Lewis's book *Patriarchal Plantations of St. Simons Island* (illustrated by Mildred Huie), there is a vivid description of life as it was at Cannon's Point in the years before Couper's death in 1850: "There were formal dinners and balls, with the ladies in silk, the men in well-cut suits of the richest of English and Scottish materials. . . . It was an excellent way of life . . . Here were broad verandahs, beautiful gardens, dignity of manners and dress, cosmopolitan entertainment that included the poorest of kin folk and titled noblemen and statesmen."

After the Civil War the estate went into a long decline, until at last little remained to remind the viewer of its colorful past. A ruined wall still was standing and the chimneys of the ancient kitchen, and the place could still be seen where legend said the oak had stood from which *Old Ironsides's* sternpost was cut.

Then one afternoon in the autumn of 1971, a lawyer called from Savannah. He said that the heirs of F.D.M. Strachan were at last willing to put up for sale the land that had been in the estate of the late shipping magnate for generations. Sealed bids, the lawyer said, would be received in Savannah, with the family reserving the right to reject all offers.

With the Joneses, junior and senior, Dewey Benefield rode to Cannon's Point, looked over the 447 acres of high land, the 1000 acres of marsh, the ruins brooding in the winter sun. Twice before the company had bought an old plantation, dead as this one, and restored it to life. Retreat, at the south of the island, was the site of the Sea Island Golf Course, and the community there grew up around it. Hamilton Plantation, on Gascoigne Bluff, had become Epworth-by-the-Sea. But what could be done here to make these ancient acres live again? None of the three at the moment knew. All they knew was that they wanted the place, to make sure it would be developed in a manner worthy of its history.

It was Bill Jones, Jr., who worked out the bid that Sea Island Company would offer. Their competing bidders, he figured, would be the two other big land owners and developers on Saint Simons—the Ashmore brothers and Evans and Mitchell. Somehow, the figure $2,500 an acre kept popping into his mind. One of the others, he felt sure, would make this as its bid. So, to $2,500 he added $12.50 for a total of $2,512.50 an acre for the high land.

For the marsh land he bid nothing, for under a new law protecting the marshes there was no way it could be developed. Quickly, on a little pocket calculator, he did his figuring—$2,512.50 an acre for 447 acres of high land. The little light at the top blinked out the figure that was to be his bid—$1,123,087.50. The Ashmores bid $750,000; Evans and Mitchell an even million.

Adjoining Cannon's Point there was another piece of land that the Joneses for a long time had wanted to add to their own. Its name in history was Lawrence Plantation, and it was part of John Couper's holdings, which he passed on to his daughter, Anna, whose British husband, Captain John Fraser, managed it for a number of years. After the War Between the States, the plantation came into the hands of Anna Gould Dodge, who traded it to a family named Taylor for lands the Taylors owned near Frederica.

It was known as Taylor's Fish Camp in 1971, when the Sea Island Company bought Cannon's Point, and it was presided over by Mrs. R.A. Taylor, a wonderful old lady who had been running the fishing camp since her husband died. Bill Jones, Jr., loved to fish and to talk about fishing, and so did Mrs. Taylor, and over the years the two had become fast friends. She was highly pleased when the Joneses bought Cannon's Point, and when Bill Jones, Jr., made the offhand remark that if she would sell him her place he would be happy to buy it, she readily agreed. The price per acre was roughly the same as he had paid for Cannon's Point. The transaction totaled half a million dollars, including a comfortable modern home he bought for Mrs. Taylor in a more populated area of Saint Simons.

Though Jones, Benefield, and the others had no idea how they would develop their new holdings for the long pull, there were some things that obviously needed doing at the moment. The ruins of the old Couper mansion at Cannon's Point, the tabby foundations of the original residence and the massive brick chimneys that had served the old kitchens, had to be stabilized — protected by concrete from the rain and changing temperatures that had been crumbling them slowly for years.

Merely to preserve old walls and chimneys, however, was not enough for Bill Jones, Sr.'s, inquiring mind. He wanted to know how the people who built those structures had lived, what records of their life had they left behind other than yellowed letters dim with time and weathered aphorisms carved on gravestones at Christ Church? For guidance he called on his friend Charles (Chuck) H. Fairbanks, who had shared with him and Mrs. Cate the original archaeological research at Frederica. At the time of the Frederica research Chuck Fairbanks was with the National Park Service. By the time Sea Island Company bought Cannon's Point, he had left federal service and was head of the Department of Anthropology and Archaeology at the University of Florida. When Bill Jones asked him if he and his students would like to do a "dig" at Cannon's Point, he accepted eagerly. For here was one of the most fascinating areas along all the Georgia coast, changed but little since the Civil War. Working out an arrangement with Dewey Benefield whereby his students could be housed and fed in the staff dormitory at the Cloister, Fairbanks brought in twenty graduate students at a time, over a period of more than two years. The result was a flow of scholarly papers touching on many aspects of life at Cannon's Point, from prehistoric Indian days to the Civil War. One interesting story was told by the kitchen middens of plantation days, containing in separate piles the refuse thrown out from the big house, the overseers' quarters, and the slaves' cabins. These showed clearly a difference in diets, utensils used, and life styles. All ate meat and fish, but as might be expected, the master ate better grades of each. Fresh beef and pork were served at the big house; the slaves and the overseers ate salt meat and dried beef. The master ate trout; the slaves ate mullet and catfish. The big house often served venison and wild turkey; the slaves ate 'coon and possum and occasionally deer.

The overseers ate more nearly like the slaves than like the master. The digging at Cannon's point turned up some puzzles, too. At the bottom of the big house well three antique coins were found. One that could be identified had been minted at Alexandria during the reign of Trajan who ruled Rome from A.D. 98 to 117. Another was a Roman copy of a Greek coin from Corinth. The only logical explanation was that John Couper, who gathered plants and shrubs from all over the world, also had a coin collection, which Yankee troops had come upon and scattered when they occupied the place during the Civil War.

Equally interesting but even more puzzling were the relics left by the aboriginal Indians. Little trace of them was found on solid land, but a short distance into the marsh lay a ring of shells, estimated by one of Mr. Fairbanks's scholars to be between 1500 and 2000 years old. By its location and its size, it seemed to be a relic of a tribe of South American Indians called the Arawak. If so, it was the furthest north that archaeological evidence of these tribes had been found. Whether it was a ceremonial ring, a fortress, or a living area where dwellers in houses built on stilts threw their shells is still a matter of debate. Other digging at scattered locations in the marsh area has turned up trash piles — broken shells mostly — dating back 4000 years.

The historic sites were marked and mapped, so that whatever might be created here in future years, the places of archaelogical interest would be preserved. Here Bill Jones, Sr., seems to combine his sense of history with his unfailing interest in what good things the future will bring — a cast of mind which at seventy-five is still the motivating force in his life. The Cannon's Point lands, along with Taylor's Fish Camp, will go into Sea Island Company's land bank for now. But when the time does come for development — ten, twenty, thirty years from now — there is the possibility that what is built there will be reminiscent of its days of glory. The old "big house," with its great chimneys of English brick, its tabby and brick foundations, its wooden upper stories, wide verandahs, and many-flowered gardens, could be restored as a hotel. The slave cabins could be re-erected as guest houses, and there is plenty of deep water in the Hampton River for a yacht basin when development does begin. (The movie company shooting the loading of the slave ship for the movie *Roots* found this to be an ideal site, and the movie *Conrack* was also shot nearby.) No place, either on Saint Simons or Sea Island, would offer house sites with more beautiful views of the marsh. The Cannon's Point highland is a peninsula, falling away on either side to a marshland that is like a great sea rippling with its own pattern of changing colors.

All development of Cannon's Point and Taylor's Fish Camp will wait, however, until a turn of the economic tide indicates that Sea Island Company's slow-but-sure building projects can be resumed. Other developers are moving in on other areas of north Saint Simons. At Butler's Point, for example, a new sub-division is being carved out. And both Joneses are aware that there is an increasing pressure from outsiders to open up new areas of development on Saint Simons, just as there is a strong and growing outcry from local residents to keep things as they are forever. So far, Sea Island Company has followed its ancient pattern of making plans for the future, being ready to move when the time comes, but taking no hasty or ill-considered steps. In the files in Dewey Benefield's office are detailed plans for developing the twenty-seven acres adjacent to the intersection of Frederica Road and the Sea Island Causeway. Under its revised charter the company can, when it wishes, create here a high-class boutique-type shopping area, tentatively called Sea Island Cross-roads. It would nestle back in the trees, its small shops blending with the landscape. These plans have been put away for awhile. There are plans, too, for a medical center, an office building to house doctors and dentists. All these must wait until the time is right, the land held, as at Cannon's Point, in a land bank. It is possible, of course, that taxes will remain so high that no company can afford to let its land lie unused.

The Sea Island Company is not an eleemosynary institution. It is a family business, on which many people, employees as well as stockholders, depend for a livelihood. In the past, recognizing its special situation and its special needs, it imposed an extra three mill tax on its properties on Sea Island, to pay the county for such special services as the causeway police station. With its more recent purchases on Saint Simons, the company now owns some 5,000 undeveloped acres on that island. And what happens in the future depends on how long the company feels it can continue to pay exorbitantly high taxes on that land. Glynn County, like every other county in Georgia, now taxes open and empty land at its so-called "highest and best use." Under this interpretation the company finds itself paying ever greater amounts in property taxes, which in some years are more than it nets in profit. By persuasion, argument, and every legal means, the Sea Island Company is trying to convince the politicians that this tax policy is fatal to orderly development—that eventually it will result in Saint Simons being covered with condominiums, motels, filling stations, and quick-food eateries, thus losing its quiet charm.

While hopefully awaiting favorable tax action, the company is doing some solid development that should help the company keep its head above the rising tax waters. Just as in the early days the "friendly little Cloister" carried the financial burden for the whole Sea Island operation, an addition to the hotel is now under way, the biggest single addition of rooms in the hotel's history. South of the Beach Club, on land where the old casino once stood, the company is adding thirty-six additional luxury rooms in a three-story central building flanked by two-story wings. The job will cost roughly $1.6 million, and the construction will be undertaken in such a way that scientists, knowledgeable on such matters, agree that no damage will be done to the fragile ecosystem of the dunes.

Bill Jones, Sr., in his first ten years, had to cope with a lack of money brought on by depression. Bill Jones, Jr., in his first decade as head of the company, has had to cope with problems growing out of inflation, taxes, and the untimely passing of men who served his father with consummate skill in their own fields of hotel management. The death of Jim Compton in 1974 was followed with unexpected suddenness by the passing of Dick Everett. Everett, the Cloister's resident manager and historian, was an urbane, witty, sometimes sharp-tongued man known to every Cloister guest over a period of twenty-odd years, and liked by nearly all of them. He also was an indefatigable worker who demanded the same dedication from his staff. In October 1974 he showed up at the office of Dr. Howard Taylor, the Sea Island doctor-in-residence at the time, saying that he was feeling "a little tired." This was unusual on his part, for always, in the past, he had stubbornly refused to have the annual physical checkup the company provided for its key employees. Taylor examined him, found his blood pressure high, and noted an irregular rhythm in his heartbeat. Taylor gave him medicine for his blood pressure and asked that he see a cardiac specialist about the arrhythmic beat. Everett took the medicine, but he refused to see the doctor. Less than two months later, on the night of January 13, 1975, Dr. Raymond F. Spanjer, the new Sea Island physician-in-residence, got a call from Mrs. Everett. Dick had come home from the hotel fairly late, she said, eaten dinner at home, and on rising from the table he had seemed to faint. By the time Dr. Spanjer had gotten there—only a few minutes later—he was dead. The ambulance came quickly and carried him to the hospital. The diagnosis was cardiac failure.

The illness of Irv Harned gave long range warning, but death came with equal suddenness. In 1966 the Cloister's manager, known and held in deep affection by thousands of people all over the nation, had had a mild heart attack. He had gone under the care of Dr. Bruce Logue, of Emory, a frequent guest at the Cloister, and for a decade he had done very well. Then, on February 21, 1977, while sitting in his office at the hotel, he suffered a sudden loss of vision in the lower half of his left eye. He called Spanjer, who saw him at once and put him on the plane to Atlanta. There Dr. Robert Smith operated on the left carotid artery to facilitate the flow of blood through that artery. Harned, though, was found to be suffering from a severe generalized hardening of the arteries, and the doctors discovered an abdominal aortic aneurysm. Again, surgery followed, the weakened blood vessel being replaced by a dacron plastic tube. This worked well, and he soon was back at Sea Island, running his job as before. Frequently though, he complained of headaches, and his blood pressure still was high. One afternoon in June 1977, he was meeting with Dewey Benefield and other directors of the company in Dewey's office, when he excused himself, saying that his head was hurting. That night, at 4 a.m., Dr. Spanjer got a call from Stella Harned. Irving, she said, seemed unconscious in his bed. She could not rouse him. Spanjer's cottage was only a few streets away, but by the time he got there, Irv Harned was dead. Again the cause was cardiac failure.

No man over the years had meant more to the Cloister guests than Irving Harned, and none had left a more lasting mark on the hotel and its operations than had he. Harned was a Quaker, Pennsylvania born and steeped in the Quaker tradition of innkeeping. In 1933, when Norman Pancoast brought the twenty-five-year-old Harned to Sea Island, he had already had some years of experience in the resort hotel business, plus a two-year stint at the famous hotel school at Cornell University. His rise at Sea Island was rapid. Pancoast left in 1934, and an older man, C.W. Wannop, who had managed resort hotels in the Flagler chain, was brought in to run the Cloister in the winter season. In the summer Irv Harned took over. Summer was the wedding season in the South, and Harned, knowing how desperately the little hotel was struggling to survive, was smart enough to make a special appeal to honeymooners. They were greeted on arrival by Harned in person and were given special attention by all hands. Records were kept, and every thousandth couple was given a day's room and board on the house. When the total got up to 7000 – meaning seven days complimentary – it was obvious that Harned was about to give the house away, so he stopped the progression. Now each thousandth couple gets a week's free room and board. Nobody knows who the winners are until the "honeymooners dinner" (another Harned innovation) at which the winners are announced. Those on each side of the even thousand get one day free as a consolation prize. One weekend was particularly memorable It was just before the Korean War and there were ninety-six couples in the hotel.

Rates were low in Harned's first days – $13 a day, for two people, American plan. Harned came up with the idea of a seven-day $7 sports ticket – golf, tennis and the use of a bicycle, all for a dollar a day. Swimming at the Beach Club was fifty cents extra. After some deliberation for fear the Cloister's image as a family resort might be damaged, Harned had introduced the cruise idea. Steamship lines out of New York, Boston and Baltimore worked out plans whereby they could bring down a hundred or so young secretaries or schoolteachers, at a special rate, for three days at the Cloister. This plan made the cover of *Life,* with a picture story inside, and it kept the house full week after week.

Harned also introduced the idea of the manager's cocktail party. Every Thursday evening in the clubrooms, newly-arrived guests were welcomed by Harned and his wife, Stella, a process by which he came to know, personally, people from all over the United States. And, equally important to the Cloister guests, they came to know and like him and his wife.

The most important heritage that Harned left was the spirit of friendly service with which he imbued the staff. Under his management the wages paid employees, and the fringe benefits they received, were among the higher in the hotel business. He also did small thoughtful things. Maids were not required to turn down the beds on Sunday night. They could go to church instead. As a result, though hotel workers are a notoriously migrant species, there has been relatively little turnover at the Cloister. A large part of the staff today are people who have been there for from five to thirty-five years and more. Cloister service runs in families. Three generations of one family, a mother and daughter and granddaughter, serve together in the dining room. Another mother, her daughter and two sons serve — as passer, waitress, captain and busboy.

Not only the loyalty of the staff to their jobs, but the genuine affection they seem to feel for the people they serve is another Harned heritage. The smiling friendliness of the captains, the waiters and waitresses, and the passers in the dining rooms, the deft and cheerful service of the people behind the reception desk, the bellmen who bring the ice, the maids who come in to turn the covers down at night, all linger in the memory of the Cloister guest long after he has gone.

The deaths of Jim Compton and Dick Everett and Irv Harned, all coming in so short a span, threw a burden of responsibility on the shoulders of young Bill Jones. Fortunately, though, he proved to have his father's touch for picking good men as replacements. As a money manager he chose Dennie McCrary, who soon proved to be as skilled in this field as Jim Compton had been. McCrary was a native of Macon, a graduate of the U.S. Naval Academy (he later transferred to the Air Force as a procurement officer), and had also earned his master's degree in business administration at Harvard. He came to Sea Island from Hilton Head, where until 1972 he was executive vice-president of the

Sea Pines Company. In April 1975, in a small office next to Bill Jones, Jr., he took over his duties as a vice-president, responsible for finances and long-range planning. About then, Bummy Baumgardner, Sea Island's landscape architect and grounds keeper from the earliest days, decided to retire from all his duties except landscape planning. This necessitated a search for a horticulturist, and Bill Gibson, Jones's personnel director and talent scout, soon came up with a name. At Athens, a young Mississippian named Ralph Graham for seven years had kept the University of Georgia grounds beautifully groomed and barbered, bright with flowers in their season, with lawns green and lush beneath old trees. In the process he earned his master's degree in horticulture. At Sea Island since 1974, Graham has done the landscaping and the planting for all Sea Island Company's properties and maintains most of the 300 private homes that make up the cottage colony.

Harned himself, nearly a decade before his death, had begun the process of strengthening many departments on which the hotel depended. In 1970 he had hired away from Emory University a gruffly amiable gentleman named Charles W. Hayes, who had been that institution's director of purchasing for a quarter century. Hayes now buys, stores, and keeps ready-to-hand everything the company uses except foods and beverages—his purchases ranging from fine china to heavy machinery.

Harned actually had picked his own successor several years before his death, when his heart problems told him that his years of work were nearing their end. His choice was Ted Wright—Edward Truman Wright, Jr.—a man whose background was similar to Harned's own. Wright, like Harned, came from an old-line, innkeeping Quaker family. Born in New York, he, like Harned, had grown up in and around the resort hotel business, first at Lake Placid, and then at White Sulphur Springs, West Virginia, where his father, Truman Wright, was for many years manager of the famous Greenbrier. His introduction to hotel keeping in the deep South came early. After graduating from Westtown, a Quaker high school near Philadelphia, and before going to Cornell Hotel School, he came to the Cloister for a year. Here he worked as a storeroom clerk, a spot from which he was able to learn in some detail the multitude of different items a hotel must keep on hand, particularly how much they weighed when being moved about.

His appetite for innkeeping whetted by what he had seen at the Cloister, he moved on to Cornell Hotel School. He finished in 1958 and came out to practice his new skills in the Navy, coming back to Georgia to serve as mess treasurer of the BOQ's and Officers Club at Glynco, just a grackle's flight away from the Cloister. He moved on then to the Greenbrier, for a six-year graduate course under his father, as sales and convention coordinator, and finally as assistant manager. From there he went with the Marriott chain, from whom, for six years, Irv Harned attempted to bring him back to Georgia as his assistant, with the almost ironclad guarantee that he would in time become Harned's successor as manager of the Cloister. Wright, however, being, as he described it, "fat and happy" with Marriott, stayed on with that chain, working first in Washington, D.C., later in Dallas and in Houston, and finally at the Camelback Inn at Scottsdale, Arizona. It was an experience which convinced him that the resort hotel business was the trade he'd like to follow the rest of his life.

Harned's offer, of course, was still open; and on a long Labor Day weekend in 1976, Ted and Rachel Wright came to Sea Island, to see the place and let the place see them. They met the Joneses and the executive committee; they talked, met the staff, got a glimpse of what the future might hold for them. In effect, they worked out all the details of Wright's transfer to Georgia. It would be within the coming year, giving Marriott ample time to find his replacement. Then, in May 1977, he went to the Green-brier to accept for Camelback Inn the Mobile Travel Guide Five Star Award, the Pulitzer Prize of the resort hotel business. Dewey Benefield was there to accept the same award for the Cloister. They talked. It was obvious that if Ted Wright was to come to the Cloister he should come soon. Irv Harned by now was desperately ill, and Mike Derkacz was filling in for him as manager. Ted Wright went back to Arizona to hand in his resignation. A few days later he got a phone call from Bill Jones, Jr. Could Wright come as soon as possible? Irving Harned was dead. On July 8, 1977 Ted Wright took over as manager of the Cloister.

Over the years, Bill Jones, Sr., had given much thought to what should be done about this little place that he, and his friends with their special skills and talents, had brought into being here. What would be best, in the long run, for the children and the grand-children for whom, in actuality, he had created this place? There were several alternatives. He could sell it—all of it, beach and marsh and duneland, hotel and condominiums and beach club—to one of the great hotel chains which often, over the years, had put out feelers in this direction. Then he could divide the sale price with the children who were the shareholders and let them use the money as they wished. Or he could convert it into a public corporation, with its shares traded on the open market, but with the current Sea Island management continuing, with its special expertise, to run the place. Would not this be a way of having one's cake and eating it too—holding to old time-tested values, while letting the open market increase the value of a share of stock? Or should it remain close-held, a family company, managed with the idea of profit in mind, but always keeping in the forefront the idea of "This Happy Isle." Holding confidently to the idea that Bill and Howard Jones, and Dewey Benefield, Dennie McCrary, and Ted Wright could meet the challenge of the times until, perhaps, even a third generation of Joneses might come along to take their place.

This last, it seems, is the course that has been chosen as the Sea Island Company goes into its second half century. To change with changing times, but never to change the basic direction laid down by Howard Coffin so long ago. In 1928 Coffin looked around him and said: "Here is a country lovely and unspoiled. Here is a simple and satisfying restfulness, . . . a place to charm the mind while nature mends nerves worn thin by living too fast and too hard. Here, in short, is peace, and play, and freedom." These are the treasures Sea Island has offered over the past fifty years. These are the treasures it hopes to offer for generations yet to come.

The End

EPILOGUE

As I come to the end of this Sea Island history, I find my mind crowded with memories . . . the sight of a young father leading his tiny son, scared but trusting in his daddy, down the beach and into the gentle surf . . . of the soft glow of the dining room at night, and an old couple, stooped and wrinkled, coming down the steps holding hands like lovers . . . of the beach at midnight, under a great gold moon that shines down upon a cavalcade of singing horsemen . . . of the beach at dawn on Easter morning, with more than 200 people gathered on the Beach Club lawn for the first sunrise service in Sea Island's history. And far, far back in time — the earliest memory of all — of a bright afternoon in April 1935, when an earnest young journalist and his bride arrived at the Cloister to begin their honeymoon . . . and did not manage to come back again until this book was begun.

Many others, like myself, have their own memories of Sea Island. Of these many were writers, and to all and each of them I owe deep obligation. First there was Margaret Davis Cate, whose fascination with the islands' past, when translated into lectures in the clubrooms at the Cloister, first stirred a nationwide interest in such historic places as Frederica and Christ Church, Bloody Marsh and the old lighthouse site on Saint Simons.

Nobody can know this place without having read Burnette Vanstory's *Georgia's Land of the Golden Isles,* Carolyn Couper Lovell's *Golden Isles of Georgia;* Betsy Fancher's *Lost Legacy of the Golden Isles.* Nor can one's understanding be complete who has not read *Patriarchial Plantations of Saint Simons Island,* by

Miss Bessie Lewis, with its sketches of the old plantation houses by artist Mildred Huie. Here in these books are recorded the facts of history, in language that recreates the mood of times long gone. So do the works of the novelists. Ben Ames Williams's "Great Oaks" brings alive the Sapelo of plantation days. Eugenia Price's famed trilogy, *The Beloved Invader, New Moon Rising,* and *Lighthouse,* adds a new dimension to the legend and the history of Saint Simons. And all these, fact and fiction, can best be understood only after reading Count Gibson's deep-going book *Sea Islands of Georgia,* which traces their geologic history.

To all of these I turned for help. But these books in the main recorded the islands' ancient past, and my goal was different — to put down, against this historic background, the story of Sea Island's more recent history, from Howard Coffin's time to the present day.

For an understanding of these years I turned to contemporary sources — to the Joneses, Kit and Bill, of course, and to Bummy Baumgardner and Montgomery Anderson, the architect, and to Marion McKendree, and to Tobe Tyson, Percy Walters, Helen Jones and Nancy Dalton at the Beach Club. Mary Wylie McCarty was very helpful, and so particularly were the Gilbert brothers, John and James, the Sea Island Company lawyers, who knew the Sea Island story in all its ramifications.

There were other company people who shared their memories with me. Chief among them was Miss Catharine Clark, long retired. For many years she served both Bill Jones and Jim Compton as their secretary, and in truth, she knew as much as both of them about how the little company managed to survive. Others to whom I am grateful are Polly King, widow of General Edward P. King, who was at one time Sea Island's postmistress and at other times social director at the Cloister.

Many of the people who shared their memories with me and to whom I am deeply obligated had backgrounds somewhat similar to my own. They had come here first as honeymooners, long ago. Then, unlike my own experience, they kept coming back, year after year; and now, as longtime members of the cottage colony, they watch their grandchildren walk the beaches they themselves had walked when they were young. All these were helpful to me as they shared their memories. Louisa Robert Carroll remembers when her daddy, Chip Robert, filled their new cottage with political bigwigs in Franklin Roosevelt's day, and when she herself swam a flashing backstroke in the old Casino pool. Many others, like Louisa's family, are now in their fourth generation at Sea Island. Ellen Newell Bryan's children enjoy the house her father, Alfred C. Newell, built in the early days. Cobbie Carter and her husband, Skip, and their children and grandchildren, still occupy the house her father, Judge Shepard Bryan, built when Sea Island was beginning. Marion MacClanahan Wernick, living now at River Club, recalls how her Oklahoma oil-man father had *two* houses—one in which he entertained his roistering friends, the other to which he would invite quieter folk. Dede King Bartenfeld's picture albums, also covering four generations, brought life and color to the early days when primitive airplanes used Sea Island Beach as a landing place.

Backing up all these personal reminiscences were the company's own records, going back to the very first days. And here I must express my feeling of deepest obligation to today's counterpart of Catharine Clark. Her name is Rosmer Branch (Mrs. David Branch), secretary to both Joneses and to their money manager, Dennie McCrary. Across her desk flows every detail of Sea Island Company business. She knows not only where can be found the records of yesterday and last week, but the records of what was happening here fifty years ago. Whatever I needed, she found for me, from a typist who could read my hieroglyphics, to old pictures and musty letters long since laid away and forgotten.

There were others, too, on Sea Island's staff, whose help was invaluable. Billie Porter and Rachel Kelly in Properties, knew or could quickly lay hands on the history of every cottage; Annetta Williams and Betsy Daves were equally knowledgeable about the landscaping department. Phyllis Hendrix, Frances Glover, and Janette Howard in accounting, Otis Sapp in the laundry, Bill Gibson in personnel, Julian Cason in reservations, Hilary Clark and Ethel Camp, hotel and cottage housekeepers, Ann Noel, Ted Wright's secretary, all guided me as best they could through the maze of their separate departments.

Sonja Taylor, who followed the fondly remembered Laura Dunn as social director, came from the Swedish-American Lines at the request of Irving Harned. She looked upon the Cloister with fresh eyes. In the year she was there before she left to marry the distinguished business lecturer Dr. Ben Rogge, whom she met at the Cloister, she introduced many thoughtful innovations — among them was the beautifully impressive sunrise service held at the beach club at dawn on Easter morning. Social directors through the years have each contributed their own special talents to the graciousness for which the Cloister is famous. From Rosalie Hull to Sarah Daugherty to Elizabeth Thompson and Laura Dunn they endeared themselves to generations of Sea Island guests.

Life at the Cloister centers around the dining room, and from the people there — from maîtres d' on down the line to captains and waiters, passers and busboys — I received not only that service for which the Cloister is famed, but friendly insights which added greatly to my understanding, particularly of the changing guest patterns in the changing seasons, the subtle differences in the people who come here. The dining room folk, it seems, must be basic psychologists, able to read in guests' look and manner that they are angry, with each other, or at something that has displeased them outside the dining room. Their job, therefore, is not only serving people but, without seeming to do so, smoothing ruffled feathers.

So, to maître d' Jack Grant and his people—to Tom Holmes, Dorothy, Evelyn, Juanita, Barbara, Cheryl, Winston, and Eddie; to Addie, Louise, Linda, Leslie, and Bill; to Don, Greg, Charles, Mike, Cindy, Bernice, Bonnie, and Nellie Rose; and to all other swift, sure-handed, warmly friendly people whose faces I remember but whose names do not come to me now—my gratitude for your unfailing, cheerful, and understanding help.

And to Arthur and Louise Wesp of Camalier and Buckley, and to Debbie and Beth at the news stands, and to Mildred, the cheerful giantess who makes the beds—I owe my thanks.

To one other person, only indirectly connected with the company, I am also grateful, as are all who come and go in the Sea Island cottage colony. As the dining room is the focal point of the hotel guests, so is the Sea Island Post Office the focal point of the cottage dwellers, and knowing this, the company has always sought to have a very special person appointed to handle the mails there. First it was Mrs. Cate, then Mrs. King, and now it is Mrs. George Stevens—"Miss Lucy"—whose husband's great grandmother was in the 1860s the postmistress at Saint Simons. "Miss Lucy" is in the great tradition of Sea Island postal clerks. Cheerful, smiling, remembering names and faces from cottage to cottage, from year to year, she and her assistant, Richard Hicks, keep alive that friendly aura of the small town post office, the place where all the people gather once a day to swap news and gossip and friendly banter. All of which make "Miss Lucy," like the beds of brilliant flowers in front of her little office, an unforgettable part of Sea Island's special charm.

INDEX